THE SERMONS
OF JESUS THE
MESSIAH

E. KEITH HOWICK

WindRiver Publishing
St. George, Utah

Queries, comments or correspondence concerning this work should be directed to the author and submitted to WindRiver Publishing at:

authors@windriverpublishing.com

Information regarding this work and other works published by WindRiver Publishing Inc., and instructions for submitting manuscripts for review for publication, can be found at:

www.windriverpublishing.com

The Sermons of Jesus the Messiah
Copyright © 2003 by WindRiver Publishing, Inc.

Library of Congress Control Number: 2003102365
ISBN 1-886249-02-4 (previously published by Bookcraft, Inc., ISBN 0-88494-627-4)

First Printing, 1987
Second Printing, 2003

Printed on acid-free paper by Malloy, Inc., Ann Arbor MI, the United States of America

To Keith, Jr., and Brian

Key to Abbreviations

Abbreviation	Name of Work
Bruce	Alexander Balmain Bruce, *The Training of the Twelve* (Grand Rapids, Michigan: Kregel Publications, reprint ed., 1982).
DNTC	Bruce R. McConkie, *Doctrinal New Testament Commentary*, Vol. 1, *The Gospels* (Salt Lake City: Bookcraft, 1975).
Ed	Alfred Edersheim, *The Life and Times of Jesus the Messiah* (Grand Rapids, Michigan: Wm. B. Eerdmans Publishing Company, reprinted December 1981).
Ed Temple	Alfred Edersheim, *The Temple: Its Ministry and Services As They Were at the Time of Jesus Christ* (Grand Rapids, Michigan: Wm. B. Eerdmans Publishing Company, reprinted 1982).
Farrar	Frederic W. Farrar, *The Life of Christ*, 2 vols. (New York: E. P. Dutton and Company, 1874).
Geikie	Cunningham Geikie, *The Life and Words of Christ*, revised ed., 2 vols. (New York: D. Appleton and Company, 1891, 1894).
HC	Joseph Smith, Jr., *History of The Church of Jesus Christ of Latter-day Saints*, ed. B. H. Roberts, 7 vols. (Salt Lake City: The Church of Jesus Christ of Latter-day Saints, 1955).
JC	James E. Talmage, *Jesus the Christ* (Salt Lake City: Deseret Book Company, 1959).
Josephus	Flavius Josephus, *Josephus: Complete Works*, trans. William Whiston (Grand Rapids, Michigan: Kregel Publications, 1971).

Miracles   E. Keith Howick, *The Miracles of Jesus the Messiah* (Salt Lake City: Bookcraft, 1985).

MD   Bruce R. McConkie, *Mormon Doctrine,* (Salt Lake City: Bookcraft, 1966).

MM   Bruce R. McConkie, *The Mortal Messiah,* 4 vols. (Salt Lake City: Deseret Book Company, 1979–81).

Parables   E. Keith Howick, *The Parables of Jesus the Messiah* (Salt Lake City: Bookcraft, 1986).

Smith   William Smith, *A Dictionary of the Bible,* rev. and ed. by F. N. and M. A. Peloubet (New York: Thomas Nelson Publishers, 1984).

TPJS   Joseph Smith, Jr., *Teachings of the Prophet Joseph Smith,* sel. Joseph Fielding Smith (Salt Lake City: Deseret Book Company, 1958).

Trench   Richard Chenevix Trench, *Notes on the Miracles of Our Lord* (Westwood, New Jersey: Fleming H. Revell Company, n.d.).

Contents

Introduction

The sermon or discourse was the principal means by which Jesus taught the "good news" of his new gospel. He emphasized his teachings through the supernatural power of his miracles,[1] and exemplified them by parables;[2] but his predominant method of teaching remained the discourse.

When we think of the discourses of Jesus we should not envision a formally prepared speech delivered in a traditional setting; rather, Jesus extemporaneously used the circumstances in which he found himself to deliver his messages. He did not confine himself to particular places or fixed times. He addressed the people in the temple and in the synagogue, but more often he was found teaching on the hillside, the lakeshore, in the streets and marketplaces, in private homes, or as he walked from place to place with the disciples, the curious, and his ever-present enemies. He was ready to teach whenever and wherever people were ready to listen.

The four Gospels record the discourses of Jesus. Matthew, Mark and Luke (commonly referred to as the synoptic Gospels or the Synoptics, because they deal with the life of Christ in a similar manner) record many miracles, all of the parables, and numerous discourses. John records several miracles but no parables, and is a primary source of the Lord's discourses. Recording only one discourse in common with the Synoptics, John devotes virtually thirteen chapters of his Gospel to fourteen discourses (twelve chapters exclusively). The remaining twenty-one discourses are scattered through the Synoptics.

In total this book discusses thirty-five discourses. Some of them are short, more like statements, and some take up entire chapters. The longest discourse, the Sermon on the Mount, is three chapters long.

The classification of the discourses in this book is my own. Their names are taken from the body of the discourse or from a common historical title. Further, they are not discussed in historical order. Although the Gospels are written in such a manner as to invite the appearance of historical continuity, it is generally accepted that none of the Gospel writers attempted to present a historical biography of Jesus; rather they assembled their materials to evidence the teaching of the kingdom of God and testify of the long-awaited Messiah.[3] For this reason it is the doctrinal teaching of the discourse that determines its classification, not its historical order.

Nevertheless, the historical setting of the discourses is important and, where possible, it is taken into consideration when interpreting them. Other considerations include related teachings and examples that the Lord rendered throughout his ministry, similar doctrines of the Old Testament, and the scriptural and historical insight that other knowledgeable writers have given on the intent and meaning of the discourses.

The body of this book is divided into seven parts and fourteen chapters. Chapter 1 introduces the concept of discourses in general, chapters 2 through 13 deal with specific discourses and chapter 14 discusses the general message of the discourses.

All biblical references are from the standard King James Version unless otherwise stated. The presentation of each discourse begins with the relevant scriptural text quoted in its entirety. If the discourse appears in more than one Gospel, the clearest and most thorough account is used. Please note that when any part of a quoted scripture is discussed in the same chapter it is not referenced (the whole source having been already cited). Cross-references are noted by chapter and verse only;

again no further reference is given in the text when a quotation is given from that source. Lengthy cross-references are shown in the notes at the end of the book. Cross-references to the Joseph Smith Translation of the Bible, which is sometimes referred to as the "Inspired Version," are here shown as JST.

Because the discourses are presented doctrinally rather than historically, there is no need to reconcile discrepancies in the scriptural texts except where they are obvious. Scriptural discrepancies do not discredit the authenticity of the discourses since each writer was clearly selective in what he chose to record and how he chose to record it.

The discourses introduced the kingdom of God, gave gospel instructions, answered questions, and declared Jesus as the Messiah. They were given to friends, strangers, disciples, the curious, enemies, and the Apostles. They often came as a result of controversies between Jesus and the rulers of the Jews. Jesus presented them regularly throughout his ministry, commencing with the Sermon on the Mount and concluding with those private discourses delivered to the Apostles prior to the Savior's arrest and crucifixion. His enemies questioned his competence as a teacher, but Jesus retorted by questioning their competence as listeners.

Christ's miracles caused astonishment. They made his followers wonder, and caused his enemies to question. His parables animated his teachings, bringing them down to the common man's level of comprehension. In his discourses the Master Teacher declared and explained his Messianic claim and expounded doctrines of the kingdom of God. He shaped the illustrations of his discourses into sermons that would become indelibly fixed in the memories of those who heard them.

It is hoped that the mind of the reader will be further enlightened as the sermons of Jesus, as presented herein, are revealed.

Part One

"And the Word Was Made Flesh"

Discourses 1

The discourses of Jesus were more like conversations than lectures or formal instruction periods. There were times when the Lord delivered them in the formal atmosphere of the synagogue (Matthew 4:23), but often they were merely informal conversations, frequently interrupted by questions put to Jesus by friends and enemies. Jesus would often pass over a question presented to him and substitute a great moral lesson for a direct answer, thereby making it difficult for his audience to disassociate the question asked from the principle he wanted to teach. Thus he stressed the value of both the discourse and the question.[1]

My treatment of the sermons is not the same as that of the parables[2] or the miracles.[3] The problems created by these different modes of instruction, however, are very similar. The basic conflict between Jesus and the synagogue continued throughout his entire ministry. It stemmed from Jesus' claim to be the long-awaited Messiah, but he was not the Messiah the Jews anticipated. Perhaps this conflict went even deeper; since the Jews did not believe in the "total corruption of man," they felt they had no need for a Savior.[4]

In their distorted view of the Messianic expectation the Jews

earnestly awaited the kingdom of God and the promised Messiah, but they no longer looked for the spiritual kingdom offered
by Christ. The kingdom they expected was temporally oriented
and based on material things. They wanted meat and drink and
wilderness-banquets—not manna. They wanted all the earthly
delights, "not to speak of the fabulous Messianic banquet which
a sensuous realism expected."[5] Christ fulfilled the very Law that
the Jews used to reject him. "The Pharisees had refined the Law
into a microscopic casuistry which prescribed for every isolated
act, but Jesus brought it into the compass of a living principle
in the soul."[6]

Their expectations of the Messiah had advanced beyond all
logical reality:

> The fruit-trees were every day, or at least every week or
> two, to yield their riches, the fields their harvest; the grain
> was to stand like palm trees, and to be reaped and win-
> nowed without labour. Similar blessings were to visit the
> vine; ordinary trees would bear like fruit trees, and every
> produce, of every clime, would be found in Palestine in
> such abundance and luxuriance as only the wildest imagi-
> nation could conceive.[7]

Jesus openly published his Messianic claim and carefully
taught the requirements of his new kingdom through his discourses. Many believed (John 7:31), but his candid claims and
explanations also caused many to follow him no more (John
6:66). To the believers he promised life eternal, but the disbe-
lievers were told that where he would be, they could not come
(John 7:34).

The Lord used parables to illustrate the principles he
taught[8] and made the miraculous seem commonplace in Israel.[9]
Yet the Jews' inherent course of religious experience made it all
but impossible for them to believe. Their rejection of Jesus was
not just a spur-of-the-moment frenzy, but "the outcome and
direct result of their whole previous religious development. . . .
The long course of their resistance to the prophetic message,
and their perversion of it, was itself a hardening of their
hearts."[10] They would not believe because they "loved the praise
of men more than the praise of God" (John 12:43).[11]

In his teachings Jesus used illustrations of almost every scene and object familiar to the Israelites of his day. He spoke of flowers, fields, budding trees, and the red of the lowering sky; of sunrise and sunset, wind and rain, stars, and lamps lighted in both home and temple. He used many examples of food, comparing the word of God to bread, salt, eggs, wine, water, fish, corn, and oil—things used in the Jews' everyday meals, banquets, ceremonies, and sacrifices. He was obviously familiar with the simple things of life and used them to teach the Jews about the kingdom of heaven. He sympathized with life's joys and participated in its sorrows. Although he was rejected time and time again and accused of all types of evil, he continued to teach the gospel and offer it to all who would listen to his words.

The Lord declined all outward honor and flattery. He walked among all types of men from the despised Samaritan and the outcast leper to the rulers of the temple and the synagogue. He dined with both rabbis and publicans, and he gave his precious time to heathen and chosen alike. His life was destined to influence all men's lives, yet in his ministry he was rejected by those he sought to save.

From our limited record of Christ's life, it is evident that the discourses were his most common method of teaching.[12] He used the spoken word, coupled with illustrations from life, to persuade the conscience and influence the will of those who heard him. His longest recorded discourse is the Sermon on the Mount, and while other discourses take up entire chapters (or large parts of them), most of his teachings are contained in numerous, scattered fragments.

Christ's miracles are very exciting, and his parables are alive with comparisons and interpretive possibilities. But the discourses are like a one-on-one conversation with Jesus the Messiah.

The Ministry Commenced

The Sermon on the Mount

Matthew 5, 6, and 7

Cross-references:

See Scriptural Appendix to the Sermon on the Mount

There are four recordings of the Sermon on the Mount. The source quoted in this chapter is the Gospel of Matthew. Luke also records this discourse in various chapters, but not as a complete text.[1] In addition to these two references, the Book of Mormon records that the Lord delivered the same discourse to the Nephites when he appeared on the Western Hemisphere after his resurrection. However, the most extensive and comprehensive version of the discourse is found in the Joseph Smith Translation of the Bible.[2] Although some of the changes made by Joseph were insignificant, a careful reading indicates that almost every verse was touched by the inspired mind of the first prophet of this dispensation. The Sermon on the Mount is the most lengthy of all the discourses recorded by the Gospel writers.

As recorded by Matthew, the Sermon on the Mount appears to be out of historical sequence. It would seem that a group of miracles and events which Matthew later recorded actually preceded this discourse, and that one important event, the call and ordination of the Twelve Apostles (not recorded at all by Matthew but referred to in chapter 10), definitely occurred prior to its delivery.[3]

Prior to this discourse Jesus' fame had already spread, for he had performed many miracles and had taught throughout all Galilee, "teaching in their synagogues, and preaching the gospel of the kingdom" (Matthew 4:23–24). Undoubtedly it was from these people, gathered from the densely populated shores of Galilee and from the environs of Jerusalem, Tyre, Sidon, and other parts of Decapolis, that the multitude had gathered to hear the Lord.

Luke verifies that the Savior called his Apostles before he gave this discourse. He also records that prior to this sermon Jesus went "out into a mountain to pray, and continued all night in prayer to God" (Luke 6:12). After concluding his prayer, Jesus called his disciples to him and from them he selected twelve men whom he called as his Apostles (Luke 6:13). After enumerating the names of the Twelve, Luke records that Jesus "came down and stood in the plain," and there (in the company of additional disciples, the Twelve, and "a great multitude of people") he delivered the discourse known as the Sermon on the Mount.

Luke adds that once the Lord had chosen the Twelve and had returned to the multitude, he healed their diseases (Luke 6:17). The Spirit abounded in their presence and they "sought to touch him: for there went virtue out of him, and healed them all" (Luke 6:19). It was probably the supernatural power of the Lord that brought the multitude together, and he rewarded them with even further miracles. Then he delivered the longest of his recorded discourses.[4]

Matthew indicates that this discourse was delivered on a mount, whereas Luke suggests that its setting was on a plain. We can imagine that the sequence of events occurred as follows: The evening before the delivery of the sermon Jesus went up to the mountain by himself and petitioned his Father in Heaven concerning the call of the Twelve Apostles. As the morning dawned he called his waiting disciples, who had undoubtedly tarried as they anticipated his return. After choosing the Twelve, he descended further down the mount into a natural amphitheater where the multitude patiently awaited him.[5]

Although the Lord had delivered previous discourses, Matthew uses the Sermon on the Mount as the commencement of Christ's ministry. Consequently, the sermon may be one of the most accurately recorded events in the ministry of Jesus, and perhaps he used it to officially inaugurate his new kingdom among the Jews. Before them now stood the Messiah whom the children of Israel had long awaited. But the Messiah the Jews had looked for and the kingdom of God they had anticipated were not embodied in the discourse Jesus taught that day.[6]

The Old Testament Jehovah instituted the Mosaic Law from the desolation of Mount Sinai with thundering and lightning while the Israelites stood in wondering awe. The Law was given as a teaching tool and as a schoolmaster to prepare those waiting for the Messiah to recognize him and believe in him. Now, in contrast to Sinai, the incarnate Jehovah stood on the green hillside slopes above the beautiful Sea of Galilee and inaugurated his kingdom for his chosen people. He did not abrogate the old Law:[7] the Law and the teachings of the Old Testament had been but a precursor of things to come.

The threatenings of the old Law and the fear of God demanded obedience from the Israelites through explicit rules of conduct. The new law would emphasize mercy (i.e., the love of God) so that man might come to realize the real reason for his obedience.

Jesus warned the Israelites that he came not to abolish the Law, but to obey and fulfill it. He taught that this obedience had nothing to do with the strict Levitical adherence to the letter of the Law, "but was rather a surrender of the heart and will to the innermost meaning and spirit which the commands involved. He fulfilled that olden Law by perfectly keeping it, and by imparting a power to keep it to all who believed in

Him, even though He made its cogency so far more universal and profound."[8]

This discourse contrasted the New Testament's gospel perfectness with the apostasy of the Levitical Jewishness of the day.[9] According to the theology of the Pharisees and the scribes, the chosen people were constantly striving and laboring (by strict adherence to the Law) toward the goal of entrance into God's kingdom. They accomplished this by obeying a Law which described in minute detail the duties of their mortal life.[10] But the new law went much further, requiring a far greater spiritual commitment to the future.[11]

The Sermon on the Mount portrays man's righteous relationship to God, to sin, to temptation, and to salvation.[12] It describes the disciples' entrance into a new life. Paul would later describe it as putting "off concerning the former conversation the old man, which is corrupt according to the deceitful lusts; and be renewed in the spirit of your mind; and that ye put on the new man, which after God is created in righteousness and true holiness" (Ephesians 4:22–24).

The Sermon

The kingdom of heaven was the basic text of the Sermon on the Mount. Through this sermon the Lord taught the means for reaching the kingdom and defined the glories of its citizens.[13] The sermon clearly exemplified that Christ came to found a kingdom and not a school. Its concepts contrasted sharply with the prevailing law, and detailed how counterfeit the old Law was in its moral and religious aspects. The new law emphasized sincerity of action as opposed to the empty profession of duty,[14] and Jesus was the perfect example of this concept. The sermon contained no mention of rabbis nor of the requirement of circumcision (the sign of the old Law), and it confirmed that the evidence of the new law was righteousness and love.[15]

> The teaching of their [the Jewish] Scribes was narrow, dogmatic, material; it was cold in manner, frivolous in matter, second-hand . . . with no freshness . . . no force, no fire; servile to all authority, opposed to all independence;

at once erudite and foolish, at once contemptuous and mean; never passing a hair's breadth beyond the carefully-watched boundary line of commentary and precedent . . . elevating mere memory above genius, and repetition above originality; concerned only about Priests and Pharisees, in Temple and synagogue, or school, or Sanhedrin, and mostly occupied with things infinitely little. It was not indeed wholly devoid of moral significance, nor is it impossible to find here and there, among the *débris* of it, a noble thought; but it was occupied a thousandfold more with Levitical minutiae about mint, and anise, and cummin, and the length of fringes, and the breadth of phylacteries, and the washing of cups and platters, and the particular quarter of a second when new moons and Sabbath-days began. But this teaching of Jesus [the Sermon on the Mount] was wholly different in its character, and as much grander as the temple of the morning sky under which it was uttered was grander than stifling synagogue or crowded school.[16]

Jesus approached the multitude, sat upon the ground (a customary method of teaching at that time) and "opened his mouth" to speak.[17] From that time forward his followers would never return to the lifelessness of rabbinism.

The Beatitudes

The teachings of this discourse applied not only to the Twelve but also to anyone who wished to be a true disciple of Christ. This seems to be confirmed by the additions Joseph Smith was inspired to make in his introduction to the discourse:

JST Matthew 5:3-4

3. Blessed are they who shall believe on me; and again, more blessed are they who shall believe on your words, when ye shall testify that ye have seen me and that I am.

4. Yea, blessed are they who shall believe on your words, and come down into the depth of humility, and be baptised in my name; for

| they shall be visited with fire and the Holy Ghost, and | shall receive a remission of their sins. |

Following this introduction the Lord commenced his discourse with what has become known as the "Beatitudes." Through the Beatitudes he openly contrasted his new kingdom with that of the old[18] and described the felicity of the kingdom independent of the outward conditions of temporal happiness. The individual Beatitudes enumerate and define blessed conditions of mankind. They each contain a recompense plus a reward for the suffering they describe; yet they are presented in a simple and unambiguous manner.[19]

Matthew 5:3

3. Blessed are the poor in spirit: for theirs is the kingdom of heaven.

These are the rightful heirs of the kingdom of heaven[20]—those who overcome self-righteous pride and conceit and "who come unto me [Jesus]." According to Matthew, just being poor merited an individual the kingdom of heaven, but the Joseph Smith Translation of the Bible clarifies the fact that just being poor does not mean that the kingdom is reached automatically. Even poor Saints must accept Jesus by obeying his laws, teachings, and ordinances before they can be heirs to the kingdom of heaven.[21]

Matthew 5:4

4. Blessed are they that mourn: for they shall be comforted.

Even though grief and sorrow are expressed in this life, mourning in and of itself does not bring comfort. Comfort is received through the assurance Christ has given us that we will once again be able to associate with our loved ones in the eternities. As Paul said, "If in this life only we have hope in Christ, we are of all men most miserable" (1 Corinthians 15:19). Assurance of divine comfort as promised comes from faithfully living the principles and ordinances of the gospel. Only then will they that mourn be comforted, "and God shall wipe away all tears from their eyes" (Revelation 7:17).

Matthew 5:5

5. Blessed are the meek:
for they shall inherit the
earth.

The meek are those who are righteous and live the celestial law.[22] They are willing to suffer injury rather than jeopardize their souls in contention.[23] They are promised that they will inherit the earth (D&C 88:17) and obtain mercy from the Lord (D&C 97:2).

Matthew 5:6

6. Blessed are they which   righteousness: for they shall
do hunger and thirst after   be filled.

The Joseph Smith Translation of the Bible adds a significant conclusion to this promise: it states that they which hunger and thirst after righteousness shall be filled "with the Holy Ghost." This signifies that the individual is hungering and thirsting after the righteousness of the kingdom of God and promises that the Holy Ghost will fill them with the Spirit in rich abundance.[24]

Matthew 5:7

7. Blessed are the merci-
ful: for they shall obtain
mercy.

Later in his ministry the Lord elaborated on this principle by giving the parable of the unmerciful servant.[25] If we expect God to show mercy toward us, we are required to show mercy toward our fellowman.

Matthew 5:8

8. Blessed are the pure in
heart: for they shall see God.

The pure in heart are those who have forsaken their sins, have come to an understanding of the divinity of Christ, have lived his commandments, and will ultimately be admitted into the presence of God (D&C 93:1).[26]

Matthew 5:9

9. Blessed are the peace-
makers: for they shall be
called the children of God.

There is no doubt that there is great merit in saving yourself and your fellowman from worldly strife, and certainly those who accomplish this feat can be numbered among the children of God.[27] But there is a greater peace that can be obtained through the gospel, for the very work of righteousness is peace, "and the effect of righteousness quietness and assurance for ever" (Isaiah 32:17). Isaiah further points out that there is no true peace for the wicked (Isaiah 48:22). Paul declared that "the peace of God, which passeth all understanding, shall keep your hearts and minds through Christ Jesus" (Philippians 4:7).

Before his crucifixion Jesus said to the Twelve, "Peace I leave with you, my peace I give unto you: not as the world giveth, give I unto you. Let not your heart be troubled, neither let it be afraid." (John 14:27.) Having overcome the world, Jesus again declared to his Apostles that in this world they would have tribulation, and "in me ye might have peace" (John 16:33). The gospel of Jesus Christ is a gospel of peace, the inner peace that comes from knowing the way to eternal life and knowing you are valiantly involved in obtaining it.

Matthew 5:10

10. Blessed are they
which are persecuted for
righteousness' sake: for theirs
is the kingdom of heaven.

Matthew states that the persecuted are blessed when they are persecuted for righteousness' sake; but in the Joseph Smith Translation of the Bible they are blessed for being persecuted for "my name's sake." It appears that this is the fate the faithful will inherit: having forsaken the world and having come unto Christ, they are to suffer oppression.[28] Paul confirmed this teaching in his second letter to Timothy when he declared, "Yea, and all that will live godly in Christ Jesus shall suffer persecution" (2 Timothy 3:12). The Lord emphasized this point in his sermon, seemingly anticipating the suffering that would be associated with true discipleship. He knew that true disciples would be reviled and falsely accused of evil, but he told them to rejoice and be exceedingly glad, "for so persecuted they the prophets which were before you."

The Beatitudes promised great blessings, but they held no attraction for the insincere and worldly. They portrayed the kingdom in a manner that would repel all but the earnest and devoted searchers of the truth: the chaff was being fanned from the wheat. The discourse compelled the true believer to distinguish between the earthly realization of blessings and the blessings to be realized beyond the grave—between mere earthly pleasure and eternal happiness.[29]

Luke follows his rendition of the Beatitudes with a series of "woes," woes that will befall those who accept earthly conciliation over eternal rewards. His woes provide an explicit contrast between the old Law and the new.[30]

Luke 6:24

24. But woe unto you that are rich! for ye have received your consolation.

The first woe was a warning to the rich, for if they counted their reward in earthly possessions, they had received their "consolation."

Luke 6:25

25. Woe unto you that are full! for ye shall hunger.

To those who felt that the Law of Moses filled their needs (causing them to look no further) Jesus said, "Woe unto you that are full! for ye shall hunger"—this because of their rejection of the gospel he so readily offered.

Luke 6:25 continued

25. Woe unto you that
laugh now! for ye shall
mourn and weep.

To those who felt secure in their own righteousness under the Law of Moses and laughed or scoffed at Christ's message, he warned of impending mourning and weeping. In the Book of Mormon Nephi warned that there would be many who would say, "Eat, drink, and be merry, for tomorrow we die; and it shall be well with us." And others will Satan "pacify, and lull them away into carnal security, that they will say: All is well in Zion; yea, Zion prospereth, all is well—and thus the devil cheateth their souls, and leadeth them away carefully down to hell." (2 Nephi 28:7, 21.)

Luke 6:26

26. Woe unto you, when   you! for so did their fathers
all men shall speak well of   to the false prophets.

Last, Luke recorded Christ's warning to all those who sought only the praise of their fellowmen and basked in their deceiving flattery. To these the Lord declared, "for so did their fathers to the false prophets," thereby denoting their eventual destruction.

The Beatitudes and woes concluded the Lord's introductory phase of the discourse and opened the gates of the kingdom to all who would enter. They condemned the corrupt religious teachers of his day not only because the teachers had contaminated and changed the Law but also because their subtle casuistry and immoral additions to it had led men astray along their evil paths. Jesus strenuously opposed the idea "that strict observance of the traditions and commands of their schools in itself satisfied the requirements of God. . . . The 'hedge' round the Law had proved one of thorns, for Rabbis and people alike."[31] This was the old Israel, which because of the rabbis had sunk to a painful observance of only the letter of the Law.

The new Israel would not be characterized by the thunderings of Sinai. The Lord's disciples were not to look for a Messiah of great political strength who would take the yoke from their necks, take vengeance upon their enemies, and reign in earthly splendor. Rather they were to await a sweeter manna than the wilderness had known and eagerly anticipate the riches of poverty, the royalty of meekness, the greatness of sorrow and persecution, and all the attributes of godliness embodied in patience, humility, gentleness, and a pure love of their fellowman.

The Disciples Admonished

Having completed his introduction to the kingdom of God, Jesus turned specifically to the Apostles, and with the multitude listening in, instructed them as to their responsibilities in the ministry. Only the Apostles had been specifically called to serve, yet additional disciples, after developing a testimony of the gospel and the Lord's kingdom, would assume other duties as they were added to the ministry.

The next four verses of this discourse draw a series of quick comparisons. The responsibility to which the comparisons relate is implicit, yet they emphasize the fact that all disciples of Jesus must extend the Lord's teachings to those who have not yet heard them.[32]

Matthew 5:13

13. Ye are the salt of the earth: but if the salt have lost his savour, wherewith shall it be salted? it is thenceforth good for nothing, but to be cast out, and to be trodden under foot of men.

Jesus first compared the disciples to salt, the great preservative of his day—they were to be the "salt" of the earth. To the Jews salt specifically symbolized fidelity and hospitality—it was an evidence of their covenant with the Lord, and it was used in every meat offering under the Law. (See Leviticus 2:13; Numbers 18:19; 2 Chronicles 13:5.) The salt had to be pure; no additives or mixtures of any kind were allowed. Any object which adulterated the salt caused it to lose its savor.

The disciples would lose their savor if they became fainthearted or slothful or if they broke the commandments. Such an occurrence caused the disciples to become adulterated, and if unrepentant, to lose their worth to the kingdom of God. They would thenceforth be "good for nothing but to be cast out and trodden under foot of men."

Matthew 5:14-15

14. Ye are the light of the world. A city that is set on an hill cannot be hid.

15. Neither do men light a candle, and put it under a bushel, but on a candlestick; and it giveth light unto all that are in the house.

Jesus next commanded the disciples to be the "light of the world." He expected them to be perfect examples of righteousness,[33] and by their words, as well as by their teachings, to declare the gospel to all people.[34] The Lord enumerated two examples to emphasize this point: a city on a hill could not be hidden; and men do not light candles with the intent of hiding them under bushels.

The Lord concluded these two instructions by admonishing, "Let your light so shine before men, that they may see your good works, and glorify your Father which is in heaven" (Matthew 5:16). Perhaps with this in mind, Paul admonished the Philippian Saints that "those things, which ye have both learned, and received, and heard, and seen in me, do" (Philippians 4:9).

The Law of Moses Compared

Matthew 5:17-20

17. Think not that I am come to destroy the law, or the prophets: I am not come to destroy, but to fulfil.

18. For verily I say unto you, Till heaven and earth

pass, one jot or one tittle
shall in no wise pass from the
law, till all be fulfilled.

19. Whosoever therefore
shall break one of these least
commandments, and shall
teach men so, he shall be
called the least in the kingdom of heaven: but whoso-
ever shall do and teach them,

the same shall be called great
in the kingdom of heaven.

20. For I say unto you,
That except your righteousness shall exceed the righteousness of the scribes and
Pharisees, ye shall in no case
enter into the kingdom of
heaven.

Jesus emphasized the continuity between the Law of Moses
and the new gospel he was promulgating by declaring that he
had not come to destroy the Law but to fulfill it. Although no
destruction of the old Law would occur, the new gospel eliminated the mundane parts of the Law that the Jews so meticu-
lously adhered to. The Messiah's gospel did not cast away the
sacred truths of the Law, but rather enlarged upon them and
clarified them. The Law of Moses had been a schoolmaster: its
rites and ceremonies had provided the simple people of previous ages with the material symbols they needed to cling to.[35] It
was, as it were, the childhood stage of a religion that Jesus
would now bring to maturity.

Paul used a like comparison when writing to the Corin-
thian Saints. He chided them for not progressing and for still
needing to be fed with "milk, and not with meat" (1 Corinthians 3:2). He stated, "When I was a child, I spake as a child,
I understood as a child, I thought as a child: but when I became
a man, I put away childish things" (1 Corinthians 13:11).

The Law had been a sacred, moral command from Sinai—
an apparatus to teach God's requirements to the children of
Israel. The ancient prophets had drawn pure and exalted concepts from it, often anticipating the teachings of Christ yet to
come. But the Law had been given for only one purpose, which
Paul clearly stated to the Galatians: "Wherefore the law was
our schoolmaster to bring us unto Christ" (Galatians 3:24). Jesus
had respect for the Law of Moses for he was the fulfillment of
it, but he condemned its corruption by the religious leaders and

teachers of his day, and warned the disciples that their "righteousness [should] exceed the righteousness of the . . . Pharisees."

The Lord now decisively demonstrated the superiority of the gospel over the Law of Moses. He proceeded to contrast the two laws—at the same time criticizing the Pharisaic abuses implemented by tradition and literalism. He did not enumerate every facet of the Law, yet step by step in the examples he used he went from the outward observance (indicated by the traditions of the elders) to the higher concepts taught by the gospel.

Matthew 5:21-26

21. Ye have heard that it was said by them of old time, Thou shalt not kill; and whosoever shall kill shall be in danger of the judgment:

22. But I say unto you, That whosoever is angry with his brother without a cause shall be in danger of the judgment: and whosoever shall say to his brother, Raca, shall be in danger of the council: but whosoever shall say, Thou fool, shall be in danger of hell fire.

23. Therefore if thou bring thy gift to the altar, and there rememberest that thy brother hath ought against thee;

24. Leave there thy gift before the altar, and go thy way; first be reconciled to thy brother, and then come and offer thy gift.

25. Agree with thine adversary quickly, whiles thou art in the way with him; lest at any time the adversary deliver thee to the judge, and the judge deliver thee to the officer, and thou be cast into prison.

26. Verily I say unto thee, Thou shalt by no means come out thence, till thou hast paid the uttermost farthing.

Murder

The sin of murder was condemned under both the Law of Moses and the gospel, but according to the traditions of the elders, only homicide was punishable under the Law of Moses. The guilty person was not only in danger of the judgment of God but also, in some cases, the Sanhedrin. The subtle change in this penalty caused the Jews to fear the Sanhedrin's punishment more than God's.[36] Thus the literalism of the Law had narrowed the concept of the crime for which a man could be punished.

The gospel, on the other hand, not only condemned the act of murder itself, but also the intent or passion that led to the act.[37] Thus, even feelings of anger with one's fellowman were unacceptable. Not only was the hand that struck the blow censured but also the heart that hated and precipitated the blow.

There was no approval for unholy and contemptuous feelings, nor for any language that conveyed improper sentiments toward another person. Matthew leaves the impression that only anger expressed "without a cause" was sinful; however, the Joseph Smith Translation omits these words, leading to the conclusion that in *no* instance is one justified in showing anger to another.[38]

The Lord emphasized this principle by giving an example that the Jews would have readily understood. Part of their daily lives—indeed their very existence—involved the procedure of presenting gifts at the altar of God; but the new law permitted no one to present a gift to God if he was at odds with any one of his fellowmen; if he did so he would be under the influence of the adversary.

Adultery

Matthew 5:27-30

27. Ye have heard that it was said by them of old time, Thou shalt not commit adultery:

28. But I say unto you, That whosoever looketh on a woman to lust after her hath committed adultery with her already in his heart.

29. And if thy right eye offend thee, pluck it out, and cast it from thee: for it is profitable for thee that one of thy members should perish, and not that thy whole body should be cast into hell.

30. And if thy right hand offend thee, cut it off, and cast it from thee: for it is profitable for thee that one of thy members should perish,

and not that thy whole body
should be cast into hell.

Adultery was the second example that the Lord used to
compare the old Law with the new. As with murder, both laws
prohibited it, but now the spirit of the law would extend to the
conception of the act rather than just to the act itself—so much
so that it was better to be blind than to look lustfully upon
another, or to be maimed than to abuse the law of chastity.
Thus, an unclean glance was a virtual commission of the trans-
gression, one which required the offender to mortify himself
symbolically rather than allow guilty thoughts to imperil his
soul. In this specific manner the Lord instructed the chosen
people and those who would be his disciples that sin originated
in the heart (or mind), and that no self-restraint was too great
an effort when spiritual salvation was endangered.

Divorce

Matthew 5:31–32

31. It hath been said,
Whosoever shall put away his
wife, let him give her a writing of divorcement:

32. But I say unto you,
That whosoever shall put
away his wife, saving for the
cause of fornication, causeth
her to commit adultery: and
whosoever shall marry her
that is divorced committeth
adultery.

Because of the liberal divorce laws the Pharisees practiced,
the Lord unsparingly condemned them. The Pharisaic law of
divorce was so shamefully loose that "if any one see a woman
handsomer than his wife, he may dismiss his wife and marry
that woman."[39] Other reasons for divorce included a woman's
going out in public without having shrouded her face with a
veil, and a husband's general displeasure with his wife's behav-
ior. Some maintained that if the wife had badly cooked the
food, or oversalted or overroasted it, or even if the wife became
grievously ill, it was grounds for divorce.[40]

Divorce had become so scandalous among the Jews that
"even to their heathen neighbours . . . the Rabbis were fain to

boast of it as a privilege granted to Israel, but not to other nations!"[41] The Lord swept aside these frivolous and sinful reasonings and declared that only for the sin of infidelity could one justify divorce.

Jesus later reiterated this same principle, as recorded in Matthew 19:9, and even his disciples, recognizing how strictly he applied this law, questioned the Savior concerning it. Jesus acknowledged the difficulty that this law imposed but emphasized that it was possible to comply with it.

Although the Church today recognizes civil divorce and cancellation of temple sealings, it strenuously teaches the sanctity of the marriage covenant and stresses that neither marriage nor divorce should be entered into lightly.

Oaths

Matthew 5:33–37

33. Again, ye have heard that it hath been said by them of old time, Thou shalt not forswear thyself, but shalt perform unto the Lord thine oaths:

34. But I say unto you, Swear not at all; neither by heaven; for it is God's throne:

35. Nor by the earth; for it is his footstool: neither by Jerusalem; for it is the city of the great King.

36. Neither shalt thou swear by thy head, because thou canst not make one hair white or black.

37. But let your communication be, Yea, yea; Nay, nay: for whatsoever is more than these cometh of evil.

The Jews indulged themselves in the taking of endless oaths by which they conducted not only business relationships but also family affairs. They swore by the sun and the temple, Jerusalem, the prophets, and their own heads. The taking of oaths had reached such a refined state that under certain conditions even perjury was sanctioned.[42] But now the Lord cautioned them in all their communications, advocating moderation in speech and forbidding the use of profanity and oaths.[43]

He pointed out that the simple truth was sufficient and an oath could neither enhance nor detract from it.[44]

Retaliation

Matthew 5:38–48

38. Ye have heard that it hath been said, An eye for an eye, and a tooth for a tooth:

39. But I say unto you, That ye resist not evil: but whosoever shall smite thee on thy right cheek, turn to him the other also.

40. And if any man will sue thee at the law, and take away thy coat, let him have thy cloke also.

41. And whosoever shall compel thee to go a mile, go with him twain.

42. Give to him that asketh thee, and from him that would borrow of thee turn not thou away.

43. Ye have heard that it hath been said, Thou shalt love thy neighbour, and hate thine enemy.

44. But I say unto you, Love your enemies, bless them that curse you, do good to them that hate you, and pray for them which despitefully use you, and persecute you;

45. That ye may be the children of your Father which is in heaven: for he maketh his sun to rise on the evil and on the good, and sendeth rain on the just and on the unjust.

46. For if ye love them which love you, what reward have ye? do not even the publicans the same?

47. And if ye salute your brethren only, what do ye more than others? do not even the publicans so?

48. Be ye therefore perfect, even as your Father which is in heaven is perfect.

The Lord now turned his attention to the vengeful part of the Law of Moses, wherein so much emphasis had been placed upon the doctrine of "an eye for an eye" that the second great commandment had been practically eliminated. The enjoyment of life and the desire for unbroken prosperity caused the Jews to interpret God's tolerance of their vengeful ancestors to mean that they themselves were justified in seeking by any means an abundance of worldly comforts and continuous success in all their undertakings so as to be triumphant and victorious over their enemies.[45] But under the higher law Jesus enunciated there were no grounds for this self-righteous justification for retaliation. Jesus had placed the second great commandment in its proper position.

The gospel would now require its disciples to suffer persecution without resistance rather than do evil to any man (although they still had the right to self-protection).[46] Love was now to replace fear and the true disciple was to avoid contention.[47] Patience and meekness were to replace retaliation, for righteousness would conquer sin. The Lord followed this command with examples: if a person smites us on the cheek, we should turn to him the other also; if a person sues us at the law and takes our coat, we should give our cloak also.[48] If someone compels us to go a mile, we should go two.[49] The Lord then concluded with the requirement that we should give to him that borrows and not turn away.

After receiving these examples, the disciples could no longer hate their enemies and feel justified. The Lord admonished them to love their enemies, bless those who cursed them, do good to those who hated them, and pray for those who despitefully used and persecuted them. By so doing the disciples would become true children of the Father.

It is true that in Moses' time retaliation was acceptable before God under certain circumstances, but the Pharisees and Sadducees had corrupted the Law and had made hasty retaliation the rule of the day. Individual rights superseded the rights of others, and deliberate revenge was the usual practice rather than compassion. The Jews had forgotten the law of "love thy neighbor" (Leviticus 19:18), and taught that it was a duty to hate the heathen and the Samaritan. Eventually the Pharisees hated the publicans, and the rabbis hated the priests, and the Pharisees and Sadducees hated the common people because they did not know the Law.[50] So pervasive was this doctrine of retaliation that it invaded their personal lives—to the extent that each could have his own private enemies and could hate and injure them with total justification of the Law. This doctrine sharply divided the nation into classes, and excluded all other people as heathens.[51]

The Lord swept away this abrogation of the second great commandment by stating, "For if ye love them which love you, what reward have ye?" The Old Testament often commended kindness and mercy (Exodus 23:4, 5; Psalm 7:5; Proverbs 24:17; 25:21; Job 31:29–30), and it also sanctioned revenge and triumph over the fall of an enemy (Psalm 7:6, 54:7); but the Lord introduced a new era by teaching the concept of universal love without distinction of any kind. He would later elaborate on this principle in the parable of the Good Samaritan, where he taught that we should be a neighbor to all who are in need of help.[52]

The Lord concluded this portion of his discourse with a sweeping commandment: "Be ye therefore perfect, even as your Father which is in heaven is perfect." Jesus was commanding all men to be perfect in doing God's will while on the earth. True, some elements of perfection (for example, the resurrection and glorification of the body) would be left until a later time, but in this life the Lord's disciples were to obey all the commandments. Jesus had outlined the way to perfection, and he expected the disciples to follow it.

Citizenship Requirements for Christ's New Kingdom

At this point in his discourse, Christ's comparisons of the old and the new law strongly criticized the Pharisaic traditions of his day; and his subsequent teachings would carry this criticism much deeper into the ancient Jewish law. In the following four examples he specifically outlined the requirements of citizenship in his "new" kingdom and taught the disciples that the spiritual reasoning for obedience to the Law was more important than the mere temporal observance of it.[53]

Almsgiving

Matthew 6:1–4

1. Take heed that ye do not your alms before men, to be seen of them: otherwise ye have no reward of your Father which is in heaven.

2. Therefore when thou doest thine alms, do not sound a trumpet before thee, as the hypocrites do in the synagogues and in the streets, that they may have glory of men. Verily I say unto you, They have their reward.

3. But when thou doest alms, let not thy left hand know what thy right hand doeth:

4. That thine alms may be in secret: and thy Father which seeth in secret himself shall reward thee openly.

In this section Jesus first noted what almsgiving had become, then he explained what it should be. Alms (or acts of charity toward one's fellowman) were not to be given in order to receive the praises of men; therefore, giving was not automatically meritorious before God. He denounced ostentatious and hypocritical displays of "charity," concluding that if alms were given in this manner, the giver had already received his reward.[54] The test in almsgiving was not the amount given (as the amount was inconsequential in spiritual terms), but the degree of sincerity which prompted the almsgiver. Alms should be given in secret with no thought of reward.

Prayer

Matthew 6:5–13

5. And when thou prayest, thou shalt not be as the hypocrites are: for they love to pray standing in the synagogues and in the corners of the streets, that they may be seen of men. Verily I say unto you, They have their reward.

6. But thou, when thou prayest, enter into thy closet, and when thou hast shut thy door, pray to thy Father which is in secret; and thy Father which seeth in secret shall reward thee openly.

7. But when ye pray, use not vain repetitions, as the heathen do: for they think that they shall be heard for their much speaking.

8. Be not ye therefore like unto them: for your Father knoweth what things ye have need of, before ye ask him.

9. After this manner therefore pray ye: Our Father which art in heaven, Hallowed be thy name.

10. Thy kingdom come. Thy will be done in earth, as it is in heaven.

11. Give us this day our daily bread.

12. And forgive us our debts, as we forgive our debtors.

13. And lead us not into temptation, but deliver us from evil: For thine is the kingdom, and the power, and the glory, for ever. Amen.

Jesus next moved to the topic of prayer. The practice of daily prayer had become formal and mechanical in Judah at Christ's time. The Jews had specifically defined both the hours for praying and the manner in which one prayed. In many instances the Jews used memorized prayers. Many prayed in the streets clothed in their broad phylacteries, while others prayed in the synagogues, making merit out of the duration of their prayers.[55] For Jesus' disciples such hypocritical prayers—often wordy and filled with illustrations and repetitions—were forbidden. If the heart is found wanting, prayer is a mere form and a worthless parade.[56]

In this discourse Jesus provided a pattern of prayer for his disciples and the world which has come to be known as the Lord's Prayer. Through it he instructed us how to pray and what to pray for. We commence our prayers by addressing the Father, thus subjecting our will to his.

The Lord recognized our need for daily sustenance, so he instructed us to pray for it—as Amulek put it, to pray over our flocks and our fields and all things that we require for our livelihood upon the earth (Alma 34:20-25).

Jesus next directed attention to our need for God's mercy. The Joseph Smith Translation of the Bible expresses that need more clearly in Matthew than does the same passage in the King James Version. It states, "And forgive us our trespasses, as we forgive those who trespass against us." In this statement

Jesus defined two relationships pertaining to sin (trespasses): first, our relationship with our Father in Heaven (wherein he required us to completely rely upon him to gain forgiveness of our transgressions); and second, our relationship with our fellowman (defined later in the Lord's parable of the unmerciful servant).[57] The Lord clearly taught us in his sample prayer that our being forgiven was dependent upon the forgiveness we extended to our fellowman.

In Matthew it states that we should not be led into temptation, but the Joseph Smith Translation clarifies this even further by stating, "and suffer us not to be led into temptation," again emphasizing our reliance upon the Father to deliver us from all evil (for God would never lead us into temptation). Paul taught this reliance when he declared, "There hath no temptation taken you but such as is common to man: but God is faithful, who will not suffer you to be tempted above that ye are able; but will with the temptation also make a way to escape, that ye may be able to bear it." (1 Corinthians 10:13.)

The Lord closed his sample prayer by glorifying the Father forever; we in turn are admonished to do all things in the name of Jesus Christ (Moses 5:8), and thus we close our prayers in this manner. Then the Lord again reiterated the importance of forgiving our fellowmen their trespasses if we expect God to forgive us: "For if ye forgive men their trespasses, your heavenly Father will also forgive you: But if ye forgive not men their trespasses, neither will your Father forgive your trespasses" (Matthew 6:14–15).

Although the Lord provided a form and a model to teach us how we can express our thoughts to our Father in Heaven, the teaching emphasis was not on the form, but rather on the underlying purpose of prayer. We should not use prayer as a means for acquiring the praise of other men. The Lord gave it to us as a method of opening our hearts to God and receiving wisdom and help from him. Again Christ stressed the spirit rather than the outward observance of the Law.

Fasting

Matthew 6:16-18

16. Moreover when ye fast, be not, as the hypocrites, of a sad countenance: for they disfigure their faces, that they may appear unto men to fast. Verily I say unto you, They have their reward.

17. But thou, when thou fastest, anoint thine head, and wash thy face;

18. That thou appear not unto men to fast, but unto thy Father which is in secret: and thy Father, which seeth in secret, shall reward thee openly.

Moses commanded the people to fast only on the Day of Atonement[58] (Leviticus 16:29), but the Pharisees had added many other days; "when fasting, they strewed their heads with ashes, and neither washed nor anointed themselves nor trimmed their beards, but put on wretched clothing, and showed themselves in all the outward signs of mourning and sadness used for the dead."[59] In this manner they sought the applause and recognition of others and also the credit or gain they supposed would come to them as a result of their outward showing of godliness, but all such pretense was abhorrent to Jesus.

Fasting, as the Lord taught, was not to be a public virtue but a private self-denial—anything else was hypocrisy.

Worldly Wealth and Needs

Matthew 6:19-34

19. Lay not up for yourselves treasures upon earth, where moth and rust doth corrupt, and where thieves break through and steal:

20. But lay up for yourselves treasures in heaven, where neither moth nor rust doth corrupt, and where thieves do not break through nor steal:

21. For where your treasure is, there will your heart be also.

22. The light of the body is the eye: if therefore thine eye be single, thy whole body shall be full of light.

23. But if thine eye be evil, thy whole body shall be full of darkness. If therefore the light that is in thee be darkness, how great is that darkness!

24. No man can serve two masters: for either he will hate the one, and love the other; or else he will hold to the one, and despise the other. Ye cannot serve God and mammon.

25. Therefore I say unto you, Take no thought for your life, what ye shall eat, or what ye shall drink; nor yet for your body, what ye shall put on. Is not the life more than meat, and the body than raiment?

26. Behold the fowls of the air: for they sow not, neither do they reap, nor gather into barns; yet your heavenly Father feedeth them. Are ye not much better than they?

27. Which of you by taking thought can add one cubit unto his stature?

28. And why take ye thought for raiment? Consider the lilies of the field,

how they grow; they toil not, neither do they spin:

29. And yet I say unto you, That even Solomon in all his glory was not arrayed like one of these.

30. Wherefore, if God so clothe the grass of the field, which to day is, and to morrow is cast into the oven, shall he not much more clothe you, O ye of little faith?

31. Therefore take no thought, saying, What shall we eat? or, What shall we drink? or, Wherewithal shall we be clothed?

32. (For after all these things do the Gentiles seek:) for your heavenly Father knoweth that ye have need of all these things.

33. But seek ye first the kingdom of God, and his righteousness; and all these things shall be added unto you.

34. Take therefore no thought for the morrow: for the morrow shall take thought for the things of itself. Sufficient unto the day is the evil thereof.

Although Jesus had already contrasted the riches of the world with spiritual wealth, he concluded this portion of his discourse by emphasizing the transitory nature of worldly wealth when compared with the riches of eternity.[60] He stated that we cannot serve two masters at the same time, and that where our desires are, there will our true treasure be. The things of the world must be subservient to the things of heaven.

Jesus declared that God knows our needs. He illustrated this by citing examples of the fowls of the heaven and the lilies of the field, proclaiming that all of Solomon's glory was not comparable to these. The Lord stated that man should take no thought for the needs of this earth life; the disciples responded by murmuring among themselves, as this was a very difficult law for them to obey. They tried to excuse their disobedience of it because they sincerely felt they needed worldly things (see JST Matthew 6:36). Jesus acknowledged this need but stated that his Father in Heaven already knew the things they required.

The Joseph Smith Translation of the Bible states, "Wherefore, seek not the things of this world but seek ye first to build up the kingdom of God, and to establish his righteousness, and all these things shall be added unto you" (JST Matthew 6:38).

As the Lord's discourse drew to a conclusion, he again gave the disciples and the multitude a list of instructions and warnings regarding their duty toward their fellowman. He began with instructions on how to judge.

Judgment

Matthew 7:1–5

1. Judge not, that ye be not judged.

2. For with what judgment ye judge, ye shall be judged: and with what measure ye mete, it shall be measured to you again.

3. And why beholdest thou the mote that is in thy brother's eye, but considerest not the beam that is in thine own eye?

4. Or how wilt thou say to thy brother, Let me pull out the mote out of thine eye; and, behold, a beam is in thine own eye?

5. Thou hypocrite, first cast out the beam out of thine own eye; and then shalt thou see clearly to cast out the mote out of thy brother's eye.

This subject is recorded in verses 1 through 9 of the Joseph Smith Translation of Matthew 7, and it differs significantly from the same passage in the King James Version. The latter records that we should not judge, lest we be judged, while the Joseph Smith Translation declares that we should not judge "unrighteously," but "judge righteous judgment." With this in mind, the example of the mote and beam that Jesus gave takes on more meaning, for he gave it as a warning for us to take note of our own spiritual condition when we feel inclined to judge others.

After giving this example, Jesus specifically instructed the disciples to admonish the Jewish leadership (i.e., the Pharisees, priests, Levites, and scribes) that "they teach in their synagogues, but do not observe the law, nor the commandments; and all have gone out of the way, and are under sin" (JST Matthew 7:6). Jesus specifically instructed the disciples to call these leaders to repentance, declaring that the kingdom of heaven had come unto them.

This counsel is also applicable in our day. Judgment often takes place—and the Lord's admonition remains in effect. We should judge cautiously, for the Lord highly disapproved of prejudiced or unsupported judgments. If we apply this counsel to the Lord's admonitions on charity and mercy, we can conclude that if we make errors of judgment, we should make them on the side of mercy. The Lord clearly warned the disciples (and all who heard his voice) that their own house must be in order before they could judge the house of another.

What to Teach

Matthew 7:6–8

6. Give not that which is holy unto the dogs, neither cast ye your pearls before swine, lest they trample them under their feet, and turn again and rend you.

7. Ask, and it shall be given you; seek, and ye shall find; knock, and it shall be opened unto you:

8. For every one that asketh receiveth; and he that seeketh findeth; and to him

that knocketh it shall be
opened.

After discussing how his disciples should call the chosen people to repentance (particularly their leadership) the Lord informed them which doctrines of the kingdom they should teach. He did not outline a specific program of instruction, but he did warn them not to teach the "mysteries" of the kingdom. The Apostles were yet young in the ministry and the Lord cautioned them that "the world [could not] receive that which [they themselves were] not able to bear." If they taught these "mysteries," it would be like casting pearls before swine, which would only cause problems for the new kingdom. If they taught doctrines without understanding, the Lord warned them that those they were teaching would "turn again and rend [them]." Jesus wanted those who heard his doctrine to verify its truthfulness by asking God. By so doing, he promised them, they would discover that the kingdom of God had in fact already come to them.

Acceptance of the Kingdom

Matthew 7:9-14

9. Or what man is there of you, whom if his son ask bread, will he give him a stone?

10. Or if he ask a fish, will he give him a serpent?

11. If ye then, being evil, know how to give good gifts unto your children, how much more shall your Father which is in heaven give good things to them that ask him?

12. Therefore all things whatsoever ye would that men should do to you, do ye even so to them: for this is the law and the prophets.

13. Enter ye in at the strait gate: for wide is the gate, and broad is the way, that leadeth to destruction, and many there be which go in thereat:

14. Because strait is the gate, and narrow is the way, which leadeth unto life, and few there be that find it.

The disciples asked Christ to help them prepare to answer

the questions they expected to receive from the Jewish leadership as they went forth to teach them his doctrine. "They will say unto us," the disciples explained, "We ourselves are righteous, and need not that any man should teach us. . . . We have the law for our salvation, and that is sufficient for us." (JST Matthew 7:14–15.) Jesus taught his disciples to handle comments like this by citing various examples, such as:

"What man among you, having a son, and he shall be standing out, and shall say, Father, open thy house that I may come in and sup with thee, will not say, Come in, my son; for mine is thine, and thine is mine?

"Or what man is there among you, who, if his son ask bread, will give him a stone?

"Or if he ask a fish, will he give him a serpent?" (JST Matthew 7:17–19.)

The Lord was pointing out that the Jews knew how to be good to one another when there was a need. Accordingly, he queried if their Father in Heaven would not fulfill their spiritual needs as they fulfilled the earthly requests of their children.

The Savior concluded this part of his sermon with the admonition known as the Golden Rule, wherein he commanded all men to treat one another as they would be treated. The Father wants all of his children to enter the gate that leads to his kingdom. The way is narrow and strait and requires belief and repentance; whereas the wide, broad way (which is easier and requires no repentance or belief) leads only to destruction.

False Prophets

Matthew 7:15–23

15. Beware of false prophets, which come to you in sheep's clothing, but inwardly they are ravening wolves.

16. Ye shall know them by their fruits. Do men gather grapes of thorns, or figs of thistles?

17. Even so every good tree bringeth forth good fruit; but a corrupt tree bringeth forth evil fruit.

18. A good tree cannot bring forth evil fruit, neither can a corrupt tree bring forth

good fruit.

19. Every tree that bringeth not forth good fruit is hewn down, and cast into the fire.

20. Wherefore by their fruits ye shall know them.

21. Not every one that saith unto me, Lord, Lord, shall enter into the kingdom of heaven; but he that doeth the will of my Father which is in heaven.

22. Many will say to me in that day, Lord, Lord, have we not prophesied in thy name? and in thy name have cast out devils? and in thy name done many wonderful works?

23. And then will I profess unto them, I never knew you: depart from me, ye that work iniquity.

Jesus warned that there would be both false and true prophets (or disciples) preaching the word of God, and from his instructions it appears that it will always be so.[61] Both the false and the good prophets will be known by their works. Many will profess knowledge of the Lord and his kingdom and will claim they are serving him; but on judgment day only good works will be accepted, and those who performed bad (or evil) works, even in the name of Christ, will be cast out.

The teachings of this discourse indicate that to be a true disciple one must accept the gospel (as taught by the Savior), repent of his iniquities, be baptized, receive the Holy Ghost, and, by keeping every standard of the Church, righteously endure to the end.[62]

Conclusion

Matthew 7:24–29

24. Therefore whosoever heareth these sayings of mine, and doeth them, I will liken him unto a wise man, which built his house upon a rock:

25. And the rain descended, and the floods came, and the winds blew, and beat upon that house; and it fell not: for it was founded upon a rock.

26. And every one that heareth these sayings of mine, and doeth them not, shall be likened unto a fool-

ish man, which built his
house upon the sand:

27. And the rain
descended, and the floods
came, and the winds blew,
and beat upon that house;
and it fell: and great was the
fall of it.

28. And it came to pass,
when Jesus had ended these
sayings, the people were
astonished at his doctrine:

29. For he taught them as
one having authority, and
not as the scribes.

The Lord ended his sermon by giving a general admonition
to those who had heard or would hear his instructions. He
stated in simple terms that those who built their houses upon a
rock were those who heard and lived the gospel. They could
withstand the fiery darts of the adversary (or the trials of life
that would come upon them). However, he who heard Christ's
words and did not do them was like the foolish man who built
his house upon the sand, and when adversity and temptation
came, the house (the man) was destroyed.

The scripture now records that the people were astonished
at Christ's doctrine, for he taught them as one having authority
and not as the scribes. But this should not be surprising, since
his teachings were clear and concise, even though the Jews considered him to be unlearned and untrained. His coherent teachings dispelled the cobwebbery of Phariseeism and brought an
end to the verbal trifling and sophistries of the Jews.

His admonitions and teachings dealt with faith, hope, and
charity: they were concerned with the destiny of the soul. There
were no definitions, no explanations, no meticulous scholastic
systems or philosophical theorizing, and no mazes of difficult
and dubious decisions. His precepts touched the human heart
and appealed to the consciousness of the spirit. He spoke as no
other man had spoken. With solemn warning he indicated that
life was a struggle between worldly attractions and spiritual
values.

Although he taught in concepts totally familiar to the people
of his time, his kingdom was in complete contrast to contem-
porary Jewish thought. He taught with perfect understanding
when he expounded that the spirit must match the action of the

Law. Whether the Jews recognized it or not, the kingdom of God had come unto them from one having authority.

New Leadership 3

It had been approximately a year since Jesus was baptized and had entered his public ministry,[1] and his miracles and teachings had already made him famous in the immediate environs of Jerusalem and Galilee. Even in these early stages of his ministry it was quite clear that those of the ruling class (the rabbis, teachers, Pharisees, scribes, and all the learned Jews of his day) deemed themselves better than Jesus and the disciples that followed him. Pride did not allow them to become his disciples; therefore, they excluded themselves from the opportunity of leadership in the Lord's new kingdom. New wine would not be placed into old bottles, nor new cloth into old garments (Matthew 9:16–17).

The "educated" men of Christ's day, prejudiced and perverted in their adaptation and interpretation of the Law of Moses, would not change, so the Lord could not look to these authorities for leadership in his new kingdom.[2] But the time had come for him to select his Apostles: his ministry would be short, and he needed to train some of his disciples in the doctrine he was restoring. These prospective leaders needed the opportunity to teach and become fellow laborers in the work of salvation so that upon Christ's death they could continue in the promulgation of the Church upon the earth.

Some of those whom Christ would select as his Apostles had been occasional companions of Jesus in his early ministry, particularly on festive occasions. Some were with him at the marriage in Cana (John 2:2), some at his first Passover in Jerusalem when he visited the scene of John the Baptist's ministry (John 2:13; 3:22–23), and some stayed with him on his journey through Samaria (John 4:1–27). But as to the exact time and place of their selection, no accurate information is available.[3]

The Call of the Twelve

Luke records that before selecting the Twelve Apostles, the Lord spent the entire night in seclusion and prayer (Luke 6:12). When dawn came, he (having received the counsel of his Father in Heaven) called his disciples to him. From those who had been with him through the early stages of his ministry he chose twelve and, as Luke specifically states, he named them Apostles (Luke 6:13).

These men would now serve with him continually (much like apprentices) to learn their duty from both his public discourses and the private intimacy of his fellowship. In this way they would each gain a testimony of him and would learn what they must do and what they must teach to be witnesses and ambassadors of the Lord Jesus Christ. The training of the Twelve became a prominent part of Christ's ministry.[4] Although these men were not of the learned and authoritative class of Christ's day, they had been disciples prior to being called. They believed in him and, perhaps to some degree, recognized his divine calling as the long-awaited Messiah. It is doubtful, however, that they fully understood the significance of the Savior's work at this early stage.[5] "It is evident by the later remarks of many of them, and by the instructions and rebuke they called forth from the Master, that the common Jewish expectation of a Messiah who would reign in splendor as an earthly sovereign after He had subdued all other nations, had a place even in the hearts of these chosen ones."[6]

All of Christ's Apostles came from common stock, were utterly devoid of social consequence, and might generally be classified as illiterate[7] because of their lack of training in the schools of the day. But to Jesus they were his little ones, his children, his servants, and his friends (Matthew 10:42; John 13:16; 21:5).

The word *apostle* comes from the Greek *Apostolos*, which means "one who is sent." In selecting twelve to be sent to magnify his kingdom before the world, Christ fell back upon the rustic, simple, sincere, and energetic men of Galilee (with the exception of Judas Iscariot, the one Judean). They all needed to learn, but they were receptive souls, imbued with humility and eagerness to serve. Jesus was content with them, and devoutly thanked his Father in Heaven for giving them to him.

The names of the Twelve Apostles appear in four different places in the New Testament. Each of the three Synoptics name them, and the book of Acts (Acts 1:13) enumerates them again— excluding Judas Iscariot, who had committed suicide (Matthew 27:5)—at the ascension of Jesus. There are differences in these accounts, and it is not possible to discern an exact order pertaining to the seniority of the Twelve in the Quorum. It is interesting to note, however, that they always appear in groups of four:

Peter, James, John and Andrew. Peter is always listed as the first and chief Apostle in the Quorum of the Twelve. In Matthew and Luke, Andrew is listed second; in Mark and Acts, James and John take the second and third positions, and Andrew is fourth.

Although the Quorum of the First Presidency of the Church may not have been established as such in the early New Testament days (i.e., as a quorum separate from that of the Twelve Apostles), it is evident that Peter was the President of the Church, and that James and John stood in the positions of first and second counselor, respectively.[8]

The Gospel writers undoubtedly mention Andrew in this first group of four for two reasons: (1) he was the brother of

Peter, and (2) he learned of the Lord before Peter, and it was he who later introduced Peter to him.

Philip, Bartholomew, Thomas, and Matthew. Philip is always listed at the beginning of this group. After him the order varies: Mark and Luke list the order enumerated above, while Matthew and Acts give differing orders.

It is interesting to note that Bartholomew, Thomas, and Matthew are identified with second names in the scriptural text: Bartholomew is also known as Nathanael, Matthew has the second name of Levi, and Thomas is also known as Didymus (signifying a twin).

James, Thaddaeus, Simon, and Judas Iscariot. In this group James, the son of Alpheus (also known in scriptural history as James II, or James the Less), always heads the list, and Judas Iscariot always ends it. Thaddaeus is also known as Lebbaeus and Judas (not Iscariot); and Simon is also known as Zelotes or the Canaanite.

The first group of Apostles is the best known, the second group is next, and the last group is the least known (except for Judas Iscariot). Peter always comes at the head of the Quorum and Judas Iscariot is always at the end.

The prophets of the New World saw these twelve Apostles in a vision of the coming of the Messiah in the flesh. Father Lehi "saw twelve others following him [Jesus], and their brightness did exceed that of the stars in the firmament" (1 Nephi 1:10). Nephi also saw "twelve others following him. And it came to pass that they were carried away in the Spirit from before my face, and I saw them not." (1 Nephi 11:29.)

There is no question that the number twelve was significant and not just a random number selected by the Savior. It symbolically represented the twelve tribes of Israel.[9] Little detail is available on the lives of the Lord's Twelve Apostles, but one can assume that all of them (with the exception of Judas Iscariot) served the Lord faithfully. Without attempting to create a personality for each of these men that does not exist, note the following information:

Peter. Although Peter is the common name by which we know the Lord's senior Apostle, his given name was Simon (2 Peter 1:1). Apparently (because of character traits known by the Lord) Jesus changed his name to Peter, or Cephas in Aramaic (John 1:42, Matthew 16:18). He was the son of Jonah or Jonas and is the first-named Apostle in all three of the Synoptics.

Peter was married (Matthew 8:14) and was a fisherman by trade. He was a partner with James, John, and his brother Andrew. They owned their own boats and employed others to help them in the business (Mark 1:16-20; Luke 5:10). His early home was in Bethsaida on the west shore of Galilee (John 1:44). At some time during the Lord's ministry, however, he moved to Capernaum (Matthew 8:14; Mark 1:29; Luke 4:38).

That Peter was prosperous materially seems evident, for when he mentioned the breadth of the sacrifice he had made to follow the Lord, the Lord did not dispute nor deny his claim.[10] (See Mark 10:28; Luke 18:28.) He was not an ignorant man, but he was unlettered and untrained in the rabbinical schools of his day.[11] Although Peter did not write a Gospel, many believe that Mark received his information from Peter.[12]

Peter was one of the three Apostles present with the Lord on the Mount of Transfiguration (Matthew 17:1), at the raising of the daughter of Jairus (Mark 5:37), and in the Garden of Gethsemane (Matthew 26:37). He spoke for both himself and the Twelve (Matthew 16:13-19) when he confessed Jesus as the long-awaited Messiah.

Peter was impulsive and initially lacked firmness, but even from the beginning he was more than willing to give up his whole soul for the Master. He was usually the first to speak and the first to experiment upon the words of the Lord.[13] Peter boldly taught the gospel after the resurrection of Jesus, and the "reward" for his endeavors was imprisonment (Acts 12:1-19). From his own writings we learn that Peter labored in Babylon (1 Peter 5:13), which is more likely a name Peter used to refer to Rome than the city on the Euphrates. Peter's greatness is affirmed in the book of Acts, where it tells of some Saints who thought so highly of him that they "brought forth the sick into the streets, and laid them on beds and couches, that at the least the shadow of Peter passing by might overshadow some of them" (Acts 5:15).

Although we do not know the exact time and method of his

death, the scriptures appear to prophesy how he would die. The Lord knew of his death (John 21:18–19) and Peter foresaw it also (2 Peter 1:14). It is generally believed that he was crucified, perhaps in Rome along with Paul during the persecutions by the Emperor Nero sometime between A.D. 64 and 68. Tradition has it that even at his death Peter felt unworthy to die in the same manner that the Lord had suffered, so his captors, adhering to his request, crucified him upside down.[14]

As a resurrected being, Peter (along with James and John) appeared to the Prophet Joseph Smith to restore the Melchizedek Priesthood to the earth in the dispensation of the fulness of times (D&C 27:12).

James. This James, the brother of John and the son of Zebedee, is sometimes referred to as James I to distinguish him from the other James in the Quorum. He, his father, and his brother John were fishermen by trade, and were in business with Peter and Andrew. The Lord gave him, along with John, the name *Boanerges*, which means "sons of thunder" (Mark 3:17). These men probably received this name because of their desire to call down fire from heaven upon certain Samaritan villages that had rejected the Lord (Luke 9:54).

Through his mother's petition James aspired (along with John) to the highest honors of the kingdom—namely, to sit by the Lord's side in heaven (Mark 10:35–41; Matthew 20:21)—and along with John and Peter he witnessed certain singular events in the life of Christ (e.g., the Master's raising of the daughter of Jairus [Mark 5:37; Luke 8:51], and the transfiguration of Jesus [Matthew 17:1–2; Luke 9:28–29]). He was near Jesus in the Garden of Gethsemane during the last moments of the Lord's life before his arrest and trial (Matthew 26:36–37), and with Peter and John he restored to earth the Melchizedek Priesthood in 1829.

James was the first apostolic martyr after the death of Jesus. He was beheaded by Herod Agrippa I near the time of the Passover, approximately A.D. 44 (Acts 12:1–2).[15]

John. John was the brother of James and one of the sons of Zebedee. He was a fisherman and was in business with his father, his brother James, and Peter and Andrew. Along with James and Peter, he also witnessed the singular events in Christ's life noted under "James" above. Like James, he aspired to the highest honors of the kingdom through the petition of his mother. The scriptures denote John as "the disciple whom Jesus loved" (John 13:23; 19:26; 20:2), indicating that he had a close, personal relationship with the Lord.

It appears that John was originally a disciple of John the Baptist (John 1:35–42),[16] but when the Baptist testified of the divinity of the Savior, John left him to follow the Messiah.

His "hot zeal" earned him (and his brother) the name *sons of thunder*. This zeal came from his intense loyalty toward Jesus.

John was perhaps the most thoughtful of the disciples. He alone of the Twelve stood at the foot of the cross, and at the request of Jesus took charge of His mother's earthly needs (John 19:25–27). We read that at the Last Supper he leaned upon Jesus' bosom (John 13:23, 25). At the miracle of the second draught of fish,[17] it was John who first recognized the Savior on the shore of Galilee after his resurrection (John 21:7).

Paul refers to his meeting with John in Jerusalem (Galatians 2:9), but he is only mentioned occasionally in Acts (Acts 3:1, 11; 4:13; 8:14). John himself tells of his banishment to Patmos because of his zeal for teaching the gospel (Revelation 1:9).

John, together with James and Peter, participated in restoring the Melchizedek Priesthood to the Prophet Joseph Smith (D&C 27:12), but unlike his two brethren, John was not a resurrected being. On the shores of Galilee he had received a special blessing from the Lord; the Savior charged him to minister to the children of the earth and blessed him that he would remain on earth until the Lord would come the second time (John 21:21–23; D&C 7).

John's unique and intimate Gospel emphasizes the Savior's Judean ministry, whereas the Synoptics stress His journeys in Galilee and Perea. John treats the life of Christ in a singular fashion, noting many events in the Savior's ministry that are not recorded by any of the other Gospel writers.

In addition to his Gospel, John wrote the book of Revelation—his vision from the Lord while exiled on the isle of Patmos. He also wrote First, Second, and Third John as general epistles to the Church.

Andrew. Andrew **was** the brother of Peter and the son of

Jonah. He is mentioned less frequently than Peter, James, or John. He also followed John the Baptist initially, but after receiving a testimony of the divinity of Jesus, he testified to his brother, Peter, that the Messiah had come (John 1:35–42). He shared in Peter's call to the ministry (Matthew 4:18–19) and was involved in one of the private interviews Jesus had with Peter, James, and John (Mark 13:3). John mentions Andrew in conjunction with the miracle of feeding the five thousand (John 6:8), and we also read that Philip asked Andrew, on behalf of some Greek converts to Judaism, to arrange a private interview with Jesus (John 12:20–22).

During the last discourse the Lord delivered, Andrew asked a question concerning the end of the world (Mark 13:3–4; Matthew 24). While there are no other authentic records of his life or death,[18] tradition has it that Andrew was widely traveled and spread the Gospel among the Scythians in what is modern-day Russia. Tradition states he was put to death upon a cross in Achaia.[19]

Philip. John 1:43–45 notes that Jesus was the one who found Philip, and Philip may have been the first to receive the call to "follow me."[20] Philip's original home was in Bethsaida. He was mentioned in the feeding of the five thousand (John 6:5–7), and it was Philip to whom some Greek converts to Judaism applied for a personal interview with Jesus (John 12:20–22). The Savior reproved him mildly for asking to see the Father (John 14:8–9), and he was present with the eleven Apostles at Jesus' ascension. Nothing else is recorded of his ministry.

Tradition has it that he was a chariot driver by profession,[21] and that he was an earnest inquirer after the truth—thoroughly acquainted with the scriptures and the Messianic promise.[22]

Philip is credited with seeking out Nathanael (Bartholomew) to inform him that the Messiah had come, and it is reported that he died in Hierapolis.[23]

Bartholomew/Nathanael. The name *Bartholomew* means "son of Tolmai,"[24] but he was called Bartholomew only at his ordination and at the Ascension. In John's Gospel he is referred to as Nathanael, the one in whom Jesus found "no guile" (John 1:45–51). Because of this comment by the Lord it is evident that he was a man of great moral strength. When Philip told him about the Lord, his comment was, "Can there any good thing come out of Nazareth?" (John 1:46). He was undoubtedly referring to the fact that generally the leaders of the Jews and the Judeans of his day despised the Galileans (including himself), considering them to be poor and ignorant. In response to his question Philip merely told Nathanael to "come and see" (John 1:46).

The reason for assuming that Bartholomew and Nathanael are the same person is that each of the three synoptic Gospels refers to Bartholomew as an Apostle, but not Nathanael; whereas the book of John names Nathanael twice as an Apostle, and makes no such reference to Bartholomew at all. In addition, the Synoptics record Bartholomew and Philip together, while in John's writings Nathanael and Philip appear together—thus the assumption that the two names describe the same man.[25]

There is no other authentic scriptural record of this Apostle's work. He is traditionally thought to have been a shepherd or a gardener.[26]

Thomas/Didymus. Didymus is the Greek equivalent of the Hebrew name for Thomas, which means "a twin."[27] From the references we have of him, it is apparent that he was a warm-hearted but melancholy individual who was ready to die for the Lord but slow to believe in his resurrection.

Thomas was ready to risk his life for the Lord when Jesus returned to Jerusalem at the request of Lazarus's sisters (John 11:16); however, as much as we would like to remember him for this loyalty and bravery, his name is usually associated with doubting—"doubting Thomas." Prone to taking somber views of things, he questioned the Lord on the eve of his crucifixion: "Lord, we know not whither thou goest; and how can we know the way?" (John 14:5). Apparently he did not know "the way," and could not believe that any of the others did either. His statement was somewhat like an apology for his ignorance; however, Jesus' response was compassionate and sympathetic: "I am the way, the truth, and the life: no man cometh unto the Father, but by me" (John 14:6).

After his resurrection the Savior appeared to the Apostles in the upper room and Thomas was not there. The scriptures give no reason for his absence. When they met together again, the other ten Apostles testified of Christ's resurrection, but Thomas was not satisfied with their testimony. It was not that he was unwilling to believe, but that he could not believe. When Jesus again appeared to the Apostles, Thomas was with them. Jesus requested that the doubting Apostle touch him so that he might believe. Thomas's doubt being satisfied, he joyfully exclaimed, "My Lord and my God."

The Lord drew an important lesson from Thomas's practical attitude when he said, "Thomas, because thou hast seen me, thou hast believed: blessed are they that have not seen, and yet have believed" (John 20:29).

Tradition has it that Thomas was killed by being run through with a lance in Persia or India.[28]

Matthew/Levi. Matthew is the son of Alpheus and one of the seven original Apostles to receive a preliminary call before his ordination to the Quorum of the Twelve. He is the author of the first Gospel in the New Testament. His second name would indicate that he was of the priestly lineage of the tribe of Levi.[29]

When Matthew received his call he gave a feast in honor of the Lord. The Pharisees publicly criticized Jesus for this (Matthew 9:9–13; Mark 2:13–17; Luke 5:27–32). The criticism came as a result of Matthew's occupation: he was a publican (or tax collector). His home was in Capernaum and he undoubtedly knew of Jesus before his call because of the many mighty works that Jesus had performed in that area.

The call of Matthew to the Twelve was probably a disconcerting event in the public view of Jesus' ministry because of Matthew's hated profession. His call would have been an additional aggravation to the Jewish leaders, but it also exemplified the Lord's total disregard of worldly opinions and his high regard for spiritual preparedness.[30]

The scriptures make no mention of Matthew's ministry; however, other secular writers indicate that his was one of the most active ministries of all the Apostles after the death of Jesus.[31]

James (James II). There appear to be three individuals named James associated with Jesus in the New Testament. The first is James I, the son of Zebedee and the brother of John. All references to this James seem to be explicit and easily identified. The second is James II, the son of Alpheus Clopas.[32] The third James is the Lord's brother (Matthew 13:55; Mark 6:3; Galatians 1:19).

Tradition has James II being younger and smaller than James, the brother of John, and it is believed that he died by being thrown down from the temple and stoned (his head being beaten with a fuller's club).[33]

Judas/Lebbaeus/Thaddaeus. This Apostle is commonly referred to as the "three-named Apostle," for obvious reasons. Matthew refers to him as Lebbaeus and Thaddaeus, Mark as Thaddaeus, and Luke as "Judas, the brother of James." The only other scriptural reference to this Apostle is in John, wherein he asked a question of the Lord during his last discourses to the Twelve before his crucifixion (John 14:22). John specifically notes that the question was by Judas, "not Iscariot." No other information is available on this Apostle.

Simon Zelotes. This is another call to the Twelve that indicates Christ's total disregard for public opinion. The name of "Zelotes" (Acts 1:13; Luke 6:15) identifies Simon with a rebellious political group led by Judas the Zealot in the days of taxation (Acts 5:37). The group was in existence twenty years before Christ's ministry began. Matthew and Mark also designate Simon as a Canaanite, but this had no reference to lineage or geographical origin. "Canaanite" is the Syro-Chaldaic equivalent of the Greek, which in English means "Zelotes."[34]

The people who belonged to this political group had an enormous zeal for the maintenance of the Mosaic ritual.[35] They were a political party of malcontents who believed in the physical restoration of the Messianic kingdom and Jewish national supremacy.[36] They used swords and daggers, while Jesus taught with the omnipotent weapon of truth.

What caused Simon Zelotes to leave the camp of Judas the Zealot in favor of Jesus is not known. He would have had to make a radical change in his political and spiritual feelings before he could have become one of the Lord's Apostles. There is no mention of him apart from his association with the Twelve, and he is as obscure as Peter is celebrated. He and Matthew were disciples of extremes. Simon had been a tax-hater and

Matthew a tax-gatherer. Simon would have been extremely patri-
otic and would have chafed under the yoke of Rome, longing
only for emancipation; Matthew would have been described as
a most unpatriotic Jew who had degraded himself by becoming
a servant to an alien ruler.

Judas Iscariot. All of the Apostles were from the province
of Galilee except Judas Iscariot. He was the only Judean among
the Twelve. His father's name was Simon (John 6:71; 13:26),
and it is believed that the family was from the town of Kerioth
in the southern borders of Judah.[37] If these facts are accurate,
Judas may have become a disciple of Jesus on one of the Lord's
early visits to Jordan (John 3:22).

Judas was the treasurer for Jesus and the Twelve, both receiving and disbursing their common funds. John records that he
was unprincipled and dishonest in this trust (John 12:6). Although
he apparently embezzled from the funds, he had undoubtedly
been entrusted with the job because he was capable of doing it.
One should not assume that he had been selected as treasurer
merely to provide the Savior with a traitor.

Perhaps Judas was initially drawn to Jesus because he believed
in him as "the Jewish Messiah" and anticipated that He would
triumph as such.[38] Yet at times he had a turning of the soul,
which is exemplified in his complaints (such as that concerning
the waste of the rich oil Mary used to anoint the feet of Jesus
before his crucifixion [John 12:1-7]). The small rebuff the Lord
issued at that time seemed to only further canker his soul. When
the Lord corrected the other Apostles in this manner, the result
was positive, but with Judas it was different. It appears that he
felt Jesus could see through him and that the Lord did not think
well of his spirit and his evil habits.

Although he was avaricious and covetous, it seems that his
betrayal of the Lord for thirty pieces of silver involved more
than a mere bargaining for money, that his deep alienation from
Christ had turned love to hate, and that he was being con-
sumed with vindictive passions. The manner of the betrayal
indicated not just a covetous man, but one that was malicious
and vengeful; not only did he betray the location of Jesus for a
price, but he personally conducted the band that would arrest
the Savior and he singled him out with an affectionate saluta-

tion (Matthew 26:49). John indicates that Satan had taken hold of Judas (John 13:2, 27). Finally, having bound himself to the devil and having betrayed the Savior of the world, Judas took his own life and was ultimately classified as a son of perdition[39] (Matthew 27:5; Acts 1:18; John 17:12).

What a melancholy end was that of Judas to an auspicious beginning! Chosen to be a companion of the Son of Man, and an eye and ear witness of His work, once engaged in preaching the gospel and casting out devils; now possessed of the devil himself, driven on by him to damnable deeds, and finally employed by a righteous Providence to take vengeance on his own crime. In view of this history, how shallow the theory that resolves all moral differences between men into the effect of circumstances! Who was ever better circumstanced for becoming good than Judas? Yet the very influences which ought to have fostered goodness served only to provoke into activity latent evil.[40]

A Charge to the Twelve

Matthew 10:1–42

1. And when he had called unto him his twelve disciples, he gave them power against unclean spirits, to cast them out, and to heal all manner of sickness and all manner of disease.

2. Now the names of the twelve apostles are these; The first, Simon, who is called Peter, and Andrew his brother; James the son of Zebedee, and John his brother;

3. Philip, and Bartholomew; Thomas, and Matthew the publican; James the son of Alphaeus, and Lebbaeus, whose surname was Thaddaeus;

4. Simon the Canaanite, and Judas Iscariot, who also betrayed him.

5. These twelve Jesus sent forth, and commanded them, saying, Go not into the way of the Gentiles, and into any city of the Samaritans enter ye not:

6. But go rather to the lost sheep of the house of Israel.

7. And as ye go, preach, saying, The kingdom of heaven is at hand.

8. Heal the sick, cleanse the lepers, raise the dead, cast out devils: freely ye have received, freely give.

9. Provide neither gold, nor silver, nor brass in your purses,

10. Nor scrip for your journey, neither two coats, neither shoes, nor yet staves: for the workman is worthy of his meat.

11. And into whatsoever city or town ye shall enter, inquire who in it is worthy; and there abide till ye go thence.

12. And when ye come into an house, salute it.

13. And if the house be worthy, let your peace come upon it: but if it be not worthy, let your peace return to you.

14. And whosoever shall not receive you, nor hear your words, when ye depart out of that house or city, shake off the dust of your feet.

15. Verily I say unto you, It shall be more tolerable for the land of Sodom and Gomorrah in the day of judgment, than for that city.

16. Behold, I send you forth as sheep in the midst of wolves: be ye therefore wise as serpents, and harmless as doves.

17. But beware of men: for they will deliver you up to the councils, and they will scourge you in their synagogues;

18. And ye shall be brought before governors and kings for my sake, for a testimony against them and the Gentiles.

19. But when they deliver you up, take no thought how or what ye shall speak: for it shall be given you in that same hour what ye shall speak.

20. For it is not ye that speak, but the Spirit of your Father which speaketh in you.

21. And the brother shall deliver up the brother to death, and the father the child: and the children shall rise up against their parents, and cause them to be put to death.

22. And ye shall be hated of all men for my name's sake: but he that endureth to the end shall be saved.

23. But when they persecute you in this city, flee ye into another: for verily I say unto you, Ye shall not have

gone over the cities of Israel, till the Son of man be come.

24. The disciple is not above his master, nor the servant above his lord.

25. It is enough for the disciple that he be as his master, and the servant as his lord. If they have called the master of the house Beelzebub, how much more shall they call them of his household?

26. Fear them not therefore: for there is nothing covered, that shall not be revealed; and hid, that shall not be known.

27. What I tell you in darkness, that speak ye in light: and what ye hear in the ear, that preach ye upon the housetops.

28. And fear not them which kill the body, but are not able to kill the soul: but rather fear him which is able to destroy both soul and body in hell.

29. Are not two sparrows sold for a farthing? and one of them shall not fall on the ground without your Father.

30. But the very hairs of your head are all numbered.

31. Fear ye not therefore, ye are of more value than many sparrows.

32. Whosoever therefore shall confess me before men, him will I confess also before my Father which is in heaven.

33. But whosoever shall deny me before men, him will I also deny before my Father which is in heaven.

34. Think not that I am come to send peace on earth: I came not to send peace, but a sword.

35. For I am come to set a man at variance against his father, and daughter against her mother, and the daughter in law against her mother in law.

36. And a man's foes shall be they of his own household.

37. He that loveth father or mother more than me is not worthy of me: and he that loveth son or daughter more than me is not worthy of me.

38. And he that taketh not his cross, and followeth after me, is not worthy of me.

39. He that findeth his life shall lose it: and he that loseth his life for my sake shall find it.

40. He that receiveth you receiveth me, and he that receiveth me receiveth him that sent me.

41. He that receiveth a prophet in the name of a prophet shall receive a prophet's reward; and he that receiveth a righteous man in the name of a righteous man shall receive a righteous man's reward.

42. And whosoever shall give to drink unto one of these little ones a cup of cold water only in the name of a disciple, verily I say unto you, he shall in no wise lose his reward.

Cross-references

Mark 3:13–19; 6:7–13;
Luke 6:12–16; 9:1–6; 12:1–12, 22–35

Having been chosen and ordained, the Twelve were now ready to become active proselyting agents in the new kingdom that Christ had established, and he prepared to send them forth to proselyte in the towns and villages of Galilee. It was to be their first mission without the Lord, and it would be a great learning experience for them. Jesus gave a discourse on this occasion that covered the following topics:

1. *Sphere of the work.* At a future time Jesus would command the Twelve to go into all the world (Matthew 28:19), but for the present they were instructed to go only to Israel, the Lord's "lost sheep." He further restricted them to their native province of Galilee. He specifically forbade them to go to the Gentiles and the Samaritans, as "their hearts were too narrow, their prejudices too strong: there was too much of the Jew, too little of the Christian, in their character."[41]

The duration of their mission is unknown, but it is unlikely that it was for any extensive period of time.[42]

2. *Nature of the work.* The Savior specifically instructed the Apostles that they should preach repentance unto the people and teach that the kingdom of God was at hand. Perhaps he restricted them so narrowly because they had such limited knowledge at the time. The Lord had given them the priesthood so they might perform miracles, and they were instructed to freely use this gift on their missions.

The Lord specifically instructed them to be cautious of men.

He knew that the ways of the Jews were such that the Apostles would have nothing to look forward to but persecution. They would be testified against, dragged before the Jewish councils and scourged in their synagogues. The work that they were to embark upon and the gospel that they were to preach would bring peace to the individual, but would divide brother against brother, father against child, and children against parents. Yet in his instructions, Jesus clearly indicated that they could win over the hearts of men through their unselfish devotion and the truth that they would teach.[43]

3. *Personal needs and comforts.* It is clear from the Lord's instructions that the Apostles were to carry neither purse nor scrip.[44] They were not to indulge in empty courtesies, but were to pay strict attention to their mission by teaching those who would receive them and casting the dust from their feet on the household or town of those who would not.[45] He intended them to sacrifice all their personal desires to follow him even though he offered no earthly reward. Their basic equipment was simple: they were to go in essentially the clothing they had on and they were not to take extra coats, shoes, or staves, to assist them in their travels. He told them, "Are not five sparrows sold for two farthings, and not one of them is forgotten before God?" Obviously the Apostles were more important than sparrows. He also comforted them by explaining that even the hairs on their heads were numbered to the Father.

Perhaps the Lord required this austerity to emphasize the fact that there could be no diversions from the mission upon which they were embarking. They had no prospects except privation, persecution, and possible martyrdom; but he told them to walk in faith, relying upon God, and he promised them that the very words which they should speak would be given to them in the hour that they were needed. They were to be fearless, yet not foolhardy; wise as serpents, but harmless as doves.[46]

It is evident that the Lord intended his Apostles to eventually abandon their formal callings and vocations and even forsake family ties for the gospel, if necessary. Through his instructions they would learn to curb their reactions to persecution and suppress even justified resentment in order to completely mold their lives to his service. They could look for a reward in heaven, but they would not find one on this earth; in this world they would be "hated of all men, for my [Christ's] name's sake." Yet even with this bleak prospect presented to them, the Apostles knew that their only fear lay in him who could destroy their souls; but the Lord assured them that his eye would be continually upon them.

4. *Results.* It would appear that Jesus chose the Twelve to go on a mission at this particular time because of the great success he had already enjoyed in his own ministry. They must have gone forth with enthusiasm for they returned with joy, noting that many multitudes had followed them. Their success was obviously considerable, but it may have been related more to their miracles than to their message. The Savior returned to Capernaum to receive the Twelve from their missions at about the same time that the news reached him of the death of John the Baptist.[47] Perhaps John's death is why the Lord cautioned the Apostles at that time not to be overly elated with their success, but their missions must have brought great joy to the Savior, in any event.

Although the Twelve were young in their callings and would yet stay with Jesus throughout his ministry, receiving much instruction from him, it was time for them to "take up their cross." They had to be willing to do whatever was necessary to promulgate the kingdom of God upon the earth. Whether they completely understood what "taking up their cross" meant at this time is not indicated, but the analogy would certainly have both impressed and terrified them;[48] as a result of this command they would "shoulder any grievous burdens placed upon their shoulders because of the cause of righteousness." [49]

The Seventy

Luke 10:1–24

1. After these things the Lord appointed other seventy also, and sent them two and two before his face into every city and place, whither he himself would come.

2. Therefore said he unto them, The harvest truly is

great, but the labourers are few: pray ye therefore the Lord of the harvest, that he would send forth labourers into his harvest.

3. Go your ways: behold, I send you forth as lambs among wolves.

4. Carry neither purse, nor scrip, nor shoes: and salute no man by the way.

5. And into whatsoever house ye enter, first say, Peace be to this house.

6. And if the son of peace be there, your peace shall rest upon it: if not, it shall turn to you again.

7. And in the same house remain, eating and drinking such things as they give: for the labourer is worthy of his hire. Go not from house to house.

8. And into whatsoever city ye enter, and they receive you, eat such things as are set before you:

9. And heal the sick that are therein, and say unto them, The kingdom of God is come nigh unto you.

10. But into whatsoever city ye enter, and they receive you not, go your ways out into the streets of the same, and say,

11. Even the very dust of your city, which cleaveth on us, we do wipe off against you: notwithstanding be ye sure of this, that the kingdom of God is come nigh unto you.

12. But I say unto you, that it shall be more tolerable in that day for Sodom, than for that city.

13. Woe unto thee, Chorazin! woe unto thee, Bethsaida! for if the mighty works had been done in Tyre and Sidon, which have been done in you, they had a great while ago repented, sitting in sackcloth and ashes.

14. But it shall be more tolerable for Tyre and Sidon at the judgment, than for you.

15. And thou, Capernaum, which art exalted to heaven, shalt be thrust down to hell.

16. He that heareth you heareth me; and he that despiseth you despiseth me; and he that despiseth me despiseth him that sent me.

17. And the seventy returned again with joy, saying, Lord, even the devils are subject unto us through thy name.

18. And he said unto them, I beheld Satan as lightning fall from heaven.

19. Behold, I give unto

you power to tread on serpents and scorpions, and over
all the power of the enemy:
and nothing shall by any
means hurt you.

20. Notwithstanding in
this rejoice not, that the spirits are subject unto you; but
rather rejoice, because your
names are written in heaven.

21. In that hour Jesus
rejoiced in spirit, and said, I
thank thee, O Father, Lord of
heaven and earth, that thou
hast hid these things from the
wise and prudent, and hast
revealed them unto babes:
even so, Father; for so it
seemed good in thy sight.

22. All things are deliv-
ered to me of my Father: and
no man knoweth who the
Son is, but the Father; and
who the Father is, but the
Son, and he to whom the
Son will reveal him.

23. And he turned him
unto his disciples, and said
privately, Blessed are the eyes
which see the things that ye
see:

24. For I tell you, that
many prophets and kings
have desired to see those
things which ye see, and have
not seen them; and to hear
those things which ye hear,
and have not heard them.

Luke is the only Gospel writer to record anything about the
mission of the seventy. He begins his record by stating that the
Lord appointed "other seventy also." There is no other record
of the call of the seventy into the mission field.[50]

Just as the number twelve signified the twelve tribes of Israel,
so too the number seventy had significance in the call of these
special witnesses to the Lord's divinity. For example:

A. When the children of Israel were in the wilderness they
refused (as a body) to enter into the presence of the Lord. Moses
selected seventy "of the elders of Israel" along with Aaron,
Nadab, and Abihu, and took them to see the God Jehovah so
that they could be special witnesses to the Israelites (Exodus
24:1–11).

B. Seventy elders of the children of Israel were to assist
Moses in judging the people (Numbers 11:16), and the Lord
empowered them with special prophetic gifts so that they could
receive the mysteries of their judgment through revelation. (Numbers 11:17).

C. The Jewish Sanhedrin (the religious authority of the time) was made up of seventy of the elders of Israel. (There were, in fact, seventy-two members in the Sanhedrin, but the other two members were the president and vice-president.)

D. The scriptural record that Israel used at the time of Christ was known by the title LXX, or seventy.[51]

E. The number seventy was also significant of the priesthood calling of the seventy (missionary work) throughout the kingdom of God upon the earth, and the Jewish leaders could not fail to recognize this. Israel also used this number to represent the world's Gentile nations; for this reason seventy oxen were sacrificed each year during the Feast of Tabernacles.[52]

Whereas Jesus had specifically restrained the Twelve from going to the gentile nations and to the Samaritans, he placed no such limitation upon the seventy. The time had come for the gospel to be spread throughout the world. Jewish exclusiveness in hearing the gospel, as set forth in Christ's instructions to the Twelve, was forever surrendered in his instructions to the seventy.

Like John the Baptist, the seventy heralded the coming of Jesus and prepared the way before him; but unlike John, they served at the end of the Lord's mission, not at the beginning. Many of the instructions the Lord gave the seventy were similar to those he had given to the Twelve, but he also gave the seventy the following directives:

"Salute no man by the way." In other words, do not take time to visit with old acquaintances, for doing so would take precious time away from their work and the Lord had much to accomplish in the short span of his ministry.

If the head of a house saluted them, they were to pause, eat, drink, and abide in that house without seeking better accommodations.

Jesus also pronounced "woes" upon various cities that had rejected his mighty works: the severity of the "woe" seemed to be in direct proportion to the amount of mighty works rejected.

The seventy returned to Jesus after completing their missions and they were filled with joy. They noted that even the devils were subject to them through the name of Jesus Christ. The Lord also had great joy, and hailed the success of the seventy as the downfall of the kingdom of Satan (perhaps referring to the specific defeat of Satan by Michael and the heavenly hosts rather than the general defeat that would occur at the end of the world).[53]

Just as the call of the seventy (and their mission) in the new Testament was a significant event in the ministry of the Savior, so, too, the call of the first seventy in the latter days was a significant event in the development of The Church of Jesus Christ of Latter-day Saints.

The first specific instructions pertaining to the call of seventy in the latter days occurred on February 8, 1835. Joseph Smith had called Brigham Young and Joseph Young to his home in Kirtland, Ohio. After referring to the call of the Twelve Apostles, he noted to Joseph Young that the Lord had made him "president of the seventies." Later that month the Prophet established and ordained both the First and Second Quorums of the Seventy in the latter days.[54]

From the limited record in Luke's Gospel and the establishment of the seventy in the latter days, it is apparent that those who fill this calling are truly special witnesses to the divinity of Jesus Christ.

> They are required to be special witnesses of the Lord Jesus Christ. It is expected of this body of men that they will have burning in their souls the testimony of Jesus Christ, which is the spirit of prophecy; that they will be full of light and of the knowledge of the truth; that they will be enthusiastic in their calling, and in the cause of Zion, and that they will be ready at any moment, when required, to go out into the world, or anywhere throughout the Church and bear testimony of the truth, preach the gospel of Jesus Christ, and set examples for the world of purity, honesty, uprightness, and integrity to the truth.[55]

Part Two

The New Law

Cleansing the Temple

4

The First Cleansing

John 2:13–25

13. And the Jews' passover was at hand, and Jesus went up to Jerusalem,

14. And found in the temple those that sold oxen and sheep and doves, and the changers of money sitting:

15. And when he had made a scourge of small cords, he drove them all out of the temple, and the sheep, and the oxen; and poured out the changers' money, and overthrew the tables;

16. And said unto them that sold doves, Take these things hence; make not my Father's house an house of merchandise.

17. And his disciples remembered that it was written, The zeal of thine house hath eaten me up.

18. Then answered the Jews and said unto him, What sign shewest thou unto us, seeing that thou doest these things?

19. Jesus answered and said unto them, Destroy this temple, and in three days I will raise it up.

20. Then said the Jews, Forty and six years was this

temple in building, and wilt thou rear it up in three days?

21. But he spake of the temple of his body.

22. When therefore he was risen from the dead, his disciples remembered that he had said this unto them; and they believed the scripture, and the word which Jesus had said.

23. Now when he was in Jerusalem at the passover, in the feast day, many believed in his name, when they saw the miracles which he did.

24. But Jesus did not commit himself unto them, because he knew all men,

25. And needed not that any should testify of man: for he knew what was in man.

John records the first cleansing of the temple by the Savior. It occurred after the marriage at Cana and after Jesus had returned to Capernaum, a city which had become known as his own (John 2:12; Matthew 4:13; 9:1).

The Passover was near, and in compliance with the Law Jesus went up to Jerusalem. The synoptic Gospels do not record this visit, for their interest was primarily with the Savior's Galilean and Perean ministries. At the time of the Passover feast the temple tax was due from "all Jews and proselytes— women, slaves, and minors excepted."[1] This was the greatest of all Jewish festivals and a time when the law required every male Israelite to present himself at the temple.

Josephus reports that Cestus once took a census of Jerusalem at the time of the Passover to inform Nero of the city's power. Cestus required the priests to number the multitude, which they did by counting the sacrifices slain at the feast. They counted 256,500 sheep and estimated that ten or eleven people would celebrate each sacrifice (it was not lawful for anyone to feast singly, and some companies were known to include as many as twenty people). The priests reported to Cestus that 2,700,200 Jews had come to the feast pure and holy. Those who were "unclean" could not sacrifice, nor could any foreigner, so the estimated figure was probably below the actual total.[2] It is no wonder, with such an enormous congregation being required to sacrifice and pay the temple tax, that the area of the temple had become heavily trafficked.

From the fifteenth to the twenty-fifth of Adar (corresponding to our months of February and March), it was the custom for the priests of the temple to set up stalls in the country towns surrounding Jerusalem to exchange the traditional currency the Judeans carried for the Galilean shekel the travelers would need to pay the temple tax while attending the Passover. After this period passed, however, the country stalls were closed and the money changers would sit within the precincts of the temple itself.[3] In addition to the exchange of funds (for which there was a charge), there was also a lively business in the selling of sacrificial animals. If an individual brought his own offering for the sacrifice, it had to be inspected (pursuant to the rabbinical law of the day), and there was also a charge for that inspection. A complicated "market" in the temple handled all business matters connected with the Passover,[4] for the greatest of the Jewish religious ceremonies had become a huge yearly fair at Jerusalem. There were booths at which poorer women bought doves to use in their ritual of purification, potters sold dishes for the Passover meal, and other vendors would cry their wares, selling such things as wine, oil, and salt.

To make matters worse, the normal traffic pattern through the city now cut through the temple courtyard instead of going around the temple, as it had in the past.[5] Also, Josephus records that Annas, the ruling high priest at the time of Christ's ministry, was a great hoarder of money. He and his sons were full of greed, avarice, and corruption, and had become exceedingly rich by violently spoiling the common priests of their official revenues and keeping the funds for themselves.[6]

Once we recognize what Jerusalem was like at the time of Christ, it is easy to understand why the Lord would call the temple "a den of robbers." Quoting Psalm 69:9 as fulfillment of prophecy, and making himself a whip of small cords,[7] he drove the sacrificial beasts through the gates of the temple into the streets of the city and ordered those who sold the caged doves to take them away. The money changers fared much worse as Jesus overturned their tables (scattering their spiritually desecrating coins on the floor) and expelled them from the premises.[8] Acting as Israel's refiner and purifier (Malachi 3:1–3), the

Lord inaugurated his mission and claimed his Messiahship by declaring that the Jews had desecrated his Father's house.

The common people did not object to Jesus' clearing of the temple, because they did not approve of the business practices being carried on there;[9] and although the Jewish leadership was angry, they did not challenge what Jesus had done, for they knew that he was right! Rather than laying hands upon him or reproving him, they came to him and asked for a sign. This request, which was in essence a challenge to Christ's authority, essentially determined the manner in which they would carry on their contest with him throughout his mission. The sign they sought was the Messianic sign, or the sign of the second coming of Christ.[10] Jesus answered them by declaring the sign of his first coming (or the Resurrection) and told them that if they destroyed "this temple" he would raise it again in three days. The incredulous Jews declared that it had taken forty-six years to raise the temple, and it was not yet complete. How could Jesus claim to be able to "rear it up" in only three days? But Jesus was speaking of the resurrection of his body, and although the Jews pretended to misunderstand him, they later proved their comprehension. At his trial they testified of this claim (Mark 14:58), accusing him of blasphemy; they taunted him with the claim upon the cross (Mark 15:29–30); and finally they used it to secure the tomb where his body lay (Matthew 27:63).

In reality, it would appear that the Jews' own sense of guilt prevented them from interfering with the Master's cleansing of the temple, for they stood before him "self-convicted of corruption, avarice, and of personal responsibility for the temple's defilement."[11]

The Second Cleansing

Mark 11:15–19

15. And they came to Jerusalem: and Jesus went into the temple, and began to cast out them that sold and bought in the temple, and overthrew the tables of the moneychangers, and the seats of them that sold doves;

16. And would not suffer that any man should carry any vessel through the temple.

17. And he taught, saying unto them, Is it not written, My house shall be called of all nations the house of prayer? but ye have made it a den of thieves.

18. And the scribes and chief priests heard it, and sought how they might destroy him: for they feared him, because all the people was astonished at his doctrine.

19. And when even was come, he went out of the city.

Cross-references

Matthew 21:12–16   Luke 19:45–48

The first cleansing was a warning to the Jews, but the second cleansing was their symbolic judgment. The first cleansing occurred at the commencement of the Savior's ministry, and the final cleansing took place four days before his crucifixion. The first time he was cleansing his "Father's house," but now he had triumphantly entered Jerusalem declaring his Messiahship, and so it was also his house.[12] Although the first cleansing caused anger and motivated the Jewish leaders to ask Jesus for a sign, the final cleansing produced a desire to destroy him.

According to Mark, Jesus began the day of the second cleansing with the miracle of the fig tree,[13] which emphasized the symbolic judgment that would come upon the children of Israel (Mark 11:12–14). Although the first cleansing had cleared the temple of its several abuses, in time all the abuses were restored.[14] The degrading confusion of

the lowing of oxen, the bleating of sheep, the cries of the money-changers, and the noisy market chaffering of buyers and sellers of doves or other accessories to a ceremonial worship, filled the air with discordant sounds of the outside world, which had no right in these sacred precincts. The scene roused the same deep indignation in Jesus, as when He formally rose in His grand protest against it. He had now, in His triumphal entry, formally proclaimed His Kingdom, and would, forthwith, vindicate its rights, by once more restoring the Temple to its becoming purity; for while it stood, it should be holy.[15]

The two episodes of Christ clearing the temple contradict our traditional view of the Savior. We normally think of him as being gentle and unassertive.

> Gentle He was, and patient under affliction, merciful and long-suffering in dealing with contrite sinners, yet stern and inflexible in the presence of hypocrisy, and unsparing in His denunciation of persistent evil-doers. His mood was adapted to the conditions to which He addressed Himself; tender words of encouragement or burning expletives of righteous indignation issued with equal fluency from His lips. His nature was no poetic conception of cherubic sweetness ever present, but that of a Man, with the emotions and passions essential to manhood and manliness. He, who often wept with compassion, at other times evinced in word and action the righteous anger of a God. But of all His passions, however gently they rippled or strongly surged, He was ever master. Contrast the gentle Jesus moved to hospitable service by the needs of a festive party in Cana, with the indignant Christ plying His whip, and amidst commotion and turmoil of His own making, driving cattle and men before Him as an unclean herd.[16]

Part Three

Disciples

The Test for Those 5
Who Followed

Disciples Indeed

Mark 9:33–50

33. And he came to Capernaum: and being in the house he asked them, What was it that ye disputed among yourselves by the way?

34. But they held their peace: for by the way they had disputed among themselves, who should be the greatest.

35. And he sat down, and called the twelve, and saith unto them, If any man desire to be first, the same shall be last of all, and servant of all.

36. And he took a child, and set him in the midst of them: and when he had taken him in his arms, he said unto them,

37. Whosoever shall receive one of such children in my name, receiveth me: and whosoever shall receive me, receiveth not me, but him that sent me.

38. And John answered him, saying, Master, we saw one casting out devils in thy name, and he followeth not us: and we forbad him, because he followeth not us.

39. But Jesus said, Forbid

him not: for there is no man which shall do a miracle in my name, that can lightly speak evil of me.

40. For he that is not against us is on our part.

41. For whosoever shall give you a cup of water to drink in my name, because ye belong to Christ, verily I say unto you, he shall not lose his reward.

42. And whosoever shall offend one of these little ones that believe in me, it is better for him that a millstone were hanged about his neck, and he were cast into the sea.

43. And if thy hand offend thee, cut it off: it is better for thee to enter into life maimed, than having two hands to go into hell, into the fire that never shall be quenched:

44. Where their worm dieth not, and the fire is not quenched.

45. And if thy foot offend thee, cut it off: it is better for thee to enter halt into life, than having two feet to be cast into hell, into the fire that never shall be quenched:

46. Where their worm dieth not, and the fire is not quenched.

47. And if thine eye offend thee, pluck it out: it is better for thee to enter into the kingdom of God with one eye, than having two eyes to be cast into hell fire:

48. Where their worm dieth not, and the fire is not quenched.

49. For every one shall be salted with fire, and every sacrifice shall be salted with salt.

50. Salt is good: but if the salt have lost his saltness, wherewith will ye season it? Have salt in yourselves, and have peace one with another.

Cross-references

Matthew 18:1–11   Luke 9:46–50

This discourse has essentially the same historical introduction in all of the synoptic Gospels—there are only minor differences. Mark is used here as the primary source, but all three Synoptics are needed to acquire a complete text.

The Transfiguration of Christ (Matthew 17) and the casting out of an evil spirit from a young boy[1] occurred just prior to this sermon. After these events Jesus left the area and proceeded on his way to Capernaum (apparently in secret so that the multitudes would not follow him). While they were traveling, the Apostles began disputing which of them would be the greatest in the kingdom of heaven. Jesus took no part in their discussion, but noticed that they were contending one with another.

Throughout the early ministry of Jesus it appeared that he had favored some of the Apostles above the others. Special honors had come to Peter and he had participated in some of the Lord's conversations and miracles more often than the other Apostles; in addition, there was obviously a strong friendship between the Lord and the Apostle John.[2] These situations may have caused some of the brethren to feel that the favored Apostles would receive more in Christ's kingdom than the others.

During this journey Jesus had told the Apostles of his impending death and resurrection (Matthew 17:22-23; Mark 9:31-32). Apparently they did not really understand what was going to happen to him, and still felt that he would eventually found a great political kingdom and restore the nation of Israel to its previous greatness.[3] They obviously thought that they would be worthy of high positions in that kingdom. Lacking understanding of the Lord's mission and thinking only of their personal ambitions, they "surrendered themselves to the selfish contemplation of their prospective stations."[4] Nothing seems to have changed them from their "invincible belief that He would soon proclaim Himself as the Messiah in the Jewish sense, and found a great political kingdom."[5]

Jesus did not enter into their conversation—or perhaps he was not close enough to participate, since the Apostles were trailing behind him at this point. Finally, perceiving the thought in their hearts, he asked them, "What was it that ye disputed among yourselves by the way?" But as Mark records, the Apostles "held their peace." Then, taking a small child in his arms for emphasis, Jesus proceeded to teach them the requirements for entrance into the kingdom of God.

First, he explained that to qualify for the kingdom of heaven one must become as a little child—not that one has to become childish, but that true greatness is exemplified by some childlike character traits. A child knows nothing of the distinctions

of rank so coveted by humanity. Children are unpretentious
and humble. The Lord stressed this in the Joseph Smith Translation of the Bible, wherein it states: "Whosoever shall humble
himself like one of these children, and receiveth me, ye shall
receive in my name" (JST Mark 9:34).

To be great in the kingdom of God—even to gain the kingdom at all—it is necessary to be humble, for "what children are
unconsciously, that Jesus requires His disciples to be voluntar-
ily and deliberately."[6] The Lord's Apostles had confused the
nuances of the Mosaic Law (as taught by the Pharisees and rulers of the Jews) with the Lord's message. Jesus emphasized that
moral fitness alone would secure entrance into the kingdom.
Entrance would not be based on earthly claims, whether they
were of legal decree, national privilege (as taught by the Pharisees), or (as in the case of the Twelve) a sacred calling. All of
these qualifications would be worthless without the humble,
moral fitness personified in the young child upon Christ's knee.

Second, the Lord declared that the Apostles should receive
little children not only in the literal sense, but in the sense that
children represent the weak, insignificant, and helpless quali-
ties in all mankind. The Lord warned his Apostles (and through
them all of us) that they should not offend his children with
worldly ambitions—even the ambitious spirit that the Twelve
had been evidencing.

As yet, the refining powers of the gospel had not operated
in the lives of the Apostles: they still had to be converted,
"changed from their carnal and fallen state to a state of righteousness, becoming again pure and spotless as they were in
their infancy. Such is the state of those who become heirs of
salvation."[7]

The Lord then described the punishment for offending his
children, a punishment which the Twelve should have been familiar with for the Romans had actually used it on some of the
leaders of a previous Judean insurrection in Galilee. (The Romans
had hung large millstones around the necks of the Jewish rebels
and thrown them into the sea of Galilee.)[8] Take special note
that the Lord did not say there would be no offenses against the
children of his kingdom; he was well aware of the nature of
man. But he stated strongly, "Woe to that man by whom the

offence cometh! . . . It were better for him that a millstone were hanged about his neck, and that he were drowned in the depth of the sea." The Lord elaborated this point by stating that it was better to have a member of the body cut off than to have that member cause the eternal loss of the soul. Mark adds that even offending members of the kingdom would have to be cut off to insure that the kingdom was incorruptible.

In Mark's report of this discourse he gives special emphasis to the use of salt. This would have conveyed special meaning to the Apostles. They knew the importance of salt in the proper worship of Jehovah under the Law of Moses. Every sacrifice for the altar had to be salted (Leviticus 2:13), for it symbolized the incorruptibility of the sacrifice. Thus, the Lord compared an errant soul to salt that had lost its savor, saying that if he would not repent, he would be cut off[9] (D&C 64:12-13).

At this point in the discourse John interrupted and asked a question about someone the Apostles had observed casting out devils in the name of the Lord, even though he was not one of Jesus' disciples. Jesus responded with an interesting comment. He said, "For he that is not against us is on our part," and he told the brethren that they should not curtail the man's activities. Perhaps the man had witnessed the goodness of the Lord and the results of his many miracles and was simply imitating that goodness, not really understanding the Messiah or his kingdom: yet assuredly he would have to come to that understanding in order to acquire salvation. No further information is given in the scriptures as to who the man was or anything about him.

John's question being resolved, the Lord moved to the third and last point of his discourse. He concluded that if anyone despised or injured one of his little ones (his disciples) they were totally out of harmony with the mind of heaven.

Suddenly the Apostles realized that the distinctions of knowledge, merit, and worth—so heavily emphasized by the Jews of their day—were not enough. They needed a simpler and more unconscious form of humility. Submission to the commandments and requirements of God would merit the kingdom. No one who desired Christ's love could deliberately offend or heartlessly condemn a brother—however insignificant he seemed to be.

This was the point that Jesus wished to impress upon his disciples. He wanted them to understand that self-interest was inconsistent with the dictates of the kingdom. They must exercise the charity that he was exemplifying to them. They must be simple and earnest in their faith and have absolute trust in him.

To the Twelve

Matthew 20:17–28

17. And Jesus going up to Jerusalem took the twelve disciples apart in the way, and said unto them,

18. Behold, we go up to Jerusalem; and the Son of man shall be betrayed unto the chief priests and unto the scribes, and they shall condemn him to death,

19. And shall deliver him to the Gentiles to mock, and to scourge, and to crucify him: and the third day he shall rise again.

20. Then came to him the mother of Zebedee's children with her sons, worshipping him, and desiring a certain thing of him.

21. And he said unto her, What wilt thou? She saith unto him, Grant that these my two sons may sit, the one on thy right hand, and the other on the left, in thy kingdom.

22. But Jesus answered and said, Ye know not what ye ask. Are ye able to drink of the cup that I shall drink of, and to be baptized with the baptism that I am baptized with? They say unto him, We are able.

23. And he saith unto them, Ye shall drink indeed of my cup, and be baptized with the baptism that I am baptized with: but to sit on my right hand, and on my left, is not mine to give, but it shall be given to them for whom it is prepared of my Father.

24. And when the ten heard it, they were moved with indignation against the two brethren.

25. But Jesus called them unto him, and said, Ye know that the princes of the Gen-

tiles exercise dominion over them, and they that are great exercise authority upon them.

26. But it shall not be so among you: but whosoever will be great among you, let him be your minister;

27. And whosoever will be chief among you, let him be your servant:

28. Even as the Son of man came not to be ministered unto, but to minister, and to give his life a ransom for many.

Cross-references

Mark 10:32-45   Luke 18:31-34; 22:24-27

This discourse occurred as Jesus and his Apostles were traveling to Jerusalem for the last time. The Apostles did not immediately understand the instructions the Lord gave in this discourse, but Matthew ultimately perceived them to have been a prediction of those terrible days when the betrayal, trial, and crucifixion of Christ took place, and he recorded them from that perspective.[10]

According to Matthew's writings, the rich young ruler's question preceded this discourse. During the ensuing interview the Lord told the young ruler to sell all and follow him, concluding that it was very difficult for a rich man to enter the kingdom of heaven (Matthew 19:16-24). This conclusion had amazed the Lord's disciples, and it motivated Peter to ask what the Apostles would receive since they had forsaken all to follow Jesus. The Lord acknowledged that they had given up all and promised them that eventually they would sit upon thrones of glory and judge the twelve tribes of Israel (Matthew 19:28). Perhaps the moment of elation this promise elicited caused the Apostles to be "completely possessed by romantic expectations, their heads giddy with the sparkling wine of vain hope; and as they drew nigh the holy city their firm conviction was, 'that the kingdom of God should immediately appear.' "[11] The Lord dampened their spirits by warning them for the third time of his impending death and resurrection[12]—yet they still failed to comprehend.[13]

This continuous misunderstanding by the Twelve might be

explained by their continued reluctance to accept the truth after having been taught the advent of a glorious, politically power- ful Messiah in their youth: they undoubtedly found it difficult to accept the fact that they were following the Savior to the cross and to the grave.[14]

While the Lord's warning was still fresh in the Apostles' minds, Salome, the mother of James and John (and Mary's sis- ter), petitioned Jesus for a favor. The request itself was evi- dence that none of the Lord's disciples understood the things which he had been teaching them concerning his coming death and resurrection[15] (Luke 18:34). Salome's request was ambi- tious: she wanted her sons to sit "one on thy right hand, and the other on thy left, in thy glory."

With the prediction of the death and resurrection of the Savior still fresh in their memories, the timing of this request seems to be incredible; yet the Lord received the petition with unbelievable patience and tenderness, as if it had come merely as a result of the love of a mother for her devoted sons. He answered them without rebuke by asking James and John if they were willing to "drink of the cup that I shall drink of," to which these zealous followers readily agreed. But this honor was not his to give as a result of mere favoritism. Such honors had to be earned.

When the ten heard what James and John were aspiring to, they were "moved with indignation against the two brethren." At this point in the Lord's ministry it would appear that at least some of the Twelve were harboring feelings of self-importance and sought to elevate themselves one above another.

These twelve, special men, who should have been closely united in the last solemn hours before the Lord's crucifixion, had been distracted from his teachings by thoughts of aggran- dizement and future glory. The Lord called them together and calmly taught them that only their service would ensure their greatness in his kingdom. He used the example of the gentile kings and how they "lorded it over" their subjects, noting how differently his power should be acquired and used. He told them, "Whosoever will be great among you, let him be your minister;" and "Whosoever will be chief among you, let him be your servant." He concluded by stating that he would give his life as a ransom for others; that he had come not to be ministered to but to minister; and that those who would be great among them in his service must emulate his greatness—"not greatness through service, but the greatness of service; and, whosoever would be chief or rather 'first' among [you], let it be in service."[16]

The Testimony of Twelve

Matthew 16:13–28

13. When Jesus came into the coasts of Caesarea Philippi, he asked his disciples, saying, Whom do men say that I the Son of man am?

14. And they said, "Some say that thou art John the Baptist: some, Elias; and others, Jeremias, or one of the prophets.

15. He saith unto them, But whom say ye that I am?

16. And Simon Peter answered and said, Thou art the Christ, the Son of the living God.

17. And Jesus answered and said unto him, Blessed art thou, Simon Barjona: for flesh and blood hath not revealed it unto thee, but my Father which is in heaven.

18. And I say also unto thee, That thou art Peter, and upon this rock I will build my church; and the gates of hell shall not prevail against it.

19. And I will give unto thee the keys of the kingdom of heaven: and whatsoever thou shalt bind on earth shall be bound in heaven: and whatsoever thou shalt loose on earth shall be loosed in heaven.

20. Then charged he his disciples that they should tell no man that he was Jesus the Christ.

21. From that time forth began Jesus to shew unto his disciples, how that he must go unto Jerusalem, and suffer many things of the elders and chief priests and scribes, and be killed, and be raised again the third day.

22. Then Peter took him, and began to rebuke him, saying, Be it far from thee, Lord: this shall not be unto thee.

23. But he turned, and said unto Peter, Get thee

behind me, Satan: thou art an offence unto me: for thou savourest not the things that be of God, but those that be of men.

24. Then said Jesus unto his disciples, If any man will come after me, let him deny himself, and take up his cross, and follow me.

25. For whosoever will save his life shall lose it: and whosoever will lose his life for my sake shall find it.

26. For what is a man profited, if he shall gain the whole world, and lose his own soul? or what shall a man give in exchange for his soul?

27. For the Son of man shall come in the glory of his Father with his angels; and then he shall reward every man according to his works.

28. Verily I say unto you, There be some standing here, which shall not taste of death, till they see the Son of man coming in his kingdom.

Cross-references

Mark 8:27–38; 9:1   Luke 9:18–27

Jesus was alone with the Twelve on the coasts of Caesarea Philippi, and for perhaps the first time in a long while he had the opportunity to confidentially instruct them. He had recently delivered a memorable discourse at Capernaum, where he clearly claimed to be the "bread of life," the Son of God. This had led to the defection of many of his disciples (John 6:41–66) and had obviously raised questions in the minds of the Twelve, for Jesus had asked them, "Will ye also go away?" (John 6:67). The Pharisees and Sadducees had asked the Lord some difficult questions, and perhaps his answers had disappointed the Twelve, for he would not openly confront nor publicly challenge the Jewish leaders.[17] With these experiences fresh in the Apostles' minds, they silently set sail with their Lord across the Sea of Galilee.

With the many miracles and teachings Jesus had thus far produced in his ministry, it was obvious that he had become the talk of all Israel; but he had "neither by word nor deed . . . measured up to the popular and traditional standard of the expected Deliverer and King of Israel"[18]—even though they had seen him in the context of the prophets of old.

In their private setting Jesus asked the Twelve, "Whom do men say that I the Son of man am?" They responded that some thought he was Elijah, some Jeremiah, and others John the Baptist. Their answer did not mean that the Jews thought Christ was literally the incarnate Elijah, Jeremiah, or John the Baptist (the Jews did not believe in the transmigration of souls),[19] but rather that he was continuing the work of these prophets by preparing the way for the Messiah yet to come. Although the Jews differed on the purpose of Christ's mission, they did not regard him as an ordinary man. They recognized that he had a mission from heaven—but they would not accept him as the Messiah.[20]

Next, Christ asked his Apostles, "But whom say ye that I am?" Peter boldly stepped forward and undoubtedly spoke for all of the Twelve when he replied, "Thou art the Christ, the Son of the living God."

None of the three Synoptics agree on the exact words Peter used in this response. Mark reported that Peter said, "Thou art the Christ," and Luke reported his answer to be "the Christ of God," but the meaning is the same. The Twelve understood at that point that Jesus was the bread of life, the Son of God, the long-awaited Messiah and Savior of the world. Their belief was based upon a confirmation from the Spirit as given from the Father, and the Savior so confirmed it.

The Lord then congratulated Peter for having received the revelation necessary to confirm his belief, and promised him the keys of the kingdom of heaven. The keys which the Savior promised Peter were those of the right of presidency and the sealing power.[21] The "rock" upon which the Church would be built was not Peter (even though he was to be the first President of the Church), but was that means by which Peter and all others after him would receive the knowledge from God that Jesus was the Christ. It was upon the rock of revelation that the Lord would build his Church, and against which the gates of hell would not prevail.[22]

From this time forth the Lord instructed the Twelve more

clearly and with greater detail concerning his coming death and resurrection. Prior to this time he had borne witness of these coming events, but the witness had been couched in riddles, the meaning of which would only become clear after the Crucifixion had taken place. He had spoken of his body as a temple which, after being destroyed, would rise again in three days (John 2:19). Another time he spoke of lifting the Son of Man up like Moses had raised the brazen serpent in the wilderness (John 3:14). On yet another occasion he spoke of the separation of the bridegroom from the children of the bride chamber (Matthew 9:15), and of giving his flesh for the world (John 6:53). He said that a sign would be given, the sign of the prophet Jonas (Matthew 16:4): but now it was necessary that the Twelve, having confessed him as the Messiah, prepare themselves for the coming events. The Lord specifically taught them what was going to happen to him, and he charged them that they should not openly testify to others that they knew he was the Messiah. Perhaps this charge by the Lord—a charge similar to that given to Peter, James, and John after their experience on the Mount of Transfiguration (Matthew 17:9)—was a contributing reason why Peter denied knowing Jesus when he was challenged by the people watching the Lord's trial (Matthew 26:69–75). Undoubtedly, if the Twelve had testified of the Lord prior to his crucifixion, they would have been crucified also, and there would have been no one in authority left to carry on the Savior's work. The ministry of the Messiah in the midst of his chosen people had to continue to its inevitable end at Jerusalem.

When Peter finally realized what was going to happen to Jesus, he became greatly alarmed. He took the Lord aside and began to "rebuke" him. Jesus' response was stern, and he associated Peter with the very devil himself; for what Peter had said, undoubtedly out of love for the Lord, was in essence what the devil had said to tempt Jesus in the wilderness after he had been fasting for thirty days. Peter was essentially saying, "If thou be the Son of God, why must you suffer such a scandalous death?" Thus, Peter's ill-conceived attempt to counsel the Lord was, in fact, an effort "to tempt the Lord."[23] The Lord's response, "Get thee behind me, Satan," was a total rebuke of Peter's intentions.

The Lord used this chastisement of Peter to teach the Twelve Apostles some general principles concerning God's kingdom and true discipleship. The disciples could either choose to save their mortal lives and lose the Lord's kingdom, or lose their mortal lives through self-denial and persecution while saving their souls in heaven.[24] When the Son of Man comes again in his glory, eternal gains and eternal losses will be judged according to the deeds men have performed in his service, not according to the material successes they achieved in this life.

Jesus concluded this discourse with a reference to the blessing he would bestow on John the Beloved, for John would never taste of death. He would live to minister to people in the flesh until Christ should come again.

Part Four

Christ Declares
Himself

"I Know That Messias Cometh"

John 4:1–42

1. When therefore the Lord knew how the Pharisees had heard that Jesus made and baptized more disciples than John,

2. (Though Jesus himself baptized not, but his disciples,)

3. He left Judaea, and departed again into Galilee.

4. And he must needs go through Samaria.

5. Then cometh he to a city of Samaria, which is called Sychar, near to the parcel of ground that Jacob gave to his son Joseph.

6. Now Jacob's well was there. Jesus therefore, being wearied with his journey, sat thus on the well: and it was about the sixth hour.

7. There cometh a woman of Samaria to draw water: Jesus saith unto her, Give me to drink.

8. (For his disciples were gone away unto the city to buy meat.)

9. Then saith the woman of Samaria unto him, How is it that thou, being a Jew, askest drink of me, which am a woman of Samaria? for the

Jews have no dealings with the Samaritans.

10. Jesus answered and said unto her, If thou knewest the gift of God, and who it is that saith to thee, Give me to drink; thou wouldest have asked of him, and he would have given thee living water.

11. The woman saith unto him, Sir, thou hast nothing to draw with, and the well is deep: from whence then hast thou that living water?

12. Art thou greater than our father Jacob, which gave us the well, and drank thereof himself, and his children, and his cattle?

13. Jesus answered and said unto her, Whosoever drinketh of this water shall thirst again:

14. But whosoever drinketh of the water that I shall give him shall never thirst; but the water that I shall give him shall be in him a well of water springing up into everlasting life.

15. The woman saith unto him, Sir, give me this water, that I thirst not, neither come hither to draw.

16. Jesus saith unto her, Go, call thy husband, and come hither.

17. The woman answered and said, I have no husband. Jesus said unto her, Thou hast well said, I have no husband:

18. For thou hast had five husbands; and he whom thou now hast is not thy husband: in that saidst thou truly.

19. The woman saith unto him, Sir, I perceive that thou art a prophet.

20. Our fathers worshipped in this mountain; and ye say, that in Jerusalem is the place where men ought to worship.

21. Jesus saith unto her, Woman, believe me, the hour cometh, when ye shall neither in this mountain, nor yet at Jerusalem, worship the Father.

22. Ye worship ye know not what: we know what we worship: for salvation is of the Jews.

23. But the hour cometh, and now is, when the true worshippers shall worship the Father in spirit and in truth: for the Father seeketh such to worship him.

24. God is a Spirit: and they that worship him must worship him in spirit and in truth.

25. The woman saith unto him, I know that

Messias cometh, which is called Christ: when he is come, he will tell us all things.

26. Jesus saith unto her, I that speak unto thee am he.

27. And upon this came his disciples, and marvelled that he talked with the woman: yet no man said, What seekest thou? or, Why talkest thou with her?

28. The woman then left her waterpot, and went her way into the city, and saith to the men,

29. Come, see a man, which told me all things that ever I did: is not this the Christ?

30. Then they went out of the city, and came unto him.

31. In the mean while his disciples prayed him, saying, Master, eat.

32. But he said unto them, I have meat to eat that ye know not of.

33. Therefore said the disciples one to another, Hath any man brought him ought to eat?

34. Jesus saith unto them, My meat is to do the will of him that sent me, and to finish his work.

35. Say not ye, There are yet four months, and then cometh harvest? behold, I say unto you, Lift up your eyes, and look on the fields; for they are white already to harvest.

36. And he that reapeth receiveth wages, and gathereth fruit unto life eternal: that both he that soweth and he that reapeth may rejoice together.

37. And herein is that saying true, One soweth, and another reapeth.

38. I sent you to reap that whereon ye bestowed no labour: other men laboured, and ye are entered into their labours.

39. And many of the Samaritans of that city believed on him for the saying of the woman, which testified, He told me all that ever I did.

40. So when the Samaritans were come unto him, they besought him that he would tarry with them: and he abode there two days.

41. And many more believed because of his own word;

42. And said unto the woman, Now we believe, not because of thy saying: for we have heard him ourselves, and know that this is indeed

the Christ, the Saviour of the
world.

This chapter deals with the first of Christ's discourses which
are formal declarations of his Messiahship. All of these discourses are found in the Gospel of John.[1] Whereas the synoptic
Gospels are set primarily in Galilee and Perea, Jerusalem and
Judea are the setting for John's Gospel. The accurate descrip-
tions emanating from the pages of his work belong to a writer
who was born and had lived among the people and places that
he was writing about. It is evident that he grew up with an
expectation of the Messiah, and that he personally experienced
the life and ministry of Jesus.[2]

Prior to this discourse Jesus had gone to Jerusalem to attend
the Passover and inaugurate his formal ministry. He had amazed
the multitudes at the Passover feast by performing many miracles (John 2:23). As his fame increased, the Pharisees began
paying greater attention to him (as they did with John the Baptist before him). Their antagonism toward Jesus and John indicated that they had been keeping a careful watch over the Lord's
new religious movement.[3]

John the Baptist had been very popular among the Jewish
people, and the scriptures note that the movement of Jesus had
caught on with even greater enthusiasm. Jesus baptized, though
"not so many as his disciples" (JST John 4:3), and it is not
unreasonable to assume that he administered all of the ordinances of the gospel as an example to the newly called Twelve.[4]

Turning from Jerusalem after the Passover feast, Jesus under-
took his first, long missionary journey through Samaria. The
Judeans would normally have detoured through Perea in order
to avoid the hostile and ignorant Samaritans, but the Galileans
would not have done so as they traveled home toward their
capital.[5]

After a hot and dusty walk that took most of the day, Jesus
arrived at the well of Jacob. He was tired from his long journey, and he rested in the shade of the well while he sent his
disciples to Sychar for food and provisions.[6]

While he was resting, a woman approached with a water
jar on her head and a long cord for lowering the jar down into

the well.[7] As she drew near, Jesus asked her for a drink of the water to quench his thirst. The woman was obviously astonished, for she immediately recognized him as a Jew. Such recognition would not have been difficult, for undoubtedly his language differed from hers and his attire would have included the blue fringes required by the Levitical Law for those who taught in the synagogues.[8] She asked Jesus why he would make such a request, "for the Jews have no dealings with the Samaritans." The Jews reserved the very name, Samaritan, as a term for reproach, and used it to describe those who were of a foreign race.[9]

After the ten tribes had been deported to Assyria, heathen transplants from various parts of the Assyrian Empire colonized Samaria (2 Kings 17:24). (A scattering of the ten tribes still remained, and perhaps other settlers from Judea.) The Old Testament notes that the lions in the land came and terrorized these colonists and slew some of them, and it further attributes the ferocity of the lions toward the colonists to the fact that they knew not the God of Israel (2 Kings 17:26). Therefore, they sent for some of the exiled priests from the tribes of Israel and added the worship of Jehovah to their worship of idols (2 Kings 17:27). Ultimately, the foreigners became more rigidly attached to the Law of Moses than the Jews.[10] The animosity between the new inhabitants of Samaria and the Jews grew more intense at the time of Ezra and Nehemiah because the Jews would not let the Samaritans participate in the reconstruction of the temple (Ezra 4:1–3).

The Samaritans built a temple of their own on Mount Gerizim, but by Jesus' time it had been destroyed. They still claimed, however, that Mount Gerizim in Samaria was more holy than Mount Moriah in Judea. They claimed Abraham and Jacob had worshipped on Mount Gerizim, and had built altars there for the blessing of the people (Deuteronomy 11:29; 27:12). Traditionally, they believed that Abraham had offered his son Isaac upon the mount and that he had met Melchizedek there returning from his wars.[11]

The Samaritans accused the Jews of "adding" to the word of God because the Jews believed in all the prophets since Moses, while the Samaritans vehemently denied their authenticity. They

believed that only the Pentateuch was inspired and that no prophets had been called since Moses. Also, they steadfastly looked
forward to the coming of an anticipated Messiah[12] (Deuteronomy
18:18). As a result of their beliefs, "the Samaritan conception
of the mission of the expected Messiah was somewhat better
founded than was that of the Jews, for the Samaritans gave
greater prominence to the spiritual kingdom the Messiah would
establish, and were less exclusive in their views as to whom the
Messianic blessings would be extended."[13]

The Samaritans favored Herod because the Jews hated him;
they would kindle small fires upon the hills in an attempt to
confuse the Jewish reckoning of the new moon and to throw
the Jewish feasts into disorder; and they also defiled the temple
at Jerusalem by strewing human bones in it at the Passover.[14]

The Jewish hatred for the Samaritans was no less intense. A
Jew could not eat food touched by a Samaritan; the Samaritans
could not be proselyted, nor would they be resurrected; no
friendships could be kindled with them, no bargains between
them were valid; testimony from a Samaritan could not be used
in a Jewish court; and if a Samaritan entered into a Jewish
household, he brought the curse of God upon that home.[15] In
spite of all of these hatreds and animosities, unavoidable inter-
action did exist between the races (the Jews inventing casuistry
upon casuistry to allow such).[16]

None of these strifes and prejudices mattered to Jesus, and
there is perhaps no greater example in all of the New Testament
than this discourse to indicate that Jesus taught the kingdom of
God wherever there was spiritual darkness. It is possible that
one reason why John included this discourse in his Gospel was
to testify to the fact that Jesus was attempting to abolish the
deep-seated enmities that exist between people.[17]

Jesus' meeting with the woman at the well occurred naturally, as did his request for a drink. He was hot and thirsty,
and the water in the well was cool. The woman had undoubtedly come to the well in the course of her normal daily routine
and, like the parable of the hidden treasure,[18] "stumbled" upon
the gospel.

When, during the course of their conversation, Jesus told
her that he could provide her with "living water," she did not

understand,[19] and she responded logically by stating that he had nothing to draw water with. Perhaps she partially understood his meaning, however, because she asked Jesus if he was greater than father Jacob who had dug the well. To this Jesus responded, "Whosoever drinketh of this water shall thirst again [referring to the well water], but whosoever drinketh of the water that I shall give him shall never thirst." But again the woman missed the spiritual analogy and thought of only how nice it would be to receive relief from the tedious chore of drawing her water from a well.

Apparently, having exhausted this line of conversation, and perhaps to further awaken a sleeping conscience of the religious instruction he was attempting to give her, the Lord abruptly changed the subject and asked the woman to call her husband: but she had no husband, and so stated. The Lord acknowledged her honest answer and declared unto her that she had in fact had five husbands and was now living with a man that was not her husband. No indication is given in the scriptural text of the status of these prior husbands, but the woman was astounded that Jesus knew these things about her and at once recognized that someone greater than an ordinary man was before her. She declared, "Sir, I perceive that thou art a prophet."[20]

Then the woman quickly turned the subject away from her personal problems and sins by asking the Lord whether it was the Samaritans or the Jews who were worshipping correctly. Jesus replied that neither worshipped correctly. He acknowledged that anciently the Jewish religion had been accurate and hers had been wrong, but now neither was right. He explained that future worship would be directed toward him, through the Spirit, and only he and his Church would dispense the truth.

With this instruction the woman's spiritual awareness expanded and she could envision the kingdom of the Messiah. She spoke eagerly of her anticipation for that kingdom. Her anxious yearning for the Messiah must have cheered the Savior's heart and for the first time, to a humble Samaritan woman, he openly disclosed, "I that speak unto thee am he."[21]

With this knowledge burning in her soul, the woman abandoned her waterpot and hurried into the city to testify that she had seen the Messiah.

The actual sequence of events in this discourse is blurred in the scriptural narrative, but John reports that at about this time the disciples returned from purchasing some meat. John notes that they were astonished when they saw Jesus in conversation with the Samaritan woman, not just because she was a Samaritan, but because relationships between the sexes were severely restricted in the Jewish culture. Women were considered inferior to men to the extent that the Talmud recorded, "No one is to speak with a woman, even if she be his wife, in the public street."[22] The Apostles did not voice their astonishment, but requested that Jesus eat the provisions they had procured. But Jesus was preoccupied—all thoughts of hunger had left his mind. He stated, "I have meat to eat that ye know not of." He could envision the results of his ministry to these people, and was undoubtedly saddened at the apparent lack of understanding on the part of his disciples. Anticipating their thoughts, he told them to not think of the harvest (yet four months away) but to "lift up your eyes and look on the fields; for they are white already to harvest."[23] The woman at the well had perceived what the disciples could not yet comprehend, for what had been rejected in Judea would now produce a spiritual harvest in Samaria.

The Samaritans flocked to see Jesus as a result of the woman's testimony.[24] They asked him to tarry with them, which he did for two days. During that time he reaped the first of his great spiritual harvests, and many Samaritan men and women gained a personal testimony of him as the Messiah.

The scriptures do not give a detailed account of what occurred during this two-day period, but from previous activity we can assume that Jesus preached the gospel and healed and comforted those who came to see him. The kingdom of God was not to be based upon tribal privilege or the narrow designation of nationality,[25] for Jesus was proclaiming that all people are equal in God's eyes and can be acceptable to him.

The Messiah They Looked For

"The Father Hath Sent Me"

John 5:17–47

17. But Jesus answered them, My Father worketh hitherto, and I work.

18. Therefore the Jews sought the more to kill him, because he not only had broken the sabbath, but said also that God was his Father, making himself equal with God.

19. Then answered Jesus and said unto them, Verily, verily, I say unto you, The Son can do nothing of himself, but what he seeth the Father do: for what things soever he doeth, these also doeth the Son likewise.

20. For the Father loveth the Son, and sheweth him all things that himself doeth: and he will shew him greater works than these, that ye may marvel.

21. For as the Father raiseth up the dead, and quickeneth them; even so the Son quickeneth whom he will.

22. For the Father judgeth no man, but hath committed all judgment unto the Son:

23. That all men should honour the Son, even as they

honour the Father. He that honoureth not the Son honoureth not the Father which hath sent him.

24. Verily, verily, I say unto you, He that heareth my word, and believeth on him that sent me, hath everlasting life, and shall not come into condemnation; but is passed from death unto life.

25. Verily, verily, I say unto you, The hour is coming, and now is, when the dead shall hear the voice of the Son of God: and they that hear shall live.

26. For as the Father hath life in himself; so hath he given to the Son to have life in himself;

27. And hath given him authority to execute judgment also, because he is the Son of man.

28. Marvel not at this: for the hour is coming, in the which all that are in the graves shall hear his voice,

29. And shall come forth; they that have done good, unto the resurrection of life; and they that have done evil, unto the resurrection of damnation.

30. I can of mine own self do nothing: as I hear, I judge: and my judgment is just; because I seek not mine own will, but the will of the Father which hath sent me.

31. If I bear witness of myself, my witness is not true.

32. There is another that beareth witness of me; and I know that the witness which he witnesseth of me is true.

33. Ye sent unto John, and he bare witness unto the truth.

34. But I received not testimony from man: but these things I say, that ye might be saved.

35. He was a burning and a shining light: and ye were willing for a season to rejoice in his light.

36. But I have greater witness than that of John: for the works which the Father hath given me to finish, the same works that I do, bear witness of me, that the Father hath sent me.

37. And the Father himself, which hath sent me, hath borne witness of me. Ye have neither heard his voice at any time, nor seen his shape.

38. And ye have not his word abiding in you: for whom he hath sent, him ye believe not.

39. Search the scriptures;

for in them ye think ye have eternal life: and they are they which testify of me.

40. And ye will not come to me, that ye might have life.

41. I receive not honour from men.

42. But I know you, that ye have not the love of God in you.

43. I am come in my Father's name, and ye receive me not: if another shall come in his own name, him ye will receive.

44. How can ye believe, which receive honour one of another, and seek not the honour that cometh from God only?

45. Do not think that I will accuse you to the Father: there is one that accuseth you, even Moses, in whom ye trust.

46. For had ye believed Moses, ye would have believed me: for he wrote of me.

47. But if ye believe not his writings, how shall ye believe my words?

This discourse constitutes a direct confrontation between Jesus and the rulers of the Jews, and is one of the few times that such a confrontation occurs. It appears from the scriptural rendering and the circumstances immediately prior to the discourse that Jesus may have anticipated making this declaration of his Messiahship before the Jewish rulers. He had previously made a public declaration of his divinity to the Samaritan woman at the well, and he had undoubtedly testified of his mission and Messiahship throughout the rest of his Galilean ministry.

At the conclusion of his mission Jesus returned to Jerusalem to attend a feast. John does not name the feast, although some have determined that it was the Feast of Purim.[1] Upon his arrival in the city, Jesus went to the pool of Bethesda and healed an impotent man who had been ill for thirty-eight years[2] (John 5:2–9). The healing was performed on the Sabbath day, which allowed the Jews to bring the specific charge of Sabbath breaking against Jesus. At the time of this healing the impotent man did not know that his benefactor was the Lord, but he later learned his name and reported it to the Jewish leadership. They proceeded to ignore the miraculous healing that had taken place and "sought to slay him [Jesus], because he had done these things on the sabbath day" (John 5:16). In response to their murderous intentions Jesus delivered the following discourse.

This discourse can be divided into three sections:
1. Christ's relationship to the Father
2. Christ's function as the judge of all men
3. Christ's personal witness of his own divinity

1. *Christ's relationship to the Father (John 5:17–21)*: After the miracle at Bethesda and the subsequent confrontation with the Jewish leaders, Jesus was charged with Sabbath breaking. He responded to this charge by stating, "My Father worketh hitherto, and I work." The Jews hallowed the Sabbath above all other days of the week. They exercised extraordinary strictness in their observance of its laws. They had developed a vast array of prohibitions and injunctions for the Sabbath, defining everything from the amount of food that one could carry to the number of letters one could write. There were special kinds of knots that one had to use that day, and if perchance a man were unfortunate enough to be buried by a cave-in on the Sabbath, rescuers could dig for him, but if they found him dead they had to leave the body in the hole—they could only remove him if he was alive.[3]

Healing on the Sabbath was strictly forbidden (Luke 13:14), but when the leaders of the Jews accused Jesus of Sabbath breaking they were ill-prepared for his defense. The Jews understood the implication of his comment and sought to kill him all the more because he had claimed that God was his Father. Jesus had declared himself io be the Messiah, and in the eyes of the Jewish leadership he had blasphemed. He had declared that his Father had always done the work of salvation on the Sabbath day, and therefore he (being the Son) could also do such work. Through this statement Jesus taught that there was a greater work to be performed than that of the Sabbath.[4] Undoubtedly shocked by Christ's claim, the Jewish leaders listened to the rest of his sermon.

Jesus first declared that even in a personal sense, God was his Father.[5] He then declared that he did nothing of himself, but only that which he had seen the Father do. Because the Father loved him, he had been shown all things that the Father had done.[6] The Lord concluded this section of the sermon by openly disclosing that his Father would raise up the dead, a power that had also been given to the Son. This is the "most comprehensive sermon in scripture on the vital subject of the relationship between the Eternal Father and His Son, Jesus Christ."[7]

2. *Christ's function as the judge of all men:* After announcing his divine commission, Jesus explained the authority that had been granted to him by the Father.[8] He boldly proclaimed that the Father had given all judgment into the hands of the Son, and that if men honored the Son they would honor the Father: but that if they honored not the Son, they would not honor the Father. By this statement Jesus again declared his equality with God. To emphasize this point he stated that those who heard his words and believed on them would have everlasting life, while those who did not would be condemned. He continued by announcing that the dead would soon hear his voice and that he had inherited from the Father the power of immortality, stating that he had "life in himself."

Then the Lord returned to the topic of the resurrection, stating that all that were in the grave would hear his voice and be resurrected: those who were good to the resurrection of life, and those who were evil to the resurrection of damnation (see also D&C 76:17). Having unquestionably affirmed the universality of the resurrection, the Lord again testified that he was doing the will of his Father.

3. *Christ's personal witness of his own divinity:* The Lord next provided six witnesses of his divinity for the angry and astonished Jewish rulers.

First, he bore his own testimony of his calling, but without other witnesses the Law of Moses disallowed such evidence, and Jesus acknowledged that. The Lord declared that the second witness was John the Baptist, and he noted how they had received John's testimony at first, but eventually rejected it. The third witness of his divinity was his own works, which he declared to be an even greater witness than John the Baptist. The fourth witness was God the Father. He stated that the Father had borne witness of him (to the condemnation of the leadership before him, for they had neither heard the Father nor had his word abide in them). He proclaimed the fifth witness of his divinity by admonishing the scholars and learned men who stood before him to search the scriptures, for "they are they which testify of me." The sixth and last witness of his divinity was the Jews' revered prophet, Moses. "For," he said, "had ye believed Moses, ye would have believed me: for he wrote of me."

The Lord was very plain in pointing out the problems the Jewish leaders were having in accepting him. He told them that their main ambition was to receive honors from one another and from their fellowman. They could believe in false Messiahs more easily than they would believe in him who had come in the Father's name. They did not believe in him because they were not of his spirit.[9] He testified to them that he did not have to accuse them before the Father, for "there is one that accuseth you, even Moses, in whom ye trust."

By this time the angry Jewish leaders were completely committed to taking the Lord's life, but in the confusion that followed his discourse he departed from Jerusalem. This was a turning point in the life of Christ. Until this discourse he had enjoyed at least a measure of tolerance and perhaps even acceptance in Jerusalem, but it was no longer safe for him there. Even in Galilee his determined enemies would watch and follow him.

The Bread of Life

John 6:22–71

22. The day following, when the people which stood on the other side of the sea saw that there was none other boat there, save that one whereinto his disciples were entered, and that Jesus went not with his disciples into the boat, but that his disciples were gone away alone;

23. (Howbeit there came other boats from Tiberias nigh unto the place where they did eat bread, after that the Lord had given thanks:)

24. When the people therefore saw that Jesus was not there, neither his disciples, they also took shipping, and came to Capernaum, seeking for Jesus.

25. And when they had found him on the other side of the sea, they said unto him, Rabbi, when camest thou hither?

26. Jesus answered them and said, Verily, verily, I say unto you, Ye seek me, not because ye saw the miracles, but because ye did eat of the loaves, and were filled.

27. Labour not for the meat which perisheth, but for that meat which endureth unto everlasting life, which the Son of man shall give unto you: for him hath God the Father sealed.

28. Then said they unto him, What shall we do, that we might work the works of God?

29. Jesus answered and said unto them, This is the work of God, that ye believe on him whom he hath sent.

30. They said therefore unto him, What sign shewest thou then, that we may see, and believe thee? what dost thou work?

31. Our fathers did eat manna in the desert; as it is written, He gave them bread from heaven to eat.

32. Then Jesus said unto them, Verily, verily, I say unto you, Moses gave you not that bread from heaven; but my Father giveth you the true bread from heaven.

33. For the bread of God is he which cometh down from heaven, and giveth life unto the world.

34. Then said they unto him, Lord, evermore give us this bread.

35. And Jesus said unto them, I am the bread of life: he that cometh to me shall never hunger; and he that believeth on me shall never thirst.

36. But I said unto you, That ye also have seen me, and believe not.

37. All that the Father giveth me shall come to me; and him that cometh to me I will in no wise cast out.

38. For I came down from heaven, not to do mine own will, but the will of him that sent me.

39. And this is the Father's will which hath sent me, that of all which he hath given me I should lose nothing, but should raise it up again at the last day.

40. And this is the will of him that sent me, that every one which seeth the Son, and believeth on him, may have everlasting life: and I will raise him up at the last day.

41. The Jews then mur-

mured at him, because he said, I am the bread which came down from heaven.

42. And they said, Is not this Jesus, the son of Joseph, whose father and mother we know? how is it then that he saith, I came down from heaven?

43. Jesus therefore answered and said unto them, Murmur not among yourselves.

44. No man can come to me, except the Father which hath sent me draw him: and I will raise him up at the last day.

45. It is written in the prophets, And they shall be all taught of God. Every man therefore that hath heard, and hath learned of the Father, cometh unto me.

46. Not that any man hath seen the Father, save he which is of God, he hath seen the Father.

47. Verily, verily, I say unto you, He that believeth on me hath everlasting life.

48. I am that bread of life.

49. Your fathers did eat manna in the wilderness, and are dead.

50. This is the bread which cometh down from heaven, that a man may eat

thereof, and not die.

51. I am the living bread which came down from heaven: if any man eat of this bread, he shall live for ever: and the bread that I will give is my flesh, which I will give for the life of the world.

52. The Jews therefore strove among themselves, saying, How can this man give us his flesh to eat?

53. Then Jesus said unto them, Verily, verily, I say unto you, Except ye eat the flesh of the Son of man, and drink his blood, ye have no life in you.

54. Whoso eateth my flesh, and drinketh my blood, hath eternal life; and I will raise him up at the last day.

55. For my flesh is meat indeed, and my blood is drink indeed.

56. He that eateth my flesh, and drinketh my blood, dwelleth in me, and I in him.

57. As the living Father hath sent me, and I live by the Father: so he that eateth me, even he shall live by me.

58. This is that bread which came down from heaven: not as your fathers did eat manna, and are dead: he that eateth of this bread

shall live for ever.

59. These things said he in the synagogue, as he taught in Capernaum.

60. Many therefore of his disciples, when they had heard this, said, This is an hard saying; who can hear it?

61. When Jesus knew in himself that his disciples murmured at it, he said unto them, Doth this offend you?

62. What and if ye shall see the Son of man ascend up where he was before?

63. It is the spirit that quickeneth; the flesh profiteth nothing: the words that I speak unto you, they are spirit, and they are life.

64. But there are some of you that believe not. For Jesus knew from the beginning who they were that believed not, and who should betray him.

65. And he said, There-fore said I unto you, that no man can come unto me, except it were given unto him of my Father.

66. From that time many of his disciples went back, and walked no more with him.

67. Then said Jesus unto the twelve, Will ye also go away?

68. Then Simon Peter answered him, Lord, to whom shall we go? thou hast the words of eternal life.

69. And we believe and are sure that thou art that Christ, the Son of the living God.

70. Jesus answered them, Have not I chosen you twelve, and one of you is a devil?

71. He spake of Judas Iscariot the son of Simon: for he it was that should betray him, being one of the twelve.

After the miracle of the feeding of the five thousand had taken place, Jesus sent the multitude away and went into the hills to pray. The multitude had recognized Christ's witness of his divinity and wanted to force him to be their political king,[10] but this was not the Lord's way. His reaction to the crowd's demands undoubtedly weakened the effect of the miracle, for "henceforth there was continuous misunderstanding, doubt, and defection among former adherents, [which gave way] to opposition and hatred unto death."[11]

From his hillside retreat Jesus could see that the Apostles (who had sailed for Capernaum) were having trouble in a storm.

He joined them, much to their astonishment, by walking on the water. The Apostles "willingly received him into the ship: and immediately the ship was at the land whither they went" (John 6:21). The next morning, when the people saw that Jesus and his disciples were gone, they also booked passage for Capernaum on ships that had sailed in during the night from Tiberias.[12]

Jesus was on his way to the synagogue in Capernaum to teach when the multitude finally caught up with him.[13] They were joined by crowds from Capernaum, for excitement must have run high as the news of the Lord's arrival spread throughout the area. The multitude from the night before asked him how he had come to Capernaum. They had seen the Apostles leave in the only boat, and they knew that the Savior was not with them. He did not answer their question, and declared that they sought him not because of the miracle but because of the food they had freely received. Jesus attempted to take them beyond their desire for material goods when he said, "Labour not for the meat which perisheth, but for that meat which endureth unto everlasting life, which the Son of man shall give unto you." He was trying to feed their spirits, not their bodies. He declared (using a well-known Jewish expression)[14] that the Son "hath God the Father sealed," and by saying this he proclaimed himself to be the Messiah and conveyed "to His hearers that for the real meat, which would endure to eternal life—for the better Messianic banquet—they must come to Him, because God had impressed upon Him His own seal of truth, and so authenticated His Teaching and Mission."[15]

Then the people asked, "What shall we do, that we might work the works of God?" For centuries they and their ancestors before them had painstakingly lived the Mosaic Law, and they were willing to add to those requirements, if necessary, to gain the kingdom of God. But it was not the Law that Jesus was referring to. He was trying to teach the multitude that the work of God was to "believe on him whom he [God] hath sent." Now the people clearly understood that he had announced himself as the Messiah, so they asked for a "sign" that they might "believe" in him.

The previous day the multitude had participated in a great sign, but they wanted an even greater one. The food that they had eaten had constituted but a single meal and the miracle was now a day old.[16] They reminded the Savior that although he had given them one meal to eat, Moses had fed their forefathers manna in the wilderness for years. Jesus quickly corrected their misinterpretation of that great miracle in the desert and reminded them that Moses had not given them the bread from heaven, but that his Father had given it. Again he declared himself to be the "bread of God" which had come down from heaven to give life unto the world.

The people continued to respond with their temporal expectation of the Messiah by asking the Lord to "evermore give us this bread." Like the woman by the well, they primarily sought to only satisfy their material needs; however, they still craved more wonders and signs.[17] They wanted Jesus to justify his Messianic claim by giving them the sign that would be associated with his second coming. They did not want a "spiritual" kingdom.

> What they waited for, was a Kingdom of God—not in righteousness, joy, and peace in the Holy Ghost, but in meat and drink—a kingdom with miraculous wilderness-banquets to Israel, and coarse miraculous triumphs over the Gentiles. Not to speak of the fabulous Messianic banquet which a sensuous realism expected, or of the achievements for which it looked, every figure in which prophets had clothed the brightness of those days was first literalised, and then exaggerated, till the most glorious poetic descriptions became the most repulsive incongruous caricatures of spiritual Messianic expectancy. The fruit-trees were every day, or at least every week or two, to yield their riches, the fields their harvest; the grain was to stand like palm trees, and to be reaped and winnowed without labour. Similar blessings were to visit the vine; ordinary trees would bear like fruit trees, and every produce, of every clime, would be found in Palestine in such abundance and luxuriance as only the wildest imagination could conceive.[18]

These were the desires the multitude expressed when they said to the Savior, "Give us this bread." Jesus would not tolerate their erroneous thoughts, so he specifically declared, "I am the bread of life." They had to look to him and believe, if they were to never hunger or thirst again. There were no requirements that they could add to their Law and no additional "works" that they should perform to gain the kingdom. He shattered their vision of temporal ease and explained to them that the Father had sent him to save them spiritually. He stated that he only did the will of the Father and those who followed him and believed would be "raised up" (a reference to the resurrection).

Then the Jews murmured at Christ. They recognized his metaphor of the bread sent by the Father, but they knew of his earthly father and mother. How could he be the Savior sent from heaven? Jesus answered them by again declaring himself as the one sent from the Father; he witnessed to them that the prophets had so taught them of his divine heritage (Isaiah 54:13), and he again told them that he was the bread of life. He emphasized the point by returning to the example of the manna eaten in the wilderness. He declared that those who had eaten this manna were now dead, but "I am the living bread which came down from heaven: if any man eat of this bread, he shall live forever: and the bread that I will give is my flesh, which I will give for the life of the world." Christ gave his life so that all mankind could live again. When we "eat of his flesh" we accept him as the Savior and live our lives in obedience to his commandments. But the literal-minded Jews immediately questioned how any man could eat of Jesus' flesh. Jesus responded by insisting that "except ye eat the flesh of the Son of man, and drink his blood, ye have no life in you." By accepting the Lord and living the commandments of his gospel, it was possible for them to cleanse their souls and come to a spiritual oneness with the Father.

The allusion to food and drink was commonly used metaphorically in the schools and synagogues of Christ's time.[19] Jesus often used these metaphors in his sermons, and while we may not always understand the significance of his examples, the Jews would have.[20] "Their failure to comprehend the symbolism of Christ's doctrine was an act of will, not the natural consequence of innocent ignorance."[21] To eat of his flesh and drink of his blood meant to keep his commandments and believe and accept him as the literal Son of God and Savior of the world.[22]

Christ was instructing the Jews how they could make him an "abiding part" of their spirits, even as the food they ate was assimilated into the tissues of their bodies.[23] The Lord was making an open declaration to the Jews that they must unconditionally accept him as the Savior by being obedient to the laws and ordinances of his gospel. But the Jews' preconceived notions of the Messiah, their dreams of political glory, and their desire for a luxurious, carefree life-style were in severe conflict with Christ's discourse, and it caused a turbulent discussion among them. Some contended for the literal interpretation of his words, while others espoused the metaphorical.[24] But the mere fact that they continued to strive for the meaning of Christ's message indicates that at least to some degree, they *did* understand the Savior when he declared that he was the Son of God.

This was the Savior's last discourse at Capernaum, and it proved to be an extraordinary test of faith.[25] Some of the Lord's disciples finally recognized that he would never be the great political leader they were looking for. Their national glory would not be restored through him, and he would not usher in the times of luxury and idleness they had been eagerly anticipating.[26] Those gathered in the synagogue to hear him had trouble accepting his doctrine. As they murmured among themselves, Jesus perceived their thoughts and asked them point-blank, "Doth this offend you?" He then openly declared that he would again ascend to "where he was before," and reiterated that it was "the spirit that quickeneth; the flesh profiteth nothing: the words that I speak unto you, they are spirit, and they are life."

The Lord's popularity had grown and flourished from the time John the Baptist had begun preaching, but since John's fateful murder it had faded, and now the people had to decide whether he was indeed the Messiah. They had seen his works and his works seemed to prove his Messiahship in spite of the arguments against them.[27] But even though they wanted to make him their earthly king, he would not become such. Instead, he attacked their traditionalism,[28] and his death would eventually become the stumblingblock of the nation. (1 Corinthians 1:23.)

Jesus spoke only of self-sacrifice and inward purity, while the Jews expected great glory and material wealth.[29] "This was not the Messiah Whom the many—nay, Whom almost any—

would own."[30] And so there was a parting of the ways, and many of Christ's disciples "walked no more with him." They began to see clearly what Jesus stood for, and they did not like it. Apparently even the Twelve were concerned by this sermon and Jesus asked them, "Will ye also go away?" Perhaps they were not able to totally comprehend the Lord's doctrine, but none of them deserted him.[31] It must have been deeply rewarding to the Savior when Peter stepped forward and said, "Lord, to whom will we go? thou hast the words of eternal life." Yet Jesus sadly declared that one of them was a devil (speaking of Judas Iscariot).

Like a great fan, the discourse on the bread of life separated the true believers from the non-believers: and like the grain tossed on the thrashing room floor, the winnowing breeze blew away the chaff, leaving only the good wheat behind.

The Light of the World

John 8:1–59

1. Jesus went unto the mount of Olives.

2. And early in the morning he came again into the temple, and all the people came unto him; and he sat down, and taught them.

3. And the scribes and Pharisees brought unto him a woman taken in adultery; and when they had set her in the midst,

4. They say unto him, Master, this woman was taken in adultery, in the very act.

5. Now Moses in the law commanded us, that such should be stoned: but what sayest thou?

6. This they said, tempting him, that they might have to accuse him. But Jesus stooped down, and with his finger wrote on the ground, as though he heard them not.

7. So when they continued asking him, he lifted up himself, and said unto them, He that is without sin among you, let him first cast a stone at her.

8. And again he stooped down, and wrote on the ground.

9. And they which heard it, being convicted by their own conscience, went out

one by one, beginning at the eldest, even unto the last: and Jesus was left alone, and the woman standing in the midst.

10. When Jesus had lifted up himself, and saw none but the woman, he said unto her, Woman, where are those thine accusers? hath no man condemned thee?

11. She said, No man, Lord. And Jesus said unto her, Neither do I condemn thee: go, and sin no more.

12. Then spake Jesus again unto them, saying, I am the light of the world: he that followeth me shall not walk in darkness, but shall have the light of life.

13. The Pharisees therefore said unto him, Thou bearest record of thyself; thy record is not true.

14. Jesus answered and said unto them, Though I bear record of myself, yet my record is true: for I know whence I came, and whither I go; but ye cannot tell whence I come, and whither I go.

15. Ye judge after the flesh; I judge no man.

16. And yet if I judge, my judgment is true: for I am not alone, but I and the Father that sent me.

17. It is also written in your law, that the testimony of two men is true.

18. I am one that bear witness of myself, and the Father that sent me beareth witness of me.

19. Then said they unto him, Where is thy Father? Jesus answered, Ye neither know me, nor my Father: if ye had known me, ye should have known my Father also.

20. These words spake Jesus in the treasury, as he taught in the temple: and no man laid hands on him; for his hour was not yet come.

21. Then said Jesus again unto them, I go my way, and ye shall seek me, and shall die in your sins: whither I go, ye cannot come.

22. Then said the Jews, Will he kill himself? because he saith, Whither I go, ye cannot come.

23. And he said unto them, Ye are from beneath; I am from above: ye are of this world; I am not of this world.

24. I said therefore unto you, that ye shall die in your sins: for if ye believe not that I am he, ye shall die in your sins.

25. Then said they unto him, Who art thou? And Jesus saith unto them, Even

the same that I said unto you from the beginning.

26. I have many things to say and to judge of you: but he that sent me is true; and I speak to the world those things which I have heard of him.

27. They understood not that he spake to them of the Father.

28. Then said Jesus unto them, When ye have lifted up the Son of man, then shall ye know that I am he, and that I do nothing of myself; but as my Father hath taught me, I speak these things.

29. And he that sent me is with me: the Father hath not left me alone; for I do always those things that please him.

30. As he spake these words, many believed on him.

31. Then said Jesus to those Jews which believed on him, If ye continue in my word, then are ye my disciples indeed;

32. And ye shall know the truth, and the truth shall make you free.

33. They answered him, We be Abraham's seed, and were never in bondage to any man: how sayest thou, Ye shall be made free?

34. Jesus answered them, Verily, verily, I say unto you, Whosoever committeth sin is the servant of sin.

35. And the servant abideth not in the house for ever: but the Son abideth ever.

36. If the Son therefore shall make you free, ye shall be free indeed.

37. I know that ye are Abraham's seed; but ye seek to kill me, because my word hath no place in you.

38. I speak that which I have seen with my Father: and ye do that which ye have seen with your father.

39. They answered and said unto him, Abraham is our father. Jesus saith unto them, If ye were Abraham's children, ye would do the works of Abraham.

40. But now ye seek to kill me, a man that hath told you the truth, which I have heard of God: this did not Abraham.

41. Ye do the deeds of your father. Then said they to him, We be not born of fornication; we have one Father, even God.

42. Jesus said unto them, If God were your Father, ye would love me: for I proceeded forth and came

from God; neither came I of myself, but he sent me.

43. Why do ye not understand my speech? even because ye cannot hear my word.

44. Ye are of your father the devil, and the lusts of your father ye will do. He was a murderer from the beginning, and abode not in the truth, because there is no truth in him. When he speaketh a lie, he speaketh of his own: for he is a liar, and the father of it.

45. And because I tell you the truth, ye believe me not.

46. Which of you convinceth me of sin? And if I say the truth, why do ye not believe me?

47. He that is of God heareth God's words: ye therefore hear them not, because ye are not of God.

48. Then answered the Jews, and said unto him, Say we not well that thou art a Samaritan, and hast a devil?

49. Jesus answered, I have not a devil; but I honour my Father, and ye do dishonour me.

50. And I seek not mine own glory: there is one that seeketh and judgeth.

51. Verily, verily, I say unto you, If a man keep my saying, he shall never see death.

52. Then said the Jews unto him, Now we know that thou hast a devil. Abraham is dead, and the prophets; and thou sayest, If a man keep my saying, he shall never taste of death.

53. Art thou greater than our father Abraham, which is dead? and the prophets are dead: whom makest thou thyself?

54. Jesus answered, If I honour myself, my honour is nothing: it is my Father that honoureth me; of whom ye say, that he is your God:

55. Yet ye have not known him; but I know him: and if I should say, I know him not, I shall be a liar like unto you: but I know him, and keep his saying.

56. Your father Abraham rejoiced to see my day: and he saw it, and was glad.

57. Then said the Jews unto him, Thou art not yet fifty years old, and hast thou seen Abraham?

58. Jesus said unto them, Verily, verily, I say unto you, Before Abraham was, I am.

59. Then took they up stones to cast at him: but Jesus hid himself, and went

out of the temple, going   them, and so passed by.
through the midst of

The Feast of Tabernacles (where this discourse took place) was one of the three annual festivals wherein every male Israelite was to present himself (if possible) before the Lord in the temple at Jerusalem.[32] It was held on the fifteenth day of the seventh month (called Tishri, corresponding to September or the beginning of October), and began five days after the day of Atonement (wherein the sins of Israel were to be removed and its covenant with God restored). The feast celebrated the completion of the harvest and the abundance Jehovah had given his chosen people, and it was to be kept by a sanctified nation.[33] The joyful feast also commemorated Israel's hope for the conversion of the heathen, and directed the Jews' thoughts forward to the coming of the Messiah.[34]

Traditionally the people lived in outdoor "booths" while they attended this feast, in remembrance of Israel's wanderings in the wilderness (Leviticus 23:42–43). The booths were erected throughout Jerusalem, and residents and visitors alike lived in them during the feast. It was a requirement of all who came to the feast that they spend the first night in the city: after that they could sleep elsewhere as long it was within a Sabbath day's journey of the temple.[35] Jesus did not participate in this custom, for the scripture notes that he came to the feast late (John 7:10, 14). Presumably he stayed with friends on the Mount of Olives, or perhaps with Mary, Martha, and Lazarus at their home in Bethany.

This feast was rich in tradition and symbolism. During the first night of the feast four great candelabra were filled with oil and lighted. They burned throughout each night of the celebration, providing light for the courts of the temple and illuminating "every court in Jerusalem."[36] The light from the candelabra represented the light of Jehovah, and the Midrash[37] specifically referred to Jehovah as the "Enlightener." The Midrash further recorded the words, "the light dwelleth with him,"[38] applying them specifically to the Messiah. The symbolic meaning of this portion of the celebration was in the "express Messianic expectation of the Rabbis."[39]

Jesus constantly used the circumstances of life to enhance the understanding of those who heard him, and in this sermon he used an analogy that the Pharisees in particular and the people in general could not misunderstand. He came to the temple early, before dawn had broken. The four giant candelabra were still glowing in the inner courts of the temple, piercing the darkness of night, when the sun rimmed the crest of the Mount of Olives. It may have been at this point that Jesus announced his Messiahship to those around him (including the proud Pharisees and rulers of the Jews) by declaring, "I am the light of the world." It was the Lord's intention to teach those who accompanied him that morning, so he proceeded on to the area in the temple that custom had designated for that purpose.[40] This great discourse on the light of the world is found in the eighth chapter of John, and it falls into three definite parts:

Part One

John 8:1–11

The Pharisees brought a woman to Jesus and accused her of adultery—taken in the very act![41] Under Jewish law they could stone her (and her consort) to death for this crime. They asked Jesus what he would do to punish the woman. They were "tempting" him, hoping he would say something they could use to accuse him before their courts. The Law of Moses was clear in these circumstances; therefore, it was obvious that the Pharisees were trying to trap Christ before the people.[42]

Only the woman "taken in adultery" was brought before the Savior. Her consort was conspicuously absent. This would seem to indicate how deliberately devious the Pharisees were being, for the Law specifically required that the man be punished along with the woman if they were found guilty of adultery (Leviticus 20:10). In any case the matter involved no legal complications, since the punishment decreed by the Law of Moses had long since lapsed.[43]

Jesus stooped down and wrote on the ground with his finger, as if he had not heard the Pharisees. They continued to ask him, so he stood up and responded simply, "He that is without sin among you, let him first cast a stone at her." Then he again stooped down and wrote upon the ground. His answer totally disarmed his antagonists. His appeal to their consciences placed the burden of sin upon their shoulders, and finding themselves convicted, they slowly went out, "one by one, beginning at the eldest, even unto the last." After a moment's pause Jesus looked up and found himself alone with the woman. He asked her where her accusers were. She said no man had stayed to condemn her. Then the Lord answered compassionately, "Neither do I condemn thee: go, and sin no more."

PART TWO

John 8:12–32

The narrative of the second part of this discourse begins while Jesus was in the treasury, or the "court of the women," where thirteen silver, trumpet-shaped receptacles had been placed to receive charitable contributions.[44] Jesus began by declaring, "I am the light of the world: he that followeth me shall not walk in darkness, but shall have the light of life." As previously noted, the Lord used an analogy in his Messianic claim which would not have gone unnoticed by the Pharisees[45] (Isaiah 49:6; 60:1–3). His declaration was reminiscent of the aged prophet Simeon who, when he saw the babe Jesus brought into the temple, declared, "A light to lighten the Gentiles, and the glory of thy people Israel" (Luke 2:32).

This Messianic declaration was too much for the Pharisees and they immediately challenged Jesus; but they did not address themselves to the question of his Messiahship. Rather, they accused him of self-aggrandizement (a crime under their Law) and questioned the legality of his statement, since he had no witness to corroborate it (for their Law required that acceptable evidence be presented by two or more witnesses; Deuteronomy 17:6).

The Lord was appealing to the spiritual nature of his audience, but the Pharisees rejected that appeal and reverted to their temporal concept of the anticipated Messiah. The Pharisees were relying on the technicalities of the Law when they demanded more evidence than the Lord's own testimony. They knew full well that such a request would require the Savior to perform the Messianic sign to prove his Messiahship.[46] Their request for this sign was simply another form of the temptation presented by Satan to Jesus when he challenged, "If thou art the Christ . . . " They were obviously judging the Lord "as one suspected, and charged with guilt."[47]

Jesus was very candid in his reply to the Pharisees. He acknowledged the technicality they had raised under the Law, but clarified two points concerning it. First, although he had testified of himself, he was qualified to do so because he knew the facts of his origin and what his mission was, and he declared that the Pharisees did not. The Jewish leaders only judged pertaining to the flesh and he would judge no man in that manner, for he judged by the Spirit, which was after the manner of his Father. He declared that the second of his witnesses was his Father, who also testified of him. By saying this, Jesus overcame the requirements of the rabbinical law, for under that law the testimony of an accused was rejected only if it was not supported by a witness—if another testified in behalf of the accused, the accused could then also testify for himself.[48]

Jesus was correct in his interpretation of their law and the inquiring Pharisees recognized it, so they asked him a second question: "Where is thy Father?" Once again their thoughts were literal and not spiritual. Although they recognized the Lord's claim to the Messiahship, they continued to question the physical and not the spiritual nature of that claim: Jesus immediately silenced them by declaring that they did not know him or the Father, for had they known either of them, they would have accepted him. This exchange obviously made the Pharisees angry, but the scripture states, "No man laid hands on him; for his hour was not yet come."

The text seems to indicate that Jesus now left the treasury area and perhaps moved to one of the "porches" of the temple where his conversation could be extended to more than the

Pharisees. He told his listeners in a second declaration of his Messiahship that he would soon leave them, and because of their sins, where he went they could not come. He was referring to the spiritual nature of his kingdom, but the Pharisees again took his comments in a literal sense and asked if he would kill himself. In their blind hypocrisy they felt that this was the only way he could separate himself from them in death, for they believed that suicide warranted the darkest reaches of the grave.[49]

Jesus responded to their deliberate ignorance by plainly stating that he was from above (from heaven), and they were of "this world." They would be separated from him because they would die in their sins, and this because they would not repent and believe in him. In exasperation the unrighteous Pharisees asked, "Who art thou?" Jesus patiently responded, "Even the same that I said unto you from the beginning."

The apparent, feigned misunderstanding on the part of the Pharisees precipitated the Lord's third declaration of his Messiahship in this section of the discourse. He turned to his antagonists and declared, "When ye have lifted up the Son of man, then shall ye know that I am he, and that I do nothing of myself; but as my Father hath taught me, I speak these things." Only when they had killed him would they recognize that he spoke the truth, and that he was only doing the will of his Father in Heaven. John reports that "many believed on him" because of this open declaration and his defense under the Law. Jesus told the Jews that believed, "If ye continue in my word, then are ye my disciples indeed; and ye shall know the truth, and the truth shall make you free."

PART THREE

John 8:33–59

It is clear from the Lord's comments that the Jewish leadership were planning his death. He tried to turn them from their evil purpose by claiming his rightful station and affording them the opportunity of accepting him—but they would not. They longed for a temporal, powerful Messiah, not what they considered an ineffectual, spiritual one. To recognize Jesus as the Messiah meant that they had to acknowledge God as his Father, and that would give Jesus a moral kinship with God that they did not have. The Jews did not believe that as a result of the Fall all men had become corrupted (because of sin); therefore, they did not have a need for a spiritual Savior.[50] Their apostasy from the truth had led them to misunderstand the Fall, Moses, and the prophets; therefore, it was difficult for them to now accept what Jesus was claiming. Before they would accept him as the Messiah they wanted a direct confirmation from God, some great, temporal sign that they could not miss. They kept ignoring the spiritual application of the Lord's words and reverting back to their temporal beliefs.

Jesus told the Jews that he would make them free, but they felt that as Israelites they were already "free." It was an excommunicable offense to call any Israelite a slave.[51] With great pride they challenged Jesus' authority, declaring that they were "Abraham's seed." Jesus ignored their pomposity and stated flatly, "Whosoever commiteth a sin is the servant of sin." Then he added, "If the Son . . . shall make you free, ye shall be free indeed." Jesus was talking about freedom from sin through repentance, but the obdurate leaders were still applying his words to their temporal condition. Jesus acknowledged that they descended from Abraham, but waved aside the claim that they would inherit the kingdom as a result of that lineage. Then he openly confronted them with seeking to kill him, and he alienated himself from them even further by declaring that he only did that which he had "seen with [his] Father," and they were doing that which they had seen with their "father."

Again the Jews boastfully claimed Abraham as their father, to which Jesus boldly replied, "If ye were Abraham's children, ye would do the works of Abraham." He again reminded them that they sought to kill him, a deed not dictated by Abraham, but by their real "father." The indignant Jews recognized the association Jesus was making and declared that they had but one Father, "even God."

The anger of the Jewish leaders must have been increasing, but the Lord continued by declaring that if God was their Father they would love him [Jesus], for he proceeded forth from God himself. The Lord then asked them a simple question, perhaps expressing impatience with the Pharisees when he exclaimed, "Why do ye not understand my speech?" Without waiting for their answer the Lord candidly continued, "Ye are of your father the devil, and the lusts of your father ye will do." The angry Jews retorted with an insult: "Thou art a Samaritan, and hast a devil." They knew what the Lord meant, but rejected his appraisal of their sinful nature, "an element which Judaism had never taken into account."[52]

Jesus was trying to teach the Jews that although they were literal descendants of Abraham, they could not simply inherit salvation. By their disobedience they had become adopted sons of the devil.[53] The Lord's argument was unimpeachable, so they accused him of having a devil and being a Samaritan; they were calling him a heretic, a prince of demons, Satan, literally a "child of the devil."[54] Jesus quickly put aside this ridiculous charge by stating, "I have not a devil; but I honour my Father, and ye do dishonour me." Again he offered them eternal life, stating that if they would but keep his sayings they should "never see death." He would not be distracted from his discourse, but they again rejected the spiritual application of his words and declared that Abraham and the prophets were dead, and asked whether he therefore was greater than their father, Abraham. Again they asked him, "Whom makest thou thyself?"

The sermon now comes to a conclusion. Jesus halted the continual wrangling that had been taking place by leaving the Jews with one more open declaration of his Messiahship, forcing them to apply his discourse to their own condition by claiming Father Abraham had "rejoiced to see [His] day." The Jews were incredulous, and said, "Thou art not yet fifty years old, and hast thou seen Abraham?" Their dull, spiritual condition continued to lead them to literal interpretations, but in great strength Jesus quietly stated, "Before Abraham was, I am."

The Lord could not have stated his position more clearly. The Jewish leaders did not misunderstand his words, but chose to wilfully misinterpret them.[55] Jesus had symbolically used the sacred title of Jehovah (the Messiah) in his own behalf. Moses, the great lawgiver, had asked the Lord what he could tell the children of Israel that would prove that he (Moses) represented God. "What is his (God's) name?" Moses had asked. "I AM THAT I AM," Jehovah had responded. (Exodus 3:13-14.) John's rendering of the Lord's statement could correctly read, "Verily, verily, I say unto you, Before Abraham, was I AM."[56]

This divine declaration blinded the Pharisees with rage. They rushed to pick up stones that they might cast them at Jesus and kill him, but "his hour was not yet come." The scriptures state that he "hid" himself, "and went out of the temple, going through the midst of them, and so passed by."[57]

The Good Shepherd

John 10:1-42

1. Verily, verily, I say unto you, He that entereth not by the door into the sheepfold, but climbeth up some other way, the same is a thief and a robber.

2. But he that entereth in by the door is the shepherd of the sheep.

3. To him the porter openeth; and the sheep hear his voice: and he calleth his own sheep by name, and leadeth them out.

4. And when he putteth forth his own sheep, he goeth before them, and the sheep follow him: for they know his voice.

5. And a stranger will they not follow, but will flee from him: for they know not the voice of strangers.

6. This parable spake Jesus unto them: but they understood not what things they were which he spake unto them.

7. Then said Jesus unto them again, Verily, verily, I say unto you, I am the door of the sheep.

8. All that ever came before me are thieves and robbers: but the sheep did not hear them.

9. I am the door: by me if any man enter in, he shall be saved, and shall go in and out, and find pasture.

10. The thief cometh not, but for to steal, and to kill, and to destroy: I am come that they might have life, and that they might have it more abundantly.

11. I am the good shepherd: the good shepherd

giveth his life for the sheep.

12. But he that is an hireling, and not the shepherd, whose own the sheep are not, seeth the wolf coming, and leaveth the sheep, and fleeth: and the wolf catcheth them, and scattereth the sheep.

13. The hireling fleeth, because he is an hireling, and careth not for the sheep.

14. I am the good shepherd, and know my sheep, and am known of mine.

15. As the Father knoweth me, even so know I the Father: and I lay down my life for the sheep.

16. And other sheep I have, which are not of this fold: them also I must bring, and they shall hear my voice; and there shall be one fold, and one shepherd.

17. Therefore doth my Father love me, because I lay down my life, that I might take it again.

18. No man taketh it from me, but I lay it down of myself. I have power to lay it down, and I have power to take it again. This commandment have I received of my Father.

19. There was a division therefore again among the Jews for these sayings.

20. And many of them said, He hath a devil, and is mad; why hear ye him?

21. Others said, These are not the words of him that hath a devil. Can a devil open the eyes of the blind?

22. And it was at Jerusalem the feast of the dedication, and it was winter.

23. And Jesus walked in the temple in Solomon's porch.

24. Then came the Jews round about him, and said unto him, How long dost thou make us to doubt? If thou be the Christ, tell us plainly.

25. Jesus answered them, I told you, and ye believed not: the works that I do in my Father's name, they bear witness of me.

26. But ye believe not, because ye are not of my sheep, as I said unto you.

27. My sheep hear my voice, and I know them, and they follow me:

28. And I give unto them eternal life; and they shall never perish, neither shall any man pluck them out of my hand.

29. My Father, which gave them me, is greater than all; and no man is able to pluck them out of my

Father's hand.

30. I and my Father are one.

31. Then the Jews took up stones again to stone him.

32. Jesus answered them, Many good works have I shewed you from my Father; for which of those works do ye stone me?

33. The Jews answered him, saying, For a good work we stone thee not; but for blasphemy; and because that thou, being a man, makest thyself God.

34. Jesus answered them, Is it not written in your law, I said, Ye are gods?

35. If he called them gods, unto whom the word of God came, and the scripture cannot be broken;

36. Say ye of him, whom the Father hath sanctified, and sent into the world, Thou blasphemest; because I said, I am the Son of God?

37. If I do not the works of my Father, believe me not.

38. But if I do, though ye believe not me, believe the works: that ye may know, and believe, that the Father is in me, and I in him.

39. Therefore they sought again to take him: but he escaped out of their hand,

40. And went away again beyond Jordan into the place where John at first baptized; and there he abode.

41. And many resorted unto him, and said, John did no miracle: but all things that John spake of this man were true.

42. And many believed on him there.

The good shepherd discourse actually consists of two discourses delivered on two separate occasions. The Savior gave the first (verses 1–21) while he was at the Feast of Tabernacles (where he also delivered the previous discourse, "the light of the world," and the discourse on "how knoweth this man letters?"). The second (verses 22–42) was delivered at the Feast of Dedication.[58]

Although delivered at two different times and with two months between them, John undoubtedly placed both discourses in the same chapter because Jesus declared his Messiahship by giving the same allegory to the same people in both discourses. These two discussions comprise the last public sermon Jesus gave in his ministry.

The allegory of a shepherd appears often in the scriptures and is one the rabbis of Christ's day also used frequently. This familiar comparison would have undoubtedly caused the Jewish leadership to remember the warnings of the Old Testament prophets against false and evil shepherds. (Jeremiah 23:1-4; 25:32-38; Isaiah 56:10-12; Ezekiel 34; Zechariah 11.) One could say that the Lord was fulfilling the prophecy of Ezekiel when he delivered his sermon of the good shepherd. (Ezekiel 34:23.)

In this discourse, Jesus first refers to himself as the door to the sheepfold, and then as the shepherd—a shepherd who first watches over the sheep and later gives his life for them. The true shepherds of Israel entered into the sheepfold by the door, whereas thieves and robbers attempted entry by some other way.

The Lord appeared to be describing the Pharisees and Sadducees of his day who had attained religious leadership over the flock but who had not done so in accordance with God's requirements. Further, they refused to recognize the correct way to enter the sheepfold. Their voice was that of a stranger, not of the shepherd. True, they looked forward to the coming of the Messiah and believed that the Old Testament prophesied of his advent, but they refused to accept Jesus as that Messiah. They not only rejected him but also sought to kill him.

These would-be "shepherds" had entered the flock through the wrong door, and by their rejection of the Lord had shown themselves to be false shepherds indeed. "Never has been written or spoken a stronger arraignment of false pastors, unauthorized teachers, self-seeking hirelings who teach for self and divine for dollars, deceivers who pose as shepherds yet avoid the door and climb over 'some other way,' prophets in the devil's employ, who to achieve their master's purpose, hesitate not to robe themselves in the garments of assumed sanctity, and appear in sheep's clothing, while inwardly they are ravening wolves."[59]

Having chastized the false shepherds of Israel, the Lord again declared his Messiahship, describing himself as the good shepherd who would give his life for his sheep, while contrasting himself with the hireling shepherds who would leave the sheep to scatter at the first sign of danger. He prophesied his untimely death and his resurrection from the grave by declaring that he would provide salvation and care for the sheep.[60]

Although Jesus considered the Jews of his time as his sheep, he noted that he also had other sheep which were not of the Jewish fold. These sheep must also hear his voice, for there was but one fold and one shepherd. The other sheep Jesus spoke of were the remaining tribes of the House of Israel.

These "other" sheep included those who, under Jehovah's personal direction, had migrated from Jerusalem to inhabit the Western Hemisphere. These sheep had also been told of the Savior's coming, and were anxiously awaiting that great event which would occur after his resurrection. (Helaman 14:2-5, 20-21; 3 Nephi 11-28.) But these were not the only sheep Jesus was referring to, for he would also visit the ten lost tribes of Israel (3 Nephi 21:26).

The Jews' reaction to this doctrine differed and there was a "division among them." Some chose to not believe the Lord and, resorting to their familiar ploy, declared that he had a devil or was mad. But Jesus had opened the eyes of a blind man[61] the previous day, and this caused some to wonder and question whether a devil could open the eyes of the blind. Thus ended the part of the discourse delivered at the Feast of Tabernacles.

John states that when Jesus gave his discourse at the Feast of Dedication, he entered the temple and went to Solomon's porch. His appearance caused many of the leaders of the Jews to literally crowd around him and bar his way. They immediately began to question him, and Jesus again took up the theme of the good shepherd. This is evidence that the Jews had recognized Christ's previous claim to the Messiahship, and hemming him in with an undoubtedly hostile spirit, they demanded, "How long dost thou make us to doubt? If thou be the Christ, tell us plainly!"

Jesus had been forced to leave the Feast of Tabernacles and even Judea because of the hostility of the Jewish leadership. The question now presented to him was couched in that same hostile spirit.[62] It demanded a simple yes or no answer, but Jesus would not reply in this manner. He did not claim to be the political Messiah the people were looking for—an earthly conquerer who would save their bodies rather than their souls.[63]

The answer the Lord gave them was probably more than the Jewish leadership bargained for. He declared, "I told you, and ye believed not: the works that I do in my Father's name, they bear witness of me." Then Jesus returned to the allegory of the sheep by declaring, "Ye believe not, because ye are not of my sheep." He concluded his testimony by promising the true sheep eternal life because his Father had given him the power to do so. Then he abruptly ended with the statement, "I and my Father are one."

The rage of the Jews was instantaneous! They had asked for a direct answer and Jesus had given it. It is obvious that they found no ambiguity in his words for the scripture states that they immediately took up stones to stone him. Jesus forestalled their attack by asking them for which of his good works they would stone him? They tersely stated, "For a good work we stone thee not; but for blasphemy; and because that thou, being a man, makest thyself God." Can there be any doubt of their understanding?

With the leadership's attention focused on him, Jesus refuted the charge of blasphemy by citing the example of Israel's judges being awarded the title of "god," and "sons of the highest," because as God's representatives they had wielded his authority (Psalm 82:6). In this instance they were called gods because they did the very acts of God. Christ concluded that if these men were called gods because they did the work of God, why was it blasphemy for him, who had been sanctified and sent into the world by that same Deity, to say he was the Son of God? He testified that he did the Father's works and challenged them to compare his claim to his works. If the works were not of the Father, they were justified in not believing him; but if his works were of the Father, then they would know that "the Father is in me, and I in Him." The result of the Lord's claim was predictable, for the Jewish leaders again sought to capture him; but he "escaped out of their hand"[64] and traveled over beyond Jordan to the place where John had first baptized. Although this was the Lord's last visit to the Holy City before his crucifixion, the people had become so hostile toward him that it was again necessary for him to leave both Jerusalem and Judea.

The scriptures do not indicate how long he stayed in Perea, but his rejection by the Jewish leaders in the Holy City was at least momentarily salved by the success he enjoyed in this area of John's ministry. The scriptures state that many followed him, "and many believed on him there."

Part Five

Teaching

Baptism

John 3:1-21

1. There was a man of the Pharisees, named Nicodemus, a ruler of the Jews:

2. The same came to Jesus by night, and said unto him, Rabbi, we know that thou art a teacher come from God: for no man can do these miracles that thou doest, except God be with him.

3. Jesus answered and said unto him, Verily, verily, I say unto thee, Except a man be born again, he cannot see the kingdom of God.

4. Nicodemus saith unto him, How can a man be born when he is old? can he enter the second time into his mother's womb, and be born?

5. Jesus answered, Verily, verily, I say unto thee, Except a man be born of water and of the Spirit, he cannot enter into the kingdom of God.

6. That which is born of the flesh is flesh; and that which is born of the Spirit is spirit.

7. Marvel not that I said unto thee, Ye must be born

again.

8. The wind bloweth where it listeth, and thou hearest the sound thereof, but canst not tell whence it cometh, and whither it goeth: so is every one that is born of the Spirit.

9. Nicodemus answered and said unto him, How can these things be?

10. Jesus answered and said unto him, Art thou a master of Israel, and knowest not these things?

11. Verily, verily, I say unto thee, We speak that we do know, and testify that we have seen; and ye receive not our witness.

12. If I have told you earthly things, and ye believe not, how shall ye believe, if I tell you of heavenly things?

13. And no man hath ascended up to heaven, but he that came down from heaven, even the Son of man which is in heaven.

14. And as Moses lifted up the serpent in the wilderness, even so must the Son of man be lifted up:

15. That whosoever believeth in him should not perish, but have eternal life.

16. For God so loved the world, that he gave his only begotten Son, that whosoever believeth in him should not perish, but have everlasting life.

17. For God sent not his Son into the world to condemn the world; but that the world through him might be saved.

18. He that believeth on him is not condemned: but he that believeth not is condemned already, because he hath not believed in the name of the only begotten Son of God.

19. And this is the condemnation, that light is come into the world, and men loved darkness rather than light, because their deeds were evil.

20. For every one that doeth evil hateth the light, neither cometh to the light, lest his deeds should be reproved.

21. But he that doeth truth cometh to the light, that his deeds may be made manifest, that they are wrought in God.

Cross-reference

JST John 3:18

It was time for the Feast of the Passover, and Jesus had come to Jerusalem to attend his first Passover since the commencement of his public ministry.[1] At the beginning of this celebration Jesus had forcefully expelled the money changers and other traffickers from the temple. The Jews did nothing to stop the Lord's evictions, but they asked him for a sign of his authority to exercise such control over their customs and traditions. Jesus would not give them a public sign, but he performed many miracles among the people, which produced initial belief in him as the Savior (John 2:23).

A man named Nicodemus lived in Jerusalem at this time. He was a leader of the Jews and a member of the Sanhedrin. There may have been multiple rulers and leaders who initially believed in Christ, but the scriptures identify only Nicodemus. They generally portray the Pharisees and other Jewish leaders as being opposed to Christ, "but it [would] be strange indeed if there [were] to be found among them no exceptions to the general characteristics; strange if honesty, candour, and sensibility, [were] utterly dead among them all. Even among rulers, scribes, Pharisees, and wealthy members of the Sanhedrin, Christ found believers and followers."[2]

We hear of Nicodemus only in the Gospel of John. In addition to his nocturnal meeting with Jesus, John records Nicodemus's limited defense of the Savior before the Sanhedrin (John 7:50) and his consideration for the Lord's body at the time of His burial (John 19:39). It would seem evident that Nicodemus had an "honest desire to befriend and acknowledge One whom he knew to be a Prophet, even if he did not at once recognize in Him the promised Messiah."[3]

John's brief record indicates that Nicodemus was a Pharisee by training, and a wealthy member of the Sanhedrin. It is evident that he was sincere with the Lord, although his limited faith in Him was apparently based on miracles.[4] He was cautious by nature, and timid of character,[5] and he did not have the strength to make the sacrifices necessary to openly align himself with the Lord.

Jesus identified Nicodemus as a "master of Israel," which suggests he may have been one of the three leading officers in the Sanhedrin. The Sanhedrin consisted of seventy educated and intellectual Jewish leaders plus a president, a vice-president, and "the 'Master' or wise man" (sometimes one of the seventy).[6] The discussion between Jesus and Nicodemus reads like an outline, enumerating only the important subjects and high points and leaving obvious gaps in the conversation.[7]

The scripture reports that Nicodemus came to Jesus by night, thus veiling his initial conversation with the Lord in secrecy. In his salutation to the Lord he said, "Rabbi, we know that thou art a teacher come from God: for no man can do these miracles that thou doest, except God be with him." Nicodemus's use of the word *we* might indicate that he came as a representative of the Sanhedrin. The miracles that Jesus had performed would qualify him for such a salutation because the Jews believed in miracles and they would not have accepted a teacher of a new faith without that teacher first evidencing the miraculous.[8]

Jesus may not have been particularly impressed that one of the Jewish rulers was so addressing him, but, "we can scarcely realize the difficulties which he [Nicodemus] had to overcome. It must have been a mighty power of conviction, to break down prejudice so far as to lead this old Sanhedrist to acknowledge a Galilean, untrained in the Schools, as a Teacher come from God, and to repair to Him for direction on, perhaps, the most delicate and important point in Jewish theology."[9]

In response to Nicodemus's salutation and declaration (and perhaps also to an unrecorded question) Jesus declared, "Except a man be born again, he cannot see the kingdom of God," defining the universal requirement for entrance into the kingdom of heaven. Nicodemus, skilled in the subtle expositions of the Law and totally familiar with the scriptures, incredulously responded with a statement that showed a total lack of understanding of his own religion: "How can a man be born when he is old? can he enter the second time into his mother's womb, and be born?" Jesus ignored Nicodemus's literal interpretation of this spiritual teaching and with greater detail reiterated the fundamental requirements for entry into the kingdom of God. He again declared that all men (Jew or Gentile) must be "born again," first of water, and then of the Spirit. They had to be reborn through baptism by immersion and spiritually regenerated (by the Holy Ghost) through repentance before they could enter the kingdom of God.[10]

This undoubtedly threw Nicodemus's thoughts into a state of confusion because it put his basic beliefs in question. The Jews considered every act man performed to be either good or evil. The Jewish concept of "an eye for an eye" applied both in life and after death. When the Lord said that a man had to be born again to enter the kingdom of heaven, he was graphically explaining to Nicodemus that, although the outward observance of legal acts would be taken into account, the motive for those acts would also be considered. Nicodemus had come to Jesus "trusting implicitly to his being a Jew, as a Divine title to citizenship in the new theocracy, and thinking only of formal acts by which he might show his devotion, and increase his claim to the favour of God, here and hereafter."[11] But now he was confronted with the realization that "neither [his] national descent, nor the uttermost exactness of [his] Pharisaic observance . . . availed at all as such, to secure entrance into the kingdom of God."[12]

These teachings were strange to Nicodemus. They were beyond the scope of his Jewish background, and he exclaimed, "How can these things be?" Using the wind as an example, Jesus explained that the physical senses and intellectual learning could not give a man an understanding of the things of God. True, the physical senses could detect the wind, but they could not determine where it came from. Likewise, the physical senses could not detect spiritual confirmation of gospel principles from God.

By now Nicodemus had twice admitted his lack of understanding, causing Jesus to question his ability as the "Master of Israel." He pointedly asked Nicodemus why it was that he knew not these things. If he could not understand these simple, earthly requirements, how could he expect to know of heavenly things? This was undoubtedly a humbling and humiliating experience for Nicodemus. Jesus continued with his discourse by bearing him a personal testimony that he was the Messiah, the Son of man come down from heaven; and just as Moses lifted up a brazen serpent in the wilderness to save Israel from poisonous snakes (Numbers 21:9), so, too, would the Son of God be lifted up to provide eternal life for all who would believe on him; for the Father had sent the Son not to condemn the world, but to save it. Nicodemus must have recognized this common representation of the Messianic expectation.

Jesus continued to elaborate on the principles necessary to attain exaltation, stating that all these things had previously been taught "by the mouth of the holy prophets; for they testified of me" (JST John 3:18). The Lord did not have to condemn the people of the world; they would condemn themselves.

Light had come into the world, but men loved darkness more than light because their "deeds were evil." Nicodemus could see that the principle of judgment (taught as a present reality) would eventually be consummated before the Savior at the judgment day. Those who heard the testimony of Jesus had to decide whether or not he was the Messiah; and some believed, but many did not.

In closing this discourse Jesus enumerated the reasons why men rejected the light that had come unto them. He said that "every one that doeth evil hateth the light, neither cometh to the light, lest his deeds should be reproved. But he that doeth truth goeth to the light that his deeds may be made manifest, that they are wrought in God."

This sermon is striking evidence that even in the early days of his ministry Jesus was using plain, straightforward language to testify that he was the long-awaited Messiah.[13]

On Marriage and Divorce

Matthew 19:1–15

1. And it came to pass, that when Jesus had finished these sayings, he departed from Galilee, and came into the coasts of Judea beyond Jordan;

2. And great multitudes followed him; and he healed them there.

3. The Pharisees also came unto him, tempting him, and saying unto him, Is it lawful for a man to put away his wife for every cause?

4. And he answered and said unto them, Have ye not read, that he which made

them at the beginning made them male and female,

5. And said, For this cause shall a man leave father and mother, and shall cleave to his wife: and they twain shall be one flesh?

6. Wherefore they are no more twain, but one flesh. What therefore God hath joined together, let not man put asunder.

7. They say unto him, Why did Moses then command to give a writing of divorcement, and to put her away?

8. He saith unto them, Moses because of the hardness of your hearts suffered you to put away your wives: but from the beginning it was not so.

9. And I say unto you, Whosoever shall put away his wife, except it be for fornication, and shall marry another, committeth adultery: and whoso marrieth her which is put away doth commit adultery.

10. His disciples say unto him, If the case of the man be so with his wife, it is not good to marry.

11. But he said unto them, All men cannot receive this saying, save they to whom it is given.

12. For there are some eunuchs, which were so born from their mother's womb: and there are some eunuchs, which were made eunuchs of men: and there be eunuchs, which have made themselves eunuchs for the kingdom of heaven's sake. He that is able to receive it, let him receive it.

13. Then were there brought unto him little children, that he should put his hands on them, and pray: and the disciples rebuked them.

14. But Jesus said, Suffer little children, and forbid them not, to come unto me: for of such is the kingdom of heaven.

15. And he laid his hands on them, and departed thence.

Cross-reference

Mark 10:1–12, 13–16

This discourse takes place during Jesus' last Perean mission and before he journeyed to Jerusalem to be crucified. All three of the Synoptic writers agree on the setting; however, Luke omits the discourse and includes the miracle of the healing of ten lepers[14] (perhaps filling in gaps that he felt Matthew and Mark had omitted). All three writers note that multitudes followed Jesus, and they testify that he healed those in need. They undoubtedly made their selections from those occurrences in the ministry of Jesus which they felt were "most important or novel, or else best accorded with the plans of their respective narratives."[15]

It seems that whenever the ministry of Jesus became at all public, the Pharisees and rulers of the Jews were there, lying in wait to entrap him in his speech.[16] On this occasion the Pharisees came to deliberately provoke Jesus, that they might accuse him.[17] Jesus had met them before in this same part of the country under similar circumstances (Luke 16:14), and had answered their taunts and objections by charging them with breaking the spirit of the Law because of their views on the subject of divorce (Luke 16:17-18). The indefatigable Pharisees again took up that topic right where they had previously left off. They "tempted him" by asking the question, "Is it lawful for a man to put away his wife for every cause?" Their question required Christ to give an exposition on the Jewish law in regard to the practice of divorce, one of the most debated questions of the day.[18] The two major schools of Pharisaic Law were in contention on this point; the school of Hillel contended that a man had a literal right to divorce his wife for any cause, while the school of Shammai contended that the marriage bonds could only be broken for offenses against chastity. Although the Jews protected their women in general and discouraged divorce, it was still a very common occurrence.[19] There are two recorded instances where a rabbi desired to be married for only a single day, and then divorced.[20] Grounds for divorce had become extremely liberal, ranging from the sin of adultery to any cause which the man might assign. For instance, if a man ceased to love his wife, if he liked another woman better, or if his wife had spoiled his dinner, he could divorce her.[21]

The Jews undoubtedly asked Jesus this question because they assumed that they could easily sway him from the Mosaic doctrine and the teachings of the rabbis. They felt this was one of the most difficult questions they could ask because (1) the Old Testament was so ambiguous in explaining the institution of divorce, (2) there was strong opposition between the doctrine of the two rabbinical schools, (3) the customs and traditions throughout Israel varied radically, and (4) the Lord's answer might produce strong political implications. Jesus was in Herod's domain, the same Herod who had previously put John the Baptist to death for crying out against the illegal marriage of Herod Antipus with Herodias, Herod's brother's wife. It therefore seemed to the Pharisees that this was the perfect question whereby they could ensnare Jesus.

The Lord avoided the various cavils of the Law and the schools of his day by appealing to a higher authority—his Father. He indicated that God had made man in the beginning and had commanded him that he should leave his father and mother and "cleave to his wife" and "be one flesh." He concluded that what God had joined together, no *man* could put asunder.

Without directly stating it, Jesus condemned both of the Jewish schools of thought. He stated emphatically that man could not undo at his pleasure what God had joined together, thus indicating that divorce was an invention of man.[22]

The Pharisees responded to Jesus with a second question. They asked him, "Why did Moses then command to give a writing of divorcement," if God commanded otherwise? Jesus wasted no time in answering their question. "He saith unto them, Moses, because of the hardness of your hearts, suffered you to put away your wives: but from the beginning it was not so." In other words, Moses had permitted divorce for the protection of the wife, but this was not the original law. Originally God had declared that only for the sin of adultery could a marriage be dissolved. The Mosaic Law had become permissive because of the general unrighteousness of the people.[23]

The Lord now concluded that when the higher law was faithfully lived, no divorce was justified except in the case of unchastity. If a man put away his wife for any other reason, it was a breach of the Law; and if the man remarried, he committed adultery (as did the man who married the divorced woman). Even the Jewish Law in practice during Christ's time dictated that an adultress could not marry the man with whom she had committed adultery.[24]

This interpretation of the Law must have startled the Pharisees and convicted them in their consciences.[25] It is recorded that the Lord's answer definitely caused his disciples some consternation, and they concluded that it was better not to marry because of the potential sin involved; but the Lord disapproved of their solution—except in special cases and for different reasons.[26]

Although Jesus did not condone their view of celibacy, he did enumerate two instances where it would be natural if an individual did not marry, and a third instance where men had selected to forego marriage for the kingdom's sake. He did not necessarily consider any of these conditions to be generally better than marriage—only different. While the disciples' premise may have been wrong, their conclusion was correct—but only in exceptional cases.[27]

The principle concerning divorce, as taught by the Lord, is the same today as it was when he gave it to the Pharisees. "The Lord may allow divorces in one day among a certain people and deny them in another day among a more enlightened populace."[28] Divorce is not a part of the eternal gospel plan, regardless of the type of marriage, but the Lord does permit divorces in some circumstances and for various legitimate reasons (depending on the spiritual stability of the people involved).[29] "Under the most perfect conditions there would be no divorce permitted except where sex sin is involved. In this day divorces are permitted in accordance with civil statutes, and the divorced persons are permitted by the Church to marry again without the stain of immorality which under a higher system would attend such a course."[30]

The Lord's answer silenced the Pharisees and established for his new kingdom the law regarding family life. He changed the position of women from that of slave or toy to the status of equal rights within the family, a position they justly deserved.

Although the Lord had concluded his sermon at this point, the event that followed it augmented the principle he was teaching. Several mothers who had listened to his discussion with the Pharisees brought their little children to Jesus for a blessing.[31] In apparent disregard for the instruction they had received in a prior, similar experience, the disciples attempted to prevent the children from being brought to Jesus. Perhaps they thought that these circumstances were beneath the dignity of a great rabbi;[32] but as if to emphasize the importance of family life, the Lord again chastened the disciples and allowed the children to come unto him. He reminded the disciples that to enter the kingdom of God they must be as a little child—not in size or intellect, but in humility, receptiveness, meekness, and teachability.

The Widow's Mite

Mark 12:41–44

41. And Jesus sat over against the treasury, and beheld how the people cast money into the treasury: and many that were rich cast in much.

42. And there came a certain poor widow, and she threw in two mites, which make a farthing.

43. And he called unto him his disciples, and saith unto them, Verily I say unto you, That this poor widow hath cast more in, than all they which have cast into the treasury:

44. For all they did cast in of their abundance; but she of her want did cast in all that she had, even all her living.

Cross-reference

Luke 21:1–4

On one occasion Jesus was sitting by the treasury, watching the people make contributions. It was the Lord's last visit to the temple before his crucifixion. Earlier in the day he had fielded questions from several Jewish leaders, finally denouncing them for their unbelief.

The treasury was located in the court of the women and occupied a very large area, one capable of accommodating as high as fifteen thousand charitable souls at one time. Along the colonnades of the court were thirteen trumpet-shaped containers. Each bore inscriptions and markings denoting the reason for the contributions it contained. One was used to receive the gifts of those who were behind in their contributions. The gifts in others were used to pay for certain sacrifices or to provide incense, wood, and other items used in the temple services.[33]

Jesus had probably stopped at the court to rest after his tedious discussion with the Pharisees. As he sat, he observed the people who were depositing their gifts in the trumpets. Some gave ostentatiously, and others gave meagerly, but they were all cheerfully performing a happy duty.[34]

Josephus notes that the wealth of the temple treasury was considerable,[35] and one could easily observe that many of the rich contributed liberally; but it was apparent to the Lord that they cast in only of their excess abundance. Then a poor widow came and contributed two mites—all that she had. It was not lawful under the Jewish law for her to contribute less than two mites, and this was "all her living"; but she cast it into the treasury as her humble offering to God. Obviously the widow's contribution was a mere trifle compared with the rich offerings Jesus had observed, but he was deeply impressed with her sacrifice, and he called his disciples to him and said, "Verily I say unto you, That this poor widow hath cast more in than all they which have cast into the treasury." He stressed the fact that the attitude of the giver was greater than the gift itself.[36]

The widow exemplified the essence of charity and self-denial. Her gift was more acceptable to the Lord because of her great sacrifice and devotion.[37] She did not know that the eyes of the Master were upon her, but she truly touched his heart.

> He spake not to her words of encouragement, for she walked by faith; He offered not promise of return, for her reward was in heaven. She knew not that any had seen it— for the knowledge of eyes turned on her, even His, would have flushed with shame the pure cheek of her love; and any word, conscious notice, or promise would have marred and turned aside the rising incense of her sacrifice . . . this deed of self-denying sacrifice [was of] far more, [value] than the great gifts of their [the wealthy] 'superfluity' . . . And

though He spake not to her, yet the sunshine of His words must have fallen into the dark desolateness of her heart; and, though perhaps she knew not why, it must have been a happy day, a day of rich feast in the heart, that when she gave up "her whole living" unto God.[38]

Paul later expanded the principle Jesus was teaching to his disciples when he declared to the Corinthians: "For if there be first a willing mind, it is accepted according to that he hath, and not according to that he hath not" (2 Corinthians 8:12).

Your Fellowman

Matthew 25:31–46

31. When the Son of man shall come in his glory, and all the holy angels with him, then shall he sit upon the throne of his glory:

32. And before him shall be gathered all nations: and he shall separate them one from another, as a shepherd divideth his sheep from the goats:

33. And he shall set the sheep on his right hand, but the goats on the left.

34. Then shall the King say unto them on his right hand, Come, ye blessed of my Father, inherit the kingdom prepared for you from the foundation of the world:

35. For I was an hungred, and ye gave me meat: I was thirsty, and ye gave me drink: I was a stranger, and ye took me in:

36. Naked, and ye clothed me: I was sick, and ye visited me: I was in prison, and ye came unto me.

37. Then shall the righteous answer him, saying, Lord, when saw we thee an hungred, and fed thee? or thirsty, and gave thee drink?

38. When saw we thee a stranger, and took thee in? or naked, and clothed thee?

39. Or when saw we thee sick, or in prison, and came unto thee?

40. And the King shall answer and say unto them, Verily I say unto you, Inasmuch as ye have done it unto one of the least of these my brethren, ye have done it unto me.

41. Then shall he say also

unto them on the left hand, Depart from me, ye cursed, into everlasting fire, prepared for the devil and his angels:

42. For I was an hungred, and ye gave me no meat: I was thirsty, and ye gave me no drink:

43. I was a stranger, and ye took me not in: naked, and ye clothed me not: sick, and in prison, and ye visited me not.

44. Then shall they also answer him, saying, Lord, when saw we thee an hungred, or athirst, or a stranger, or naked, or sick, or in prison, and did not minister unto thee?

45. Then shall he answer them, saying, Verily I say unto you, Inasmuch as ye did it not to one of the least of these, ye did it not to me.

46. And these shall go away into everlasting punishment: but the righteous into life eternal.

After Jesus had completed his final conversations with the Pharisees and the leaders of the Jews in the temple (just prior to his betrayal and crucifixion), he left the temple area with his Apostles and crossed over to the Mount of Olives. There the Apostles asked questions about the prophecies the Lord had made concerning his second coming, and he responded with the Second Coming discourse recorded in Matthew chapter 24 (see chapter 10). After he had completed that discourse and had given some general instructions to his disciples, the Lord proceeded to give the parable of the ten virgins[39] and the parable of the talents.[40]

In these instructions Jesus generally alluded to the judgments that would come upon mankind because of their failure to truly love God and accept him as the Messiah. His conversation briefly touched on the first great commandment, but then he quickly moved away from that subject and instructed the Twelve on the judgment that would result from either keeping or breaking the second great commandment: i.e., to love their fellowman.

The Lord told his disciples that this judgment would occur at the time of his second coming, and then he told them how this would occur. The separation would be as simple as a shepherd dividing his "sheep from the goats." Likewise, the Lord's final judgment would also separate the sheep (the righteous) from the goats (the unrighteous). Those who were righteous and obedient he would place on his right hand, and those who were unrighteous and disobedient he would place on his left. This instruction was intended for those who called themselves disciples (or members of the Church).[41] Although the Jews believed to some degree in the principles of eternal righteousness and eternal punishment, their instructions in this area were limited.[42]

We should take literally the Lord's teachings in this discourse, because in the latter days he admonished the inhabitants of the earth that the day would eventually come when every man would receive "recompense . . . according to his work, and measure . . . according to the measure which he has measured to his fellowman" (D&C 1:10). Jesus taught his disciples by example whom they should serve and what the results of their service would be. After using the example of the sheep and the goats to represent righteous and unrighteous souls, he elaborated by telling the righteous in his example, "For I was an hungred, and ye gave me meat: I was thirsty, and ye gave me drink: I was a stranger, and ye took me in: naked, and ye clothed me: I was sick, and ye visited me: I was in prison, and ye came unto me."

The disciples were puzzled. They asked the Lord when they had fed him or given him drink. "When saw we thee a stranger, and took thee in? or naked, and clothed thee? Or when saw we thee sick, or in prison, and came unto thee?" The Lord replied "Inasmuch as ye have done it unto one of the least of these my brethren, ye have done it unto me." There were also those disciples who had been judged and found wanting in their service. They did not understand the Lord's analogy either, and questioned Jesus as to when they had failed to provide him with food, drink, or other necessities. Again the Lord responded that because they had not done it unto their fellowman, they had not done it unto him. King Benjamin admonished those who were listening to his final address that they would learn wisdom if they learned "that when ye are in the service of your fellow beings ye are only in the service of your God"[43] (Mosiah 2:17).

According to the second great commandment, we will be judged according to how we treat (or perform services for) our fellowman, and the Lord specifically stated that those who were judged in this manner would be judged as if they had performed their acts of charity for him. Our individual responsibility under the second great commandment is often referred to in scriptures (see, for example, Mosiah 4:11–19, 26; D&C 56:14–16; D&C 104:11–18). The test of true discipleship throughout the ages has always been the same. We are commanded to "remember in all things the poor and the needy, the sick and the afflicted, for he that doeth not these things, the same is not my disciple" (D&C 52:40).

At the conclusion of this discourse the Lord determined that those who observed the second great commandment would gain eternal life—a reward of inestimable value—whereas those who did not obey the second great commandment would be cast into the "unfathomable doom" of "everlasting punishment."[44]

The Jewish leaders of Christ's day had misunderstood this concept. They taught that perfect righteousness was necessary before an individual could be sealed up to eternal life, and perfect wickedness was required if a person was to be sealed to "Gehenna" or hell; those in intermediate categories had an undefined fate based on Old Testament teachings[45] (Zechariah 13:9; Daniel 12:2).

Since the restoration of the gospel this concept has been more clearly explained. The Doctrine and Covenants states that "endless torment" and "eternal damnation" are definitions for God's punishment, because "Endless" is one of God's names (D&C 19:6–12). The punishment that those on the left hand of God therefore anticipate (because of their disobedience to the second great commandment) is not endless punishment (i.e., punishment that will have no end), but punishment that is determined by God. The faithful (those on the right hand of God) will receive an inheritance based upon their charitable service toward their fellowman.

The Apostles understood what the Lord was teaching. Paul later evidenced this when he admonished the Saints in Galatia to "bear . . . one another's burdens, and so fulfill the law of Christ" (Galatians 6:2). Paul continued to instruct the Saints in several matters, but concluded, "Let us not be weary in well doing: for in due season we shall reap, if we faint not. As we have therefore opportunity, let us do good unto all men." (Galatians 6:9-10.)

Part Six

"Despised and Rejected of Men"

Question One

"Why eateth your Master with publicans and sinners?"

Matthew 9:9–13

9. And as Jesus passed forth from thence, he saw a man, named Matthew, sitting at the receipt of custom: and he saith unto him, Follow me. And he arose, and followed him.

10. And it came to pass, as Jesus sat at meat in the house, behold, many publicans and sinners came and sat down with him and his disciples.

11. And when the Pharisees saw it, they said unto his disciples, Why eateth your Master with publicans and sinners?

12. But when Jesus heard that, he said unto them, They that be whole need not a physician, but they that are sick.

13. But go ye and learn what that meaneth, I will have mercy, and not sacrifice: for I am not come to call the righteous, but sinners to repentance.

Cross-references

Mark 2:13-17   Luke 5:27-32   JST 9:18-21

It is obvious upon reading the Gospels that the Pharisees, scribes, and rulers of the Jews often came to Jesus or the disciples asking questions concerning the Lord's character, his actions, or his doctrine. While some of these questions were sincere, most were of a demeaning or critical nature as these wicked men attempted to find fault with Jesus. When the Pharisees saw Jesus at Matthew's dinner and noticed the type of guests that were there, they asked the Lord's disciples, "Why eateth your Master with publicans and sinners?" They were criticizing Jesus in an attempt to cause him public embarrassment.[1]

Matthew was holding the dinner to celebrate his call to follow Jesus. Although the scriptures would lead us to believe that Matthew and the Lord had not previously known each other, it is quite apparent that Matthew had previously (and perhaps frequently) heard Jesus teach and had perhaps witnessed his miracles,[2] for Matthew's home was in Capernaum, the city where Jesus lived in the early part of his ministry.

It is significant that Jesus would select Matthew, a publican, to be one of his disciples and one of the chosen Twelve (see chapter 2). Matthew's selection graphically denoted the Lord's total disregard for the mores of his time, since the Jews considered publicans to be vile, corrupt, and evil. They had a bad reputation among the Pharisees because of their greed and exactitude.[3] They were generally thought of as "publicans and sinners," a name indiscriminately given to usurers, gamblers, thieves, shepherds, and sellers of fruit grown on the Sabbath.[4] They were socially classified in the lower levels of the masses by the Pharisees and were considered hopelessly lost because of their "uncleanness." "It was unlawful to come into their company, even with the holy design of inducing them to read the Law, and it was defilement to take food from them, or, indeed, from any stranger, or even to touch a knife belonging to them. [They were] 'unclean' from mere ignorance, or from their callings, or from carelessness, [and] were an 'abomination,' 'vermin,' 'unclean beasts,' and 'twice accursed'."[5] This condemnation extended not only to the individuals who held the position of publican but also to their families. But Jesus was indifferent to such prejudice.

The rabbis had not yet formed an opinion about Jesus, but his participation in the evening's social activities with Matthew and his friends would have been highly irregular to them. Nothing would have been more abhorrent in their minds than to eat with publicans.[6]

Jesus overheard the question posed to his disciples and, without allowing them to respond, he quickly addressed these self-righteous "protectors of the law" by stating, "They that be whole need not a physician, but they that are sick." He admonished the Pharisees to "go . . . and learn what that meaneth." He spoke not of bodily illness, but of spiritual needs, for the Pharisees were as needy in that sense as the publicans he was eating with. While the Pharisees' question spoke of sinners and sins, Jesus' answer spoke of repentance and forgiveness. On this point rabbinism stood "self-confessedly silent and powerless as regarded the forgiveness of sins, so it had emphatically no word of welcome or help for the sinner."[7] This was the basic difference between a call to the kingdom of God and the requirements of the Pharisaic law. While the Pharisees considered themselves very religious, they were also full of pride, prejudice, and hatred—characteristics far worse than eating with "sinners."

Jesus continued his response by quoting from the Old Testament and stating that he would have mercy and not sacrifice (Hosea 6:6). As if to mimic the irony and sarcasm[8] of the Pharisee's question, he then proceeded to declare that he came "not to call the righteous, but sinners to repentance." The Pharisees' question intimated that they considered themselves whole and without sin; therefore, Jesus should go to those who would acknowledge their illness. The Pharisees had cleverly phrased their question in a way that denounced a whole category of sinners, but Jesus answered by quoting their own Law, which required that they heal the sick and call sinners to repentance.[9] Jesus left the Pharisees to make their own application of the answer he had given them. In God's eyes, all men have an equal opportunity to enter his kingdom.

Question Two

"Why do we and the Pharisees fast oft, but thy disciples fast not?"

Matthew 9:14–17

14. Then came to him the disciples of John, saying, Why do we and the Pharisees fast oft, but thy disciples fast not?

15. And Jesus said unto them, Can the children of the bridechamber mourn, as long as the bridegroom is with them? but the days will come, when the bridegroom shall be taken from them, and then shall they fast.

16. No man putteth a piece of new cloth unto an old garment, for that which is put in to fill it up taketh from the garment, and the rent is made worse.

17. Neither do men put new wine into old bottles: else the bottles break, and the wine runneth out, and the bottles perish: but they put new wine into new bottles, and both are preserved.

Cross-references

Mark 2:18–22   Luke 5:33–39

Immediately after Jesus had answered the question, "Why eateth your Master with publicans and sinners?" the Pharisees presented another question to him through the disciples of John the Baptist.[10] John was in prison at the time, and his disciples may have been confused; although John testified of the Savior as the anticipated Messiah, Jesus clearly disregarded the sacred Mosaic Law and its meticulous observance.

John had come as did the prophets of old, and his eccentric style of living may have justified his disciples' (and some of the Pharisees') punctilious observance of the Law. Their question implied that John had taught his disciples to fast and pray (seemingly in a manner similar to that observed by the Pharisees). The Law of Moses prescribed only one official fast day, the Day of Atonement[11] (Leviticus 16:29), but the rabbis had added many public and private fasts. The public fasts generally commemorated the calamities of Israel's past,[12] but the question posed to the Savior was centered around the private fast days wherein the Pharisees aimed at the highest degree of merit obtainable under the observance of their Law. They held prescribed fasts a minimum of twice a week on the second and fifth days (Monday and Thursday). They selected these days of the week because they thought that Moses had gone up on Mount Sinai for the second set of tablets on a Thursday and had returned on a Monday.[13]

The Pharisees, however, had enlarged the fast even beyond this. They celebrated it for many special occasions, believing that fasting would give them lucky dreams and the interpretations thereof, or that it would allow them to receive revelation, avert evil, or procure some good.[14] They reasoned this way because of their concept of hostility between body and spirit. They believed that the spirit could be exalted only by suppressing the body.

John's disciples' question also assumed that Jesus had not taught his disciples to pray, while John's disciples and the Pharisees prayed continually. (The topic of prayer is mentioned only in the Joseph Smith Translation of Matthew.) Nevertheless, the prayers they used were merely mechanical repetitions contrived to fit the hedge of the Law. They were tediously long and terribly depressing, with many superstitions assigned to the words. Their prayers were governed with minute rules not only to ensure the correctness of their content but also to fix the very hours they prayed.[15] At this time in his ministry, however, Jesus had given his disciples no formal rules for prayer or fasting, and in responding to the question he ignored the topic of prayer and dealt only with fasting.

Jesus did not blame John's disciples for asking this question, but he defended himself and his followers by asking another question: "Can the children of the bridechamber mourn, as long as the bridegroom is with them?" The Lord was justified in his position. "But the days will come," he added, "when the bridegroom shall be taken from them, and then shall they fast."

Jesus had come to liberate the Jews from the yoke of the Mosaic ordinances and the bondage that had been placed upon them by the traditions of their fathers. His answer clearly implied an abrogation of the rabbinical rules and numerous traditions of that Law.[16] His answer also proclaimed that he was the Messiah who had come to declare a new law, not merely reform the old one. [17] His new kingdom would not be established by patching up the old robe of Judaism. The gospel that Jesus taught was a new revelation—a new and everlasting covenant—because the rents of the old ceremonial law which Christ ignored could not be patched. Nor could the new "wine" of his kingdom be confined in the old "bottles" of Judaism.

Although Jesus had given the old Law, he avoided an open condemnation of it at this time. He treated it with indifference. Had the children of Israel been righteously observing the old Law the way the Lord gave it in the Old Testament, they would have accepted him in the meridian of time.[18]

Question Three

"Who is my mother?"

Matthew 12:46-50

46. While he yet talked to the people, behold, his mother and his brethren stood without, desiring to speak with him.

47. Then one said unto him, Behold, thy mother and thy brethren stand without, desiring to speak with thee.

48. But he answered and said unto him that told him, Who is my mother? and who are my brethren?

49. And he stretched forth his hand toward his disciples, and said, Behold my mother and my brethren!

50. For whosoever shall do the will of my Father which is in heaven, the same is my brother, and sister, and mother.

Cross-references

Mark 3:31-35   Luke 8:19-21   JST Matthew 12:44

Unlike the previous questions, Jesus posed the question, "Who is my mother?" He directed it to those who were listening to him as he sat teaching. It was apparently a request by his mother (and other members of his family) to speak with him that invoked this query. Their interruption came shortly after the Lord had responded to the Beelzebub argument[19] and could be attributed to the Pharisaic opposition "which either filled [the] relatives of Jesus with fear for His safety, or made them sincerely concerned about His proceedings."[20] The scriptures indicate that at times the Lord's family did not truly understand or accept him as the Messiah. Perhaps they were even somewhat jealous of him; but for whatever reason, their belief in him did not develop until after his resurrection.[21]

The Jews held a deep reverence for parents and family members, but the Lord's response to his family's request to speak with him indicated that he was concerned with higher spiritual relationships, not the earthly ones that may have prompted his family's concern. He would not deviate from his mission, and he would not allow family ties to interfere with his work in any way. He did not condemn his mother or his family and he meant no disrespect by his response. He treated it like he had the incident that had occurred when he was twelve years old and was found teaching in the temple. When his parents asked him at that time why he had not told them what he was doing, he informed them that he was "about his Father's business."

Jesus asked his question to emphasize the principles of the gospel he had been discussing, and to testify of his divinity.[22] He explained that all disciples would become his brothers and sisters if they did the will of the Father. Through their obedience they would experience a new birth into his "family" and become his joint heirs in heaven.

The Lord's work took precedence over the claims of his family and all other temporal things. This early teaching would take on greater importance to the Twelve when the Lord later explained that he expected a like devotion of them (Matthew 10:37; Luke 14:26).

Question Four

"What good thing shall I do, that I may have eternal life?"

Matthew 19:16–30

16. And, behold, one came and said unto him, Good Master, what good thing shall I do, that I may have eternal life?

17. And he said unto him, Why callest thou me good? there is none good but one, that is, God: but if thou wilt enter into life, keep the commandments.

18. He saith unto him, Which? Jesus said, Thou shalt do no murder, Thou shalt not commit adultery, Thou shalt not steal, Thou shalt not bear false witness,

19. Honour thy father and thy mother: and, Thou shalt love thy neighbour as thyself.

20. The young man saith unto him, All these things have I kept from my youth up: what lack I yet?

21. Jesus said unto him, If thou wilt be perfect, go and sell that thou hast, and give to the poor, and thou shalt have treasure in heaven: and come and follow me.

22. But when the young man heard that saying, he went away sorrowful: for he had great possessions.

23. Then said Jesus unto his disciples, Verily I say unto you, That a rich man shall hardly enter into the kingdom of heaven.

24. And again I say unto you, It is easier for a camel to go through the eye of a needle, than for a rich man to enter into the kingdom of God.

25. When his disciples heard it, they were exceedingly amazed, saying, Who then can be saved?

26. But Jesus beheld them, and said unto them, With men this is impossible; but with God all things are possible.

27. Then answered Peter and said unto him, Behold, we have forsaken all, and followed thee; what shall we have therefore?

28. And Jesus said unto them, Verily I say unto you, That ye which have followed me, in the regeneration when the Son of man shall sit in the throne of his glory, ye also shall sit upon twelve thrones, judging the twelve tribes of Israel.

29. And every one that hath forsaken houses, or brethren, or sisters, or father, or mother, or wife, or children, or lands, for my name's

sake, shall receive an hun-
dredfold, and shall inherit
everlasting life.

30. But many that are
first shall be last; and the last
shall be first.

Cross-references

Mark 10:17–31   Luke 18:18–30

As Jesus traveled toward Jerusalem on one of his journeys,
a young man came to him and, addressing him as "Good
Master," asked, "What good thing shall I do that I should have
eternal life?" It was not an unusual question. It was repeatedly
put to the rabbis of the day and frequently occurred in Jewish
writings.[23]

As is usual among the Gospel writers, Matthew reports the
words of the young man; Mark adds the graphic touches, noting that the young man ran to Jesus and kneeled before him;
and Luke, concerned with detail, adds that the young man was
a ruler. It was not common in Israel to be called "Good master,"[24] so the salutation addressed to Jesus was a unique one. It
appears to have been a polite compliment, which undoubtedly
is why the Lord rejected the salutation, emphasizing the distinction concerning the word *good*.[25]

After commenting on the salutation, the Lord responded to
the question by instructing the young man that to enter into
eternal life he must keep all the commandments. This answer
was too general for the rich young ruler, because he apparently
sought some specific "good work" or "task" that he might accomplish in order to enhance his ability to gain the kingdom. So he
pressed Jesus for a specific task and asked, "Which?" desiring
the Lord to enumerate some specific commandment that he might
perform. Jesus enumerated several of the commandments and
ended his instructions with, "Love thy neighbor as thyself."
With apparent sincerity the young man affirmed that he had
accomplished all of these commandments from his youth, yet
he obviously felt that there was something missing, so he asked,
"What lack I yet?"

The Lord did not question the young man's keeping of the
outward requirements of the letter of the Law; but now, dis-

cerning what the young man needed, he tailored his answer to fit that need—that the young ruler might in fact attain the kingdom of heaven. Jesus commanded him to sell all that he had, give it to the poor, and follow him.

This was not a blanket instruction intended for all disciples,[26] rather it was suited specifically to the young ruler standing before Jesus. The Lord undoubtedly directed the instruction to him because he had perceived that the young men needed it. His worldly possessions were standing in the way of his progress. This stern admonition was in conformity with several other admonitions which the Lord had given to those who would follow him. To one man he declared, "Let the dead bury the dead"; to another he explained "that when the hand had been placed to the plough they must not look back"; and to yet another he commanded that they should "hate father and mother" to be worthy of him. Beneath these requests lay the requirement that the Lord's disciples must make a total self-sacrifice for the new kingdom if the kingdom was to be successfully established upon the earth.

But this requirement was too stringent for the young ruler and only disclosed his weakness. He could not choose spiritual rewards over his earthly possessions. He was humbled before the Lord and, recognizing the great sacrifice necessary to attain the kingdom of heaven, allowed the world to get the best of him and retreated into scriptural obscurity.

Using this example Jesus continued to teach the disciples, declaring to them that it was very difficult for rich men to enter the kingdom of heaven. He declared, in fact, that it was easier for a camel to go through the eye of a needle than for a rich man to get into heaven. This saying amazed the disciples exceedingly, for they (along with the young ruler) believed that it was necessary to attain material things in this life in order to attain spiritual things in the kingdom of heaven. This was a doctrine the Jews had developed over the years from the last instructions of Moses to the children of Israel. [27] (See Deuteronomy 28:1–14.)

The stunned Apostles then turned to the Lord and asked, "Who then can be saved?" Jesus calmly responded, "With men this is impossible; but with God all things are possible." Peter now said to the Lord, "Behold, we have forsaken all, and followed thee: what shall we have therefore?" It is evident that Peter (and perhaps all the Twelve) felt that since he had done what the rich young ruler could not do (i.e., give up all to follow Jesus), he might be eligible for a reward in the kingdom of heaven, and he therefore asked the Lord what he might receive as a result of his sacrifice.

Jesus acknowledged the devotion of Peter and the Twelve and assured them that their sacrifice and continued labor would entitle them to sit upon thrones in the kingdom of his Father, where they would judge the twelve tribes of Israel. Lest any of his Apostles should become proud and neglect the work required to enter his kingdom, Jesus cautioned them and said, "Many that are first shall be last; and the last shall be first."

Question Five

"Are there few that be saved?"

Luke 13:22-35

22. And he went through the cities and villages, teaching, and journeying toward Jerusalem.

23. Then said one unto him, Lord, are there few that be saved? And he said unto them,

24. Strive to enter in at the strait gate: for many, I say unto you, will seek to enter in, and shall not be able.

25. When once the master of the house is risen up, and hath shut to the door, and ye begin to stand without, and to knock at the door, saying, Lord, Lord, open unto us;

and he shall answer and say unto you, I know you not whence ye are:

26. Then shall ye begin to say, We have eaten and drunk in thy presence, and thou hast taught in our streets.

27. But he shall say, I tell you, I know you not whence ye are; depart from me, all ye workers of iniquity.

28. There shall be weeping and gnashing of teeth, when ye shall see Abraham, and Isaac, and Jacob, and all the prophets, in the kingdom of God, and you yourselves thrust out.

29. And they shall come from the east, and from the west, and from the north, and from the south, and shall sit down in the kingdom of God.

30. And, behold, there are last which shall be first, and there are first which shall be last.

31. The same day there came certain of the Pharisees, saying unto him, Get thee out, and depart hence: for Herod will kill thee.

32. And he said unto them, Go ye, and tell that fox, Behold, I cast out devils, and I do cures to day and to morrow, and the third day I shall be perfected.

33. Nevertheless I must walk to day, and to morrow, and the day following: for it cannot be that a prophet perish out of Jerusalem.

34. O Jerusalem, Jerusalem, which killest the prophets, and stonest them that are sent unto thee; how often would I have gathered thy children together, as a hen doth gather her brood under her wings, and ye would not!

35. Behold, your house is left unto you desolate: and verily I say unto you, Ye shall not see me, until the time come when ye shall say, Blessed is he that cometh in the name of the Lord.

Jesus was on his last journey toward Jerusalem when "one" came to him and asked, "Are there few that be saved?" Although it is not known who asked the question, it would seem likely that the person was a representative of the Pharisees.[28] Perhaps the question came as a result of the Jewish teaching which emphasized that every Israelite was entitled to a portion in the kingdom of heaven; since they believed that although God had made the world for many people to live in, he had created the hereafter for only a chosen few.[29]

The Lord did not declare that many would be saved; rather he declared that many who strive for the kingdom would not make it because the way was narrow, and once they had been shut out of the kingdom they were out of it for good, even if they pleaded for entrance. The Lord was essentially rescinding the privileges that the Israelites had been claiming. He taught them that it was their spiritual accomplishments that would qualify them for entry into his kingdom. To emphasize this he noted that they would eventually see their own patriarchs and prophets (Abraham, Isaac, and Jacob) in the kingdom, while they themselves would be outside its bounds. They must press on to gain entry into the kingdom while the door was yet open to let them in, lest it be closed and they be forever barred.

Claims based on lineage would not admit the Israelites into the kingdom of God. Earthly acquisitions would not save them. Procrastination in obeying the commandments would endanger their souls; because belief in the Savior was the key that would allow them (and all men) to enter into the kingdom of heaven.[30] Jesus concluded with the warning that many whom they considered to be automatically outside of the bounds of the kingdom would enter therein, while they would be "thrust out."

Sometime later that same day the Pharisees came to Jesus and warned him to leave the area of Perea because Herod sought to kill him. Whether the warning was a ruse[31] or based on legitimate concerns[32] is unknown, but the danger was real enough. But Jesus would not hasten his work, regardless of threats. He chided Herod to the Pharisees and called him a "fox." He told the Pharisees to tell Herod that today he did cures, and he would again do them on the morrow, but on the third day he would be perfected—thus predicting his imminent death at Jerusalem. He lamented over Jerusalem and cried, "O Jerusalem, Jerusalem, which killeth the prophets and stonest them that are sent unto thee." The Savior would not be killed by Herod. Herod ruled in Perea, and prophets perished only in Jerusalem.

Jerusalem was the religious capital of the world and was like no other place. It was the Holy City and the city of the Savior's temple. It was the home of the prophets and the center of Christ's personal ministry; yet it was a city of depravity—a spiritual Sodom and Egypt (Revelation 11:8) where it was foreseen that the Son of God would be crucified (2 Nephi 10:3). After declaring the city's future desolate state, the Lord concluded this teaching sequence by prophesying of Jerusalem's glory in the latter days, in a time when the word of the Lord would again go forth out of that holy city (Isaiah 2:3).

Enemies

"What Went Ye Out for to See?"

Matthew 11:1–30

1. And it came to pass, when Jesus had made an end of commanding his twelve disciples, he departed thence to teach and to preach in their cities.

2. Now when John had heard in the prison the works of Christ, he sent two of his disciples,

3. And said unto him, Art thou he that should come, or do we look for another?

4. Jesus answered and said unto them, Go and shew John again those things which ye do hear and see:

5. The blind receive their sight, and the lame walk, the lepers are cleansed, and the deaf hear, the dead are raised up, and the poor have the gospel preached to them.

6. And blessed is he, whosoever shall not be offended in me.

7. And as they departed, Jesus began to say unto the multitudes concerning John, What went ye out into the wilderness to see? A reed shaken with the wind?

8. But what went ye out

for to see? A man clothed in soft raiment? behold, they that wear soft clothing are in kings' houses.

9. But what went ye out for to see? A prophet? yea, I say unto you, and more than a prophet.

10. For this is he, of whom it is written, Behold, I send my messenger before thy face, which shall prepare thy way before thee.

11. Verily I say unto you, Among them that are born of women there hath not risen a greater than John the Baptist: notwithstanding he that is least in the kingdom of heaven is greater than he.

12. And from the days of John the Baptist until now the kingdom of heaven suffereth violence, and the violent take it by force.

13. For all the prophets and the law prophesied until John.

14. And if ye will receive it, this is Elias, which was for to come.

15. He that hath ears to hear, let him hear.

16. But whereunto shall I liken this generation? It is like unto children sitting in the markets, and calling unto their fellows,

17. And saying, We have piped unto you, and ye have not danced; we have mourned unto you, and ye have not lamented.

18. For John came neither eating nor drinking, and they say, He hath a devil.

19. The son of man came eating and drinking, and they say, Behold a man gluttonous, and a winebibber, a friend of publicans and sinners. But wisdom is justified of her children.

20. Then began he to upbraid the cities wherein most of his mighty works were done, because they repented not.

21. Woe unto thee, Chorazin! woe unto thee, Bethsaida! for if the mighty works, which were done in you, had been done in Tyre and Sidon, they would have repented long ago in sackcloth and ashes.

22. But I say unto you, It shall be more tolerable for Tyre and Sidon at the day of judgment, than for you.

23. And thou, Capernaum, which art exalted unto heaven, shalt be brought down to hell: for if the mighty works, which have been done in thee, had been done in Sodom, it would have remained until

this day.

24. But I say unto you, That it shall be more tolerable for the land of Sodom in the day of judgment, than for thee.

25. At that time Jesus answered and said, I thank thee, O Father, Lord of heaven and earth, because thou hast hid these things from the wise and prudent, and hast revealed them unto babes.

26. Even so, Father: for so it seemed good in thy sight.

27. All things are delivered unto me of my Father: and no man knoweth the Son, but the Father; neither knoweth any man the Father, save the Son, and he to whomsoever the Son will reveal him.

28. Come unto me, all ye that labour and are heavy laden, and I will give you rest.

29. Take my yoke upon you, and learn of me; for I am meek and lowly in heart: and ye shall find rest unto your souls.

30. For my yoke is easy, and my burden is light.

Cross-reference

Luke 7:18–35

John the Baptist, as the forerunner to Christ's ministry, had borne witness of him as the Messiah—but now he was in prison, having been put there by Herod. While languishing in captivity he undoubtedly heard of the commencement of the Savior's ministry, and perhaps also of the many miracles Jesus had performed. It was from this setting that John sent two of his disciples to Jesus to ask him an interesting question: "Art thou he that should come, or do we look for another?"

Jesus responded by inviting them to listen to the things that he would say and to watch the things that he would do. After hearing the Savior's teachings and witnessing the miracles that he performed in their presence, they then returned to John and told him all that they had seen and heard. We cannot infer that John was uncertain or doubtful in his testimony of Jesus as the Messiah,[1] since the record states that when John was first imprisoned Jesus "sent angels, and . . . they came and ministered unto him [John]" (JST Matthew 4:11). But John may have become despondent in his prison environment, feeling that there was appreciably nothing left for him to do; and in his loneliness (a feeling not unlike that of Elijah and Moses of the Old Testament) he sent these disciples to the Messiah. Perhaps John hoped that his disciples might believe on Christ, as they apparently still followed him who was but the forerunner of Jesus—the true leader of the kingdom and the Messiah.[2]

After John's disciples had gone, the Lord turned his attention to the multitude and proceeded with his sermon. He first bore testimony of John, praising him in the highest terms as one whom no wind of doctrine could shake. Jesus declared boldly that although John was not wearing the soft raiment of the day, he was most assuredly a prophet, even "more than a prophet," because this man who had come in the likeness and manner of the great prophets of old was the forerunner of the kingdom of God of which the prophet Malachi had prophesied (Malachi 3:1), and was the "Elias, which was for to come."

John represented the last and greatest of the prophets of the old dispensation. He was chosen to usher in the new dispensation, and Christ now declared him to be the greatest of all the prophets that had been born of women. But so far as we know, John had performed no miracles, and the approximate length of his ministry at the time of Christ's baptism was only six months. From that time until his arrest his ministry decreased as the Savior's increased.[3] How then was he the greatest of prophets? First, the Lord entrusted him to prepare the way before His face and declare His divinity to all men. Second, it was his privilege to lead the Son of God into the waters of baptism and witness the Holy Ghost descend upon him. Third, during John's short ministry he "was the only legal administrator in the affairs of the kingdom . . . on the earth . . . holding the keys of power."[4] Then the Lord continued and declared, "He that is least in the kingdom of heaven [referring to himself] is greater than he."[5]

The Jews admitted that all of the Law and the prophets looked forward to the coming of the Messiah, but the expectancy (as prophesied in the scriptures and the Law) and the reality (as anticipated by the Jews) differed sharply, and the Lord confirmed that in this discourse.[6]

The Jews anticipated the coming Messiah to be a national hero-king who would stand at the head of a great revolt and deliver them from the bondage of Rome, destroying the heathen and establishing the Jewish theocracy as it was in the days of old.[7] The spiritual and moral slavery under which they had long been bound would not allow them to accept the Lord's spiritual kingdom. Such a kingdom could not deliver them from temporal bondage. The herald of the new kingdom and the actual Messiah that followed that herald did not satisfy their unrealistic expectations. Jesus portrayed them as "children sitting in the markets, and calling unto their fellows," declaring, "We have piped unto you, and you have not danced." Although they knew the Law and lived for the coming Messiah, they expected one who would fit the tunes that they played.

John (the first witness) had come "neither eating nor drinking," but living the austere life of the prophets of old; yet they rejected him and said, "He hath a devil." Jesus (the second witness) had come living in the normal fashion of the day, and they had accused him of being a "winebibber [and] a friend of publicans and sinners." They justified their rejection of John because he called them sinners when they thought themselves righteous; they rejected Jesus because he did not meet the qualifications of their traditions; so the Lord declared, "Wisdom is justified of her children."

Jesus next upbraided the cities and communities that had rejected him, even though he had given them a mighty witness of his divinity. Of Chorazin we know nothing; and of Bethsaida we know only that he healed a blind man (Mark 8:22–26) and the sick in general, and fed the five thousand in the immediate vicinity (Mark 6:30–46; Luke 9:10–17). But the people of those cities must have witnessed mighty works, as the Lord declared that if the same works had been done in Tyre and Sidon they would have put on sackcloth and ashes and quickly repented. He condemned Capernaum, stating that it would be "brought down to hell" because it had rejected the mighty works performed there:[8] in the day of judgment it would be more tolerable for Sodom than for Capernaum.

Following his condemnation of these wicked cities, Jesus thanked his Father for those who had believed, even though they had not come from the learned and ruling classes.

Closing the discourse, the Lord openly taught the multitude that the Father would reveal the Son and the Son would reveal the Father to those who would believe. He then freely invited the covenant people to cast off the heavy burdens, rituals, and traditions of men that the rulers of Israel had laid upon them—men who should have recognized him. He taught them that by accepting him, their burden would become light, their yoke easy, and they would find rest for their souls.

He did not speak as a prophet but as the expected Messiah, and he called upon all who would listen to repent, forsake the world, and come unto him—with the promise that if they did, their souls would enter into the rest of the Lord (D&C 84:17–25). To those who love God his commandments are easy and his burden light.[9]

Discipleship Prevented

Luke 14:25–35

25. And there went great multitudes with him: and he turned, and said unto them,

26. If any man come to me, and hate not his father, and mother, and wife, and children, and brethren, and sisters, yea, and his own life also, he cannot be my disciple.

27. And whosoever doth not bear his cross, and come after me, cannot be my disciple.

28. For which of you, intending to build a tower, sitteth not down first, and counteth the cost, whether he have sufficient to finish it?

29. Lest haply, after he hath laid the foundation, and is not able to finish it, all that behold it begin to mock him.

30. Saying, This man began to build, and was not able to finish.

31. Or what king, going to make war against another king, sitteth not down first, and consulteth whether he be able with ten thousand to meet him that cometh against him with twenty thousand?

32. Or else, while the other is yet a great way off, he sendeth an ambassage, and desireth conditions of peace.

33. So likewise, whosoever he be of you that forsaketh not all that he hath, he cannot be my disciple.

34. Salt is good: but if the salt have lost his savour, wherewith shall it be seasoned?

35. It is neither fit for the land, nor yet for the dunghill; but men cast it out. He that hath ears to hear, let him hear.

The Synoptic writers record many times that wherever Jesus went during his ministry, great multitudes followed him. At the time this discourse was given a multitude was again with him, and he stopped to instruct them. The Lord was being assailed from all sides by his enemies, and the leaders of the Jews constantly accused him of evil to discredit him.

In this discourse Jesus taught his disciples the things that would prevent them from entering his kingdom unless they were totally sincere in their belief. He did not want transitory enthusiasts—those who followed him had to be geniune disciples. He outlined the sacrifice and devotion demanded of those who would be in his service, emphasizing that their duty to God would take precedence over all temporal commitments.

A true disciple of the Lord could not expect earthly love or acceptance, but rather alienation and opposition. He therefore must be prepared to abandon (if necessary) every earthly tie. In essence the Lord warned, "Those who are not able and determined to keep the commandments are better off outside the Church."[10]

A follower could not be a disciple unless he could "hate" all family ties. This did not imply actual hatred;[11] it was a warning that the gospel took precedence over all family or personal obligations. The Lord did not promise earthly rewards for such sacrifice, and he used the analogy of "bearing his cross" to describe the reception that the disciples would receive.

A disciple must also be willing to bear the Lord's shame and give up his own life for the kingdom. To emphasize this point the Lord used two examples: First was that the builder of a tower should count his costs before beginning construction in order to ensure the tower's completion. The Lord was illustrating that a person, deciding whether to be a disciple, had to consider more than the present. He must take the cost of total commitment into account. Second, the Lord told of a king who was planning a war. Common sense dictated to the king that he must compare his forces with those of the enemy, as it was better to safely withdraw from the battle in humiliation or sue for peace than to suffer a costly defeat. He who would be a disciple must "deliberately [count] the cost, and, in view of the coming trial, ask himself whether he had, indeed, sufficient inward strength . . . to conquer."[12]

The Lord brought this discourse to a swift conclusion by declaring, "Whosoever he be of you that forsaketh not all that he hath, he cannot be my disciple." One of the multitude contended, "We have Moses and the prophets, and whosoever shall live by them, shall he not have life?" (JST Luke 14:35). Jesus countered, "Ye know not Moses, neither the prophets; for if ye had known them, ye would have believed on me . . . for to this intent they were written."

Obviously, the inquirer believed that through the Law and its demands he could attain the kingdom of heaven, for he and his ancestors before him had for centuries looked for salvation through conformity with the laws and ordinances revealed by Moses and the prophets. He therefore questioned why he should follow the teachings of Jesus. But the eternal life that the inquirer sought did not come from Moses and the prophets, and the Lord so taught. Jesus finally concluded, "For I am sent that ye might have life" (JST Luke 14:36).

Jesus then used a common proverb of his day[13] when he declared that if good salt ever lost its savour, it would thereafter be good for nothing and would be cast out. He concluded by warning, "He that hath ears to hear, let him hear."

In this discourse the Lord outlined the requirements for an aspiring disciple, emphasizing absolute self-sacrifice for his cause. In the early history of The Church of Jesus Christ of Latter-day Saints Joseph Smith described this self-sacrifice:

> Let us here observe, that a religion that does not require the sacrifice of all things never has power sufficient to pro-

duce the faith necessary unto life and salvation; for, from
the first existence of man, the faith necessary unto the enjoyment of life and salvation never could be obtained without
the sacrifice of all earthly things. It was through this sacrifice, and this only, that God has ordained that men should
enjoy eternal life; and it is through the medium of the sacrifice of all earthly things that men do actually know that
they are doing the things that are well pleasing in the sight
of God. When a man has offered in sacrifice all that he has
for the truth's sake, not even withholding his life, and believing before God that he has been called to make this sacrifice because he seeks to do his will, he does know, most
assuredly, that God does and will accept his sacrifice and
offering, and that he has not, nor will not seek his face in
vain. Under these circumstances, then, he can obtain the
faith necessary for him to lay hold on eternal life.

It is in vain for persons to fancy to themselves that they
are heirs with those, or can be heirs with them, who have
offered their all in sacrifice, and by this means obtain faith
in God and favor with him so as to obtain eternal life,
unless they, in like manner, offer unto him the same sacrifice, and through that offering obtain the knowledge that
they are accepted of him. . . .

Those, then, who make the sacrifice, will have the testimony that their course is pleasing in the sight of God; and
those who have this testimony will have faith to lay hold
on eternal life. . . . But those who do not make the sacrifice cannot enjoy this faith, because men are dependent upon
this sacrifice in order to obtain this faith; . . .

All the saints of whom we have account, in all the revelations of God which are extant, obtained the knowledge
which they had of their acceptance in his sight through the
sacrifice which they offered unto him . . . and were
enabled . . . to . . . contend against the wiles of the adversary, overcome the world, and obtain the end of their faith,
even the salvation of their souls.[14]

"The Blind Lead the Blind"

Matthew 15:1–20

1. Then came to Jesus scribes and Pharisees, which were of Jerusalem, saying,

2. Why do thy disciples transgress the tradition of the elders? for they wash not their hands when they eat bread.

3. But he answered and said unto them, Why do ye also transgress the commandment of God by your tradition?

4. For God commanded, saying, Honour thy father and mother: and, He that curseth father or mother, let him die the death.

5. But ye say, Whosoever shall say to his father or his mother, It is a gift, by whatsoever thou mightest be profited by me;

6. And honour not his father or his mother, he shall be free. Thus have ye made the commandment of God of none effect by your tradition.

7. Ye hypocrites, well did Esaias prophesy of you, saying,

8. This people draweth nigh unto me with their mouth, and honoureth me with their lips; but their heart is far from me.

9. But in vain they do worship me, teaching for doctrines the commandments of men.

10. And he called the multitude, and said unto them, Hear, and understand:

11. Not that which goeth into the mouth defileth a man; but that which cometh out of the mouth, this defileth a man.

12. Then came his disciples, and said unto him, Knowest thou that the Pharisees were offended, after they heard this saying?

13. But he answered and said, Every plant, which my heavenly Father hath not planted, shall be rooted up.

14. Let them alone: they be blind leaders of the blind. And if the blind lead the blind, both shall fall into the ditch.

15. Then answered Peter and said unto him, Declare unto us this parable.

16. And Jesus said, Are ye also yet without understanding?

17. Do not ye yet understand, that whatsoever

entereth in at the mouth goeth into the belly, and is cast out into the drought?

18. But those things which proceed out of the mouth come forth from the heart; and they defile the man.

19. For out of the heart proceed evil thoughts, murders, adulteries, fornications, thefts, false witness, blasphemies:

20. These are the things which defile a man: but to eat with unwashen hands defileth not a man.

Cross-reference

Mark 7:1–23

The enemies of Jesus recognized in the Savior a deadly threat to their traditions and position; and almost from the beginning of his ministry they followed him, spied on him, and attempted to entrap him in his words (Luke 14:1; 6:7; 20:20). From the scriptural text it would appear that the Lord had performed the miracle of the feeding of the five thousand the day before this discourse took place.[15] This miracle caused his enemies to make what they considered a serious charge against him.[16]

They asked Jesus, "Why do thy disciples transgress the tradition of the elders? for they wash not their hands when they eat bread." At first glance this appears to be a trifling accusation, but to the leadership who presented it, it was a crime as great as eating the flesh of swine.[17]

In all, the leadership of the Jews made three great charges against Christ: first, they accused him of performing his great miracles by the power of Beelzebub[18] (Matthew 12), "whose special representative—almost incarnation—they declared Jesus to be";[19] second, they charged that he was not of God because he was a sinner—it was therefore their duty to unmask him to avoid deceiving the people (John 9).[20] They did this by instituting charges, such as the one in this discourse, to prove that Jesus sanctioned breaches in the traditional Law "which, according to their fundamental principles, involved heavier guilt than sins against the revealed Law of Moses."[21] Third, they charged him with blasphemy for stating that he was equal to God (John 5:18).

The Jews considered eating with "common hands" a sin of extreme gravity, for eating "with unwashen hands was as if it had been filth."[22] Jesus treated their traditional ceremonialism with indifference and had no sympathy for a system that ignored conscience but found the essence of religion in the slavery of outward form. He immediately responded to the Pharisees' charge, but as usual did not answer it. Instead he took the offensive by accusing his antagonists of transgressing the commandments because of their traditions. He told them that they considered the washing of pots and cups and many other similar things greater than honoring their father and mother.

Their traditions dictated that by merely speaking the word *corban* (meaning "a gift") they could avoid the requirement of caring for the earthly needs of their parents. So strict was the observance of this tradition that the person saying *corban* could "prevent the person so addressed from ever deriving any benefit from that which belonged to him. And so stringent was the ordinance that . . . it [was] expressly stated that such a vow was binding, even if what was vowed involved a breach of the Law."[23]

The Lord then quoted Isaiah and indicated that the Pharisees standing before him had fulfilled the prophecy because their lips honored the God of their fathers, but their religion was the doctrine of men. He continued to upbraid the Pharisees by saying, "Full well is it written of you, by the prophets whom ye have rejected. They testified these things of a truth, and their blood shall be upon you." (JST Mark 7:10–11).

There was no salvation in the punctilious observance of their Law, even though their worship was directed toward a true God. Their worship, based upon false principles, was in vain.[24] Christ abrogated the rabbinical regulations and offerings, declaring that mercy was better than sacrifice (Matthew 9:13; 12:7). He stated, "Not that which goeth into the mouth defileth a man; but that which cometh out of the mouth, this defileth a man." No amount of soap and water can clean a man's thoughts, for "those things which proceed out of the mouth come forth from the heart; and they defile the man." For the first time Jesus openly denounced the Jewish leaders, accusing them of concerning themselves with the obedience of things instituted by men and neglecting that which God had established.

Jesus made it painfully clear to the Jews that their traditionalism was totally incompatible with the scriptures, and through its use they had made void the word of God.

The Savior's response bitterly offended the Pharisees and his disciples noted this to him. But Jesus only warned them of the fate awaiting those who reject the Father for their own doctrines. "Let them alone," he declared. "They be blind leaders of the blind. And if the blind lead the blind, both shall fall into the ditch."

This must have been a harsh attitude for the disciples to comprehend. Jesus was talking to the "elite" of Israel, and his audacity alarmed them. Peter ventured to ask the Lord to explain his comment. Jesus quickly responded with a mild rebuke and stated, "Are ye also without understanding?" Then the Lord again declared that the food going into a man could not defile him, but that which came out of his mouth and proceeded from his heart could. Jesus then cited several evils and sins as examples.

The Lord made it very clear that all things were clean to those who were spiritually cleansed. This teaching was in direct opposition to the Pharisaic belief that external purification was the key to acceptance by God. Jesus made no attempt to reconcile himself with his antagonists. It was because of their obstinacy that they refused to understand,[25] and their willful tenacity made it easy for them to reject Jesus as the Messiah.

"Beware of the Leaven of the Pharisees"

Matthew 16:5-12

5. And when his disciples were come to the other side, they had forgotten to take bread.

6. Then Jesus said unto them, Take heed and beware of the leaven of the Pharisees and of the Sadducees.

7. And they reasoned among themselves, saying, It

is because we have taken no bread.

8. Which when Jesus perceived, he said unto them, O ye of little faith, why reason ye among yourselves, because ye have brought no bread?

9. Do ye not yet understand, neither remember the five loaves of the five thousand, and how many baskets ye took up?

10. Neither the seven loaves of the four thousand, and how many baskets ye took up?

11. How is it that ye do not understand that I spake it not to you concerning bread, that ye should beware of the leaven of the Pharisees and of the Sadducees?

12. Then understood they how that he bade them not beware of the leaven of bread, but of the doctrine of the Pharisees and of the Sadducees.

Cross-reference

Mark 8:14-21

Matthew records that after the feeding of the four thousand, certain Pharisees and Sadducees came tempting Jesus, requesting a sign. They seemed to have a consuming desire to see the Lord perform miracles, and they were constantly asking him to show them the Messianic sign.[26]

The Jews constantly sought signs in connection with their religious ceremonies—signs that would guide them in their temporal choices or decisions and help them gain the things they wanted. One of these signs was connected with the conclusion of the Feast of Tabernacles. They would watch what direction the smoke from the evening sacrifice traveled and would then use that occurrence to discern what the weather would be for the coming year. If the smoke turned northward, they believed that there would be much rain and that the poor would rejoice; if the smoke turned southward, they believed that the rich would rejoice, the poor would mourn, and that there would be little rain; if the smoke turned eastward, everyone would rejoice together; and if it turned westward, all would mourn together.[27]

The Jews again failed in their attempt to involve Jesus in a

dispute, and his abrupt response left them discomforted before
the multitude. He then left with the Twelve by boat to pass
over to the other side of the Sea of Galilee in an effort to rid
himself of the sign-seekers and perhaps gain a moment of soli-
tude. Matthew notes that when they reached the other shore,
the disciples had forgotten to take any bread with them. Jesus
turned to them and said, "Take heed and beware of the leaven
of the Pharisees and of the Sadducees." But the Apostles did
not understand; they thought Jesus was referring to the fact
that they had no food. From the scriptures it appears that the
Apostles were constantly having trouble interpreting the metaphors Jesus used. For example, when Jesus talked to them of
"meat" in the discourse with the woman at the well, they thought
he was referring to the food they were seeking; later when Jesus
said that Lazarus was "sleeping," they thought Lazarus was resting, when in fact he was dead.

Jesus quickly perceived their misunderstanding and told them
they had little faith, reminding them of the two great miracles
he had performed: first, the feeding of the five thousand and,
most recently, the feeding of the four thousand.

Many of the Lord's discourses were of this type—short in
duration and tied to a particular doctrine—but often the anal-
ogies or metaphors he used confused his listeners, and at times
even the Twelve did not comprehend his meaning. This may
have indicated to Jesus that the Twelve were not yet spiritually
mature.[28] Their lack of faith made it difficult for them to discern the meaning of the Lord's instructions and so he reproved
them. Then he made his instructions clear to them.

It was not the leaven in the food he was referring to, but
the doctrine of the Pharisees and the Sadducees. The Lord was
warning the Apostles to beware of the Jewish leaders' teachings, their slander, and their misleading information. It was
their false doctrine that the Lord wanted the Apostles to shun,
so that they would not become tainted by the opposition.[29]

"How Knoweth This Man Letters?"

John 7:1–53

1. After these things Jesus walked in Galilee: for he would not walk in Jewry, because the Jews sought to kill him.

2. Now the Jews' feast of tabernacles was at hand.

3. His brethren therefore said unto him, Depart hence, and go into Judaea, that thy disciples also may see the works that thou doest.

4. For there is no man that doeth any thing in secret, and he himself seeketh to be known openly. If thou do these things, shew thyself to the world.

5. For neither did his brethren believe in him.

6. Then Jesus said unto them, My time is not yet come: but your time is alway ready.

7. The world cannot hate you; but me it hateth, because I testify of it, that the works thereof are evil.

8. Go ye up unto this feast: I go not up yet unto this feast; for my time is not yet full come.

9. When he had said these words unto them, he abode still in Galilee.

10. But when his brethren were gone up, then went he also up unto the feast, not openly, but as it were in secret.

11. Then the Jews sought him at the feast, and said, Where is he?

12. And there was much murmuring among the people concerning him: for some said, He is a good man: others said, Nay; but he deceiveth the people.

13. Howbeit no man spake openly of him for fear of the Jews.

14. Now about the midst of the feast Jesus went up into the temple, and taught.

15. And the Jews marvelled, saying, How knoweth this man letters, having never learned?

16. Jesus answered them, and said, My doctrine is not mine, but his that sent me.

17. If any man will do his will, he shall know of the doctrine, whether it be of God, or whether I speak of myself.

18. He that speaketh of himself seeketh his own glory: but he that seeketh his

glory that sent him, the same is true, and no unrighteousness is in him.

19. Did not Moses give you the law, and yet none of you keepeth the law? Why go ye about to kill me?

20. The people answered and said, Thou hast a devil: who goeth about to kill thee?

21. Jesus answered and said unto them, I have done one work, and ye all marvel.

22. Moses therefore gave unto you circumcision; (not because it is of Moses, but of the fathers;) and ye on the sabbath day circumcise a man.

23. If a man on the sabbath day receive circumcision, that the law of Moses should not be broken; are ye angry at me, because I have made a man every whit whole on the sabbath day?

24. Judge not according to the appearance, but judge righteous judgment.

25. Then said some of them of Jerusalem, is not this he, whom they seek to kill?

26. But, lo, he speaketh boldly, and they say nothing unto him. Do the rulers know indeed that this is the very Christ?

27. Howbeit we know this man whence he is: but when Christ cometh, no man knoweth whence he is.

28. Then cried Jesus in the temple as he taught, saying, Ye both know me, and ye know whence I am: and I am not come of myself, but he that sent me is true, whom ye know not.

29. But I know him: for I am from him, and he hath sent me.

30. Then they sought to take him: but no man laid hands on him, because his hour was not yet come.

31. And many of the people believed on him, and said, When Christ cometh, will he do more miracles than these which this man hath done?

32. The Pharisees heard that the people murmured such things concerning him; and the Pharisees and the chief priests sent officers to take him.

33. Then said Jesus unto them, Yet a little while am I with you, and then I go unto him that sent me.

34. Ye shall seek me, and shall not find me: and where I am, thither ye cannot come.

35. Then said the Jews among themselves, Whither will he go, that we shall not find him? will he go unto the

dispersed among the Gentiles, and teach the Gentiles?

36. What manner of saying is this that he said, Ye shall seek me, and shall not find me: and where I am, thither ye cannot come?

37. In the last day, that great day of the feast, Jesus stood and cried, saying, If any man thirst, let him come unto me, and drink.

38. He that believeth on me, as the scripture hath said, out of his belly shall flow rivers of living water.

39. (But this spake he of the Spirit, which they that believe on him should receive: for the Holy Ghost was not yet given; because that Jesus was not yet glorified.)

40. Many of the people therefore, when they heard this saying, said, Of a truth this is the Prophet.

41. Others said, This is the Christ. But some said, Shall Christ come out of Galilee?

42. Hath not the scripture said, That Christ cometh of the seed of David, and out of the town of Bethlehem, where David was?

43. So there was a division among the people because of him.

44. And some of them would have taken him; but no man laid hands on him.

45. Then came the officers to the chief priests and Pharisees; and they said unto them, Why have ye not brought him?

46. The officers answered, Never man spake like this man.

47. Then answered them the Pharisees, Are ye also deceived?

48. Have any of the rulers or of the Pharisees believed on him?

49. But this people who knoweth not the law are cursed.

50. Nicodemus saith unto them, (he that came to Jesus by night, being one of them,)

51. Doth our law judge any man, before it hear him, and know what he doeth?

52. They answered and said unto him, Art thou also of Galilee? Search, and look; for out of Galilee ariseth no prophet.

53. And every man went unto his own house.

Jesus had not been in Jerusalem for six months, and the Feast of Tabernacles was drawing nigh.[30] At this time in the

Savior's ministry Judea was no longer open to him, but he still had to present his claim to the Messiahship in the temple of the Holy City of David.

Jerusalem was the main headquarters of the Jewish priests and rabbis and also the headquarters of the institution Jesus had come to supersede. Even though the scripture reports that after a certain point he had not previously walked in Jewry because the Jews sought to kill him, the steadily deepening hostility could not keep him from declaring his Messiahship to the leaders of the "chosen people."

The Feast of Tabernacles was the third of the great annual festivals held each year in Israel. At these three feasts every male of the covenant people was to appear before the Lord. The Feast of Tabernacles fell during the seventh Jewish month on the fifteenth day (which corresponds to the latter part of September or the beginning of October).[31] It was the most joyful of all the festival seasons, and it was held at the time of year when the people were naturally full of thankfulness. The crops had been stored and the fruits gathered in. The thanksgiving of harvest and the Feast of Tabernacles "reminded Israel, on the one hand, of their dwelling in booths in the wilderness, while, on the other hand, it pointed to the final harvest when Israel's mission should be completed, and all nations gathered unto the Lord."[32] This joyful feast followed five days after the Day of Atonement, wherein the sins of Israel were removed and their "chosen" covenant with God restored.

The Lord's "brethren" urged him to go up to the feast in Jerusalem and show his mighty miracles. The "brethren" spoken of here were members of Christ's own family, the other children of Mary and Joseph, who apparently had not yet openly declared their belief in him even though they were asking him to show his signs.[33] They chided Jesus for not going openly to the feast[34] and wondered why he would not go and perform his miracles. They apparently felt like most of the Israelites who clung to the traditions that the anticipated Messiah would restore Israel to its former, national glory. They obviously did not understand the Lord, and they perhaps wondered why he stayed in Galilee if he wanted to establish his Messianic kingdom since they knew that such a kingdom would have to be established in Jerusalem.[35]

But Jesus would not attend the feast in this manner, nor would he display his powers for their pleasure; so he told them to go to the feast without him, as his "time was not yet come." After his brethren had gone, Jesus waited two more days; then he departed secretly for the feast with his chosen Twelve, traveling through Samaria toward Jerusalem. The normal hospitality afforded strangers was denied him on this trip, as the Samaritans again showed their open hostility toward the Israelites.[36]

Three groups of people attended the Feast of Tabernacles: first, the ever-present Pharisees and leaders of the Jews; second, a multitude of pilgrims (as this particular feast was predominately designated for foreign pilgrims coming from great distances in order to make their temple contributions);[37] and third, those who lived in the Holy City.

All who attended the feast anticipated that Jesus would be there, and the scripture notes that they were looking for him but could not find him. There was general disagreement among the populace concerning Christ. They did not talk openly of him for fear of the Jewish leadership, but curiosity ran high. Some indicated that he was a good man, while others rejected him. The murmuring and whispering of the crowd, as recorded in John, is different from that recorded elsewhere in the scriptures, and John appears to have felt that the people wanted to do the right thing, but were unsure what it was.

In the middle of the feast Jesus suddenly appeared in the temple and began teaching. His brethren had gone to the feast to prove themselves faithful to the Law, that they might "keep" the feast, but Jesus had gone to witness his Messiahship.

The subject of his discourse in the temple is not recorded, but the reaction to it is. The people listened in astonishment. The leaders of the Jews "knew what common unlettered Galilean tradesmen were,"[38] and they were astounded at the teachings of Jesus. In their ongoing attempt to create doubt and suspicion in the Lord's teachings, they asked the question, "How knoweth this man letters, having never learned?"

To the Jews there was only one kind of learning: theology, and only one road to it: the schools of the rabbis.[39] In those schools each student learned theology from a great teacher, but Jesus had attended none of them.[40] The question the leaders posed challenged the Lord's competence as a teacher, but the answer he gave disputed their competence as hearers. He told them that the doctrine he taught was not his, but his Father's who had sent him; they had only to do the will of the Father to know the validity of the doctrine. Jesus had bypassed the normal schools of learning (which the Jews felt could be traced from one great teacher to another on back to Moses, and thus to God himself). The Savior had received his education directly from God: he was God's messenger to the Jews.

As the discussion continued, Jesus asked, "Did not Moses give you the law, and yet none of you keepeth the law?" The Jews were breaking the Law because they sought to kill him. The people responded by stating incredulously, "Thou hast a devil: who goeth about to kill thee?" Perhaps the murderous intentions of the leaders were not known to the common people. Jesus declared that the reason for their evil intentions against him was his work on the Sabbath. He specifically referred to the healing of the impotent man[41] as the reason they sought to put him to death. They felt he was desecrating their Sabbath. Jesus defended his work by stating that they allowed the requirement of circumcision to supersede the Sabbath Law; therefore, why should they be angry at him for making a man whole on the Sabbath day. He demanded that they "judge not according to the appearance, but judge righteous judgment." This defense immediately generated belief in some of the Jews at the festival, and some acknowledged that although this was the man the leadership sought to kill, he spoke to them boldly and the leaders did nothing. They questioned whether this was the "very Christ." The crowd began to wonder if he really was the long-awaited Messiah.

The Jewish leadership quickly attempted to curtail this belief by asking another question, this time concerning the Messiah's origin. They knew where Jesus had been raised, and it was "evident that Jesus was thought of as a native of Nazareth, and that the circumstances of His birth were not of public knowledge."[42] At the time of Christ there were two divergent beliefs associated with the coming forth of the anticipated

Messiah. Some believed that the Savior would be born in Bethlehem, and they based their view on the Old Testament (Micah 5:2–3). A second group taught that the Messiah would come from an unknown source: his origin would be a mystery.[43]

Jesus now dropped all pretense and clearly declared what his mission was and from whom he had been sent: "I am not come of myself, but he that sent me is true, whom ye know not. But I know him: for I am from him, and he hath sent me." After this powerful declaration the Jews immediately "sought to take him," but they could not, for "his hour was not yet come."

Undoubtedly Jesus spent many additional hours teaching in Jerusalem, but John only records fragments of his sermons.[44] Many began to believe on him, but the Pharisees could not tolerate his success, so they sent temple officers to again try to arrest him. Jesus ignored them and closed this portion of his discourse by reiterating that he would go to his Father, "and where I am," he said, "thither ye cannot come." The leaders misunderstood this prophecy of his death and resurrection, and questioned whether or not it meant that he would go to the Gentiles.

On the last day of the Feast of Tabernacles Jesus again declared his Messiahship before all those attending the celebration. The significance of the feast helps us to understand what the Lord meant when he declared, "If any man thirst, let him come unto me and drink." On each day of the feast a priest went down to the pool of Siloam (where Jesus had healed the impotent man) and drew water into a golden pitcher. He then proceeded to the temple sacrifice area,

> . . . so timing it, that he returned just as his brethren carried up the pieces of the sacrifice to lay them on the altar. As he entered by the "Watergate," which obtained its name from this ceremony, he was received by a threefold blast from the priests' trumpets.
>
> [On the seventh day of the feast] . . . they made the circuit of the altar seven times . . . after the priest had returned from Siloam with his golden pitcher, and for the last time poured its contents to the base of the altar; after the "Hallel" had been sung to the sound of the flute, . . .

[and] just when the interest of the people had been raised to its highest pitch . . . [as] the mass of worshippers . . . were waving towards the altar quite a forest of leafy branches . . . a voice was raised which resounded through the Temple, startled the multitude, and carried fear and hatred to the hearts of the leaders.[45]

Jesus stood and cried aloud saying, "If any man thirst, let him come unto me, and drink. He that believeth on me . . . out of his belly shall flow rivers of living water."

The words the priests and the people were speaking at that point of the temple ceremony referred to the Holy Spirit, and the symbolism of the Savior's cry would have been clearly understood.[46] Jesus interpreted and fulfilled the words they spoke, thereby asserting his claim to the Messiahship[47] (Isaiah 44:3; 55:1; 58:11).

Some believed, some continued to question, and the division among the people remained. The Pharisees questioned the officers they had sent to arrest Jesus, asking why they had not brought him to them. But even the officers acknowledged that they could not resist the Lord, for he spoke not as other men. The Pharisees sitting in council strongly condemned Jesus, but Nicodemus raised a legal question: "Doth our law judge any man, before it hear him, and know what he doeth?" This precipitated a response by his fellow Pharisees. They questioned the origin of Jesus again, and without thinking, they angrily declared, "Search, and look: for out of Galilee ariseth no prophet." They ignored their legal procedures (Exodus 23:1; Deuteronomy 1:16; Deuteronomy 19:15) and apparently also overlooked the fact that at least Jonah had come from Galilee, and perhaps also Nahum, Hosea, and Elijah.[48] It was the third time that they had raised the subject of Jesus' Galilean origin, and even though he did not hail from Galilee (they apparently being ignorant of his actual birthplace), it was evidence of the enormous effect the words of Jesus had upon them.

The festival was over, the discourse had ended, the Lord's claim to the Messiahship had been asserted and rejected, "and every man went unto his own house."

The Last Controversies

Matthew 22:15–46

15. Then went the Pharisees, and took counsel how they might entangle him in his talk.

16. And they sent out unto him their disciples with the Herodians, saying, Master, we know that thou art true, and teachest the way of God in truth, neither carest thou for any man: for thou regardest not the person of men.

17. Tell us therefore, What thinkest thou? Is it lawful to give tribute unto Caesar, or not?

18. But Jesus perceived their wickedness, and said, Why tempt ye me, ye hypocrites?

19. Shew me the tribute money. And they brought unto him a penny.

20. And he saith unto them, Whose is this image and superscription?

21. They say unto him, Caesar's. Then saith he unto them, Render therefore unto Caesar the things which are Caesar's; and unto God the things that are God's.

22. When they had heard

these words, they marvelled, and left him, and went their way.

23. The same day came to him the Sadducees, which say that there is no resurrection, and asked him,

24. Saying, Master, Moses said, If a man die, having no children, his brother shall marry his wife, and raise up seed unto his brother.

25. Now there were with us seven brethren: and the first, when he had married a wife, deceased, and, having no issue, left his wife unto his brother:

26. Likewise the second also, and the third, unto the seventh.

27. And last of all the woman died also.

28. Therefore in the resurrection whose wife shall she be of the seven? for they all had her.

29. Jesus answered and said unto them, Ye do err, not knowing the scriptures, nor the power of God.

30. For in the resurrection they neither marry, nor are given in marriage, but are as the angels of God in heaven.

31. But as touching the resurrection of the dead, have ye not read that which was

spoken unto you by God, saying,

32. I am the God of Abraham, and the God of Isaac, and the God of Jacob? God is not the God of the dead, but of the living.

33. And when the multitude heard this, they were astonished at his doctrine.

34. But when the Pharisees had heard that he had put the Sadducees to silence, they were gathered together.

35. Then one of them, which was a lawyer, asked him a question, tempting him, and saying,

36. Master, which is the great commandment in the law?

37. Jesus said unto him, Thou shalt love the Lord thy God with all thy heart, and with all thy soul, and with all thy mind.

38. This is the first and great commandment.

39. And the second is like unto it, Thou shalt love thy neighbour as thyself.

40. On these two commandments hang all the law and the prophets.

41. While the Pharisees were gathered together, Jesus asked them,

42. Saying, What think ye of Christ? whose son is

he? They say unto him, The Son of David.

43. He saith unto them, How then doth David in spirit call him Lord, saying,

44. The Lord said unto my Lord, Sit thou on my right hand, till I make thine

enemies thy footstool?

45. If David then call him Lord, how is he his son?

46. And no man was able to answer him a word, neither durst any man from that day forth ask him any more questions.

Cross-references

Mark 12:13–34   Luke 20:21–43

Controversy Number One: The Tribute Money

Throughout the Lord's ministry the Jewish leadership tried unsuccessfully to entrap him in his speech, and, notwithstanding their failures, they persisted in counseling with others how they "might entangle him in his talk." This attempt to entrap Jesus was unique in that the Pharisees solicited the assistance of the Herodians (men who would have otherwise been their foes)[1] in developing their plot to ruin their "common enemy."

This was the second time that the Pharisees and the Herodians had united in an attempt to ensnare Jesus (Mark 3:6), and to this end, on the last day of the Lord's public ministry, they devised a question that they felt would lead to his downfall. It involved the relationship between religion and state. These two parties—one watching for the smallest technical infringement of the Mosiac Law and the other constantly on guard for the slightest excuse to accuse Jesus of disloyalty to the secular powers—proceeded to send a young group of zealous disciples from the Pharisees to speak to him. They flattered the Lord by addressing him as "Master" and proceeded to ply him with praise, stating that they knew he was a teacher from God, that he spoke the truth, and that he regarded not the opinions of men. They were apparently unknown to Jesus, and as yet they had not publicly evidenced personal antagonism toward him.[2] Their approach was truthful in every word, but "as uttered by those fulsome dissemblers and in their nefarious intent, it was egregiously false."³

The approach had been conceived to avoid the Savior's suspicions, to perhaps appeal to his "fearlessness and singleness of moral purpose, to induce Him to commit Himself without reserve."⁴ So these hand-picked, young scholars asked Jesus the question, "Is it lawful to give tribute unto Caesar, or not?" The snare lay in the political obligation involved. To answer incorrectly would compromise Jesus before the Roman procurator.

Their question appeared to place Jesus in an uncompromising position which would force him to answer no. Yet if he answered no the Herodians would accuse him of sedition and claim he championed rebellion. Israel was already divided on the issue of tribute. They felt that if they gave their allegiance to Caesar it would mean that they were being disobedient to Jehovah.⁵ But it would have pleased the Pharisees if Jesus had answered yes, as they could then accuse him before the populace (since the Messiah-King that Israel anticipated would never have submitted to the hated tax the tribute represented).⁶ The Pharisees were certain that the cunning question they had devised would present a threat to Jesus, no matter which way he answered.

The Lord did not evidence much patience when he replied to the Jewish leaders, "Why tempt ye me, ye hypocrites?" He then asked, "Shew me the tribute money." The Lord had no intention of being trapped by the wicked Pharisees. The Roman coinage that the Jews paid tribute with had already circulated throughout Jerusalem and Galilee. They recognized the de facto government of Rome in that they had partaken of its benefits; so in practice they had already resolved their question.⁷

Taking the coin, Jesus asked his inquisitors, "Whose is the image and superscription?" "Caesar's," they quickly responded. Without hesitation Jesus replied, "Render therefore unto Caesar the things which are Caesar's; and unto God the things that are God's."

The Lord's answer established the relationship between the spiritual and the secular responsibilities of the members of his kingdom.⁸ He was not opposing civil authority; he was simply stating that political and religious spheres could exist side-by-side and yet be distinct. His answer was neither treasonable nor a violation of the Law of Moses. Politics and religion do not have to involve nor exclude each other: they exist in different domains. The Lord's kingdom was not of this world. Those who were concerned with temporal things could demand the things of the world; but God required spiritual devotion. (D&C 58:21–22; 98:4–10; Romans 13:1–7; 1 Timothy 2:1–3; Titus 3:1; 1 Peter 2:13–17; Articles of Faith 1:12.)

The Lord's answer startled his inquisitors. He was correct in every particular, so they "marvelled and left him and went their way."

Controversy Number Two: A Question on the Resurrection

As soon as the controversy over tribute was put to rest, the Sadducees came to Jesus with a question. (The scriptures record only one other conflict between Jesus and the Sadducees [Matthew 16:1].) The Sadducees were a group of clergymen drawn from all classes of the people. They were "rich, dignified . . . affected at first only to despise the Galilean, who, like so many before Him, had stirred up commotion for the time among His rude compatriots. Even now, in Jerusalem, they were disposed to look at Him and His adherents with a lofty contempt, and to laugh the foolish rabble who listened to Him out of their fanatical dreams. His claims were, in their opinion, more silly than dangerous, and they would, therefore, bring the whole matter into contempt, by making it ridiculous."[9]

The Sadducees had carefully thought out their question. Even though they considered Jesus a fanatic, it appears that they were attempting to make him an object of ridicule.[10] Their presentation was one of icy politeness and philosophic calm, couched in a stale piece of casuistry already settled in their law.[11] Their question concerned the fate of a woman in the resurrection who had been married to her husband and (because of intervening deaths) to each of his six brothers. This question had already been resolved for the Jews, since the writings of the Talmud indicated that a wife in this situation would have the first husband.[12] But the question was an interesting one in that the Sadducees denied the existence of the resurrection (the very basis of the question), maintaining "that it is as vain to hope that a cloud which has vanished will appear again, as that the grave will give back its dead."[13]

Jesus responded to this interrogation in a manner he had used many times before. He quickly passed over the guise of the query pertaining to marriage and declared, "in the resurrection they neither marry, nor are given in marriage." Jesus knew that these questions had to be settled before the resurrection by those holding the proper priesthood authority.[14] Next, Jesus resolved the portion of the question involving the resurrection. He told the Sadducees that they were in error when they maintained that there was no resurrection, and that they did not know the scriptures or the power of God. He did not argue the scriptures with them but declared the very existence of God, using as examples their dead forefathers: Abraham, Isaac, and Jacob. He then testified of the reality and existence of the resurrection, stating that God was "not the God of the dead, but of the living." Jesus made it very clear to the Sadducees that their doctrine on the resurrection[15] was false, and he put them "to silence." Again the multitude was astonished at his doctrine.

Controversy Number Three: "What Think Ye of Christ?"

By this time Jesus had a question of his own to ask, but before he could present it a lawyer came "tempting him" and asked him which was the greatest commandment. As Matthew puts it, the lawyer's question was actually more of an introduction to Christ's question to the Pharisees and the Sadducees than an attempt to entrap him. Jesus responded quickly to the lawyer, stating that to love God was the first great commandment, and the second was like unto it, "to love thy neighbour as thyself."

The lawyer was apparently trying to make one point of the law weightier than another, but the Lord pointed out that the commandments of God were beyond the theocratic abstraction of the letter of the Law, and that the second commandment was "like unto it," because to love God was to love your fellowman. "On these two commandments hang all the law and the prophets," he explained. The things the prophets teach and the commandments we are expected to live all encourage us to love God and our fellowman, and treat them accordingly.

Jesus then took the initiative and asked the Pharisees, "What think ye of Christ? whose son is he?" They quickly responded, "The Son of David," perhaps thinking that Jesus was entering into one of their dialectic discussions. But the Lord then asked them, "How then doth David in spirit call him Lord," or in other words, how could the Messiah be David's son?

It was a question that testified of the Lord's divinity (Psalm 110:1), and he asked it to deliberately force the Pharisees to compare the Messianic prophecies with their own false concept of the coming Messiah.[16] The question was a favorite theme in Judaism, the lineage of the Messiah being a most familiar subject in their theology.[17] Jesus had now raised the issue of his own divinity by showing them that the Messiah was David's son through mortal lineage, but that as the Son of God he was exalted far above David. No man dared answer the Lord, so they remained silent; nor did they ask him any more questions from that day on.

The Final Plea

John 12:20-50

20. And there were certain Greeks among them that came up to worship at the feast:

21. The same came therefore to Philip, which was of Bethsaida of Galilee, and desired him, saying, Sir, we would see Jesus.

22. Philip cometh and telleth Andrew: and again Andrew and Philip tell Jesus.

23. And Jesus answered them, saying, The hour is come, that the Son of man should be glorified.

24. Verily, verily, I say unto you, Except a corn of wheat fall into the ground and die, it abideth alone: but if it die, it bringeth forth much fruit.

25. He that loveth his life shall lose it; and he that hateth his life in this world shall keep it unto life eternal.

26. If any man serve me, let him follow me; and where I am, there shall also my servant be: if any man serve me, him will my Father honour.

27. Now is my soul troubled; and what shall I say? Father, save me from this hour: but for this cause came I unto this hour.

28. Father, glorify thy name. Then came there a voice from heaven, saying, I have both glorified it, and will glorify it again.

29. The people therefore, that stood by, and heard it, said that it thundered: others said, An angel spake to him.

30. Jesus answered and said, This voice came not because of me, but for your sakes.

31. Now is the judgment of this world: now shall the prince of this world be cast out.

32. And I, if I be lifted up from the earth, will draw all men unto me.

33. This he said, signifying what death he should die.

34. The people answered him, We have heard out of the law that Christ abideth for ever: and how sayest thou, The Son of man must be lifted up? who is this Son of man?

35. Then Jesus said unto them, Yet a little while is the light with you. Walk while ye have the light, lest darkness come upon you: for he that walketh in darkness knoweth not whither he goeth.

36. While ye have light, believe in the light, that ye may be the children of light. These things spake Jesus, and departed, and did hide himself from them.

37. But though he had done so many miracles before them, yet they believed not on him:

38. That the saying of Esaias the prophet might be fulfilled, which he spake, Lord, who hath believed our report? and to whom hath the arm of the Lord been revealed?

39. Therefore they could not believe, because that Esaias said again,

40. He hath blinded their eyes, and hardened their heart; that they should not see with their eyes, nor understand with their heart, and be converted, and I should heal them.

41. These things said Esaias, when he saw his glory, and spake of him.

42. Nevertheless among the chief rulers also many believed on him; but because of the Pharisees they did not confess him, lest they should be put out of the synagogue:

43. For they loved the praise of men more than the praise of God.

44. Jesus cried and said, He that believeth on me, believeth not on me, but on him that sent me.

45. And he that seeth me seeth him that sent me.

46. I am come a light into the world, that whosoever believeth on me should not abide in darkness.

47. And if any man hear my words, and believe not, I judge him not: for I came not to judge the world, but to save the world.

48. He that rejecteth me, and receiveth not my words, hath one that judgeth him: the word that I have spoken, the same shall judge him in the last day.

49. For I have not spoken of myself; but the Father which sent me, he gave me a commandment, what I should say, and what I should speak.

50. And I know that his commandment is life everlasting: whatsoever I speak therefore, even as the Father said unto me, so I speak.

This is the final public discourse given by the Savior before his crucifixion. The narrative is brief and written in a style reminiscent of topic headings, summaries, or outlines, rather than a continuous report. No surrounding circumstances are given for this discourse other than that it occurred after Jesus' final entry into Jerusalem, and it appears that it was written as John's conclusion to the Lord's public ministry.

The discourse seems to stem from a request made by certain Greek proselytes for a personal meeting with Christ. Their request was directed to Philip, but he, for whatever reason, decided not to make the request to Jesus alone and solicited the assistance of Andrew, another member of the Twelve. Together they introduced the Greek proselytes to the Savior.

The Greeks may have requested the audience because they were impressed with Jesus' actions at the feast, or perhaps his fame had previously reached their nation;[18] but no reasons are

given for the requested interview. John's clipped method of recording this discourse makes it appear that Jesus is ignoring the
Greeks altogether, as he never refers to them in his comments.[19]

John reports the discourse as if Jesus had been answering
questions, but no questions are indicated. The Lord began by
declaring openly for the first time that "the hour is come that
the Son of man should be glorified" (previously he had always
stated that his hour had not yet come). This opening statement
to the Greeks anticipated the establishment of the gospel in its
future triumphs among the heathen nations, since the gospel
would eventually go to all men.[20] The Lord had previously
spoken of his coming death, and apparently they asked him
why he would die.[21] Jesus answered with an analogy, saying
that a grain of wheat must die before it could produce "much"
fruit. He was obviously alluding to the fact that he, too, must
die for his work if it was to bear fruit (the fruit of his labor, as
death to him was not a tragedy, but a triumph). John appears
to have again left out some of the Lord's comments, for in the
very next verse Jesus applied this analogy to his disciples and
followers, requiring them also to yield their lives completely to
the kingdom, emphasizing the necessity of their faithfulness to
him, and citing the blessings attached to such action.

The Lord then seemed to be caught in a moment of intro-
spection as he reflected on the ignominious circumstances of
his death. "Now is my soul troubled," he lamented, "and what
shall I say? Father, save me from this hour." But knowing that
such was not the plan of his Father, he reconciled his mind to
the inevitable by stating, "But for this cause came I unto this
hour." No one else in all of creation could have saved mankind
from sin. Jesus turned to his Father and prayed, "Father, glorify
thy name." Then a voice came from heaven, saying, "I have
both glorified it, and will glorify it again." These circumstances
were real, the actual voice of God was heard from the heavens.[22] But the people who stood by failed to understand or
recognize it—some thinking an angel had spoken to the Lord
and others perceiving his voice as thunder. Had they been spiritually in tune with the Savior and believed in him as the Messiah, they would undoubtedly have recognized the Father's voice.

Jesus (who heard his Father's words while those around him heard only sounds) testified of the Father and declared the voice had come "not because of me, but for your sakes." The Lord had openly declared to them that the Father had spoken from heaven that they might believe, yet they persisted in doubting. Jesus continued by testifying, "Now is the judgment of this world," and he concluded by stating that Lucifer, "the prince of this world," would be cast out. Through the atonement and the resurrection, Jesus would overcome the power of the devil.[23]

John abruptly moves to another point of the Lord's discourse as Jesus again testified of his impending death and his ascension to his rightful place in heaven, where he would "draw all men" to him. But the people listening (apparently others were there besides the Greeks) still failed to understand the Lord's mission, and they resorted to their historical expectations of the Messiah, declaring that the Savior would not die, but live forever. With this in mind they wanted to know why the Son of Man had to be lifted up; and then, as if to compound their misunderstanding, they asked, "Who is this Son of man?" But the time for theological discussions was over. Jesus would not enter into the controversy which their comments raised. He did, however, answer their question, declaring that while the light (meaning himself) was with them, they should walk in the light so as not to be overcome by the darkness that would surround them when he was gone.

John now enters the discussion himself, breaking off the comments of the Savior to reiterate the continuous theme he has maintained throughout his Gospel—the unbelief of the Jews. He comments that even though Jesus had performed many miracles for the Jews, "yet they believed not on him." This, he concluded, fulfilled the prophecy of Esaias, who, upon seeing the ministry of Jesus and his rejection in a vision, declared that no one would believe his report, even though "the arm of the Lord" had been revealed (Isaiah 53:1). John continued by quoting Isaiah and noting that those who had observed the powerful ministry of the Savior had blinded their eyes and hardened their hearts so that they would not be converted and healed (Isaiah 6:8-11). To emphasize the Jews' lack of commitment (even though they still looked for the Messiah), John notes that many of the rulers believed on Christ, but would not confess him for fear of being put out of the synagogue, "For they loved the praise of men more than the praise of God."

John's comments are a summation of all the reasons why the Jews rejected Christ. That rejection

> was not an isolated act, "but the outcome and direct result of their whole previous religious development. In face of the clearest evidence, they did not believe, because they could not believe. The long course of their resistance to the prophetic message, and their perversion of it, was itself a hardening of their hearts, although at the same time a God-decreed sentence on their resistance. Because they would not believe—through this their mental obscuration, which came upon them in Divine judgment, although in the natural course of their self-chosen religious development—therefore, despite all evidence, they did not believe, when He came and did such miracles before them . . . [because they] . . . loved the glory of men more than the glory of God."[24]

After his short soliloquy, John returned to the Lord's discourse and recorded the Savior's last great appeal to the multitude surrounding him. He challenged them to have faith, declaring, "He that believeth on me, believeth not on me, but on him that sent me." In other words, if you believe in Jesus Christ, you believe in God. The Lord then reiterated the purpose of his mission, declaring that he had come to save the world and not to judge it. He clarified this by stating, "He that rejecteth me, and receiveth not my words, hath one that judgeth him: the word [the gospel] that I have spoken." He pointed out that he spoke not of himself but was fulfilling the mission his Father had given him, and that the commandment, if heeded, would provide life everlasting. With this final plea he ended his discourse.

Part Seven

"It Is Finished"

"Farewell, I Will Come Again" 12

Christ's Farewell

Matthew 23:1–39

1. Then spake Jesus to the multitude, and to his disciples,

2. Saying, The scribes and the Pharisees sit in Moses' seat:

3. All therefore whatsoever they bid you observe, that observe and do; but do not ye after their works: for they say, and do not.

4. For they bind heavy burdens and grievous to be borne, and lay them on men's shoulders; but they themselves will not move them with one of their fingers.

5. But all their works they do for to be seen of men: they make broad their phylacteries, and enlarge the borders of their garments,

6. And love the uppermost rooms at feasts, and the chief seats in the synagogues,

7. And greetings in the markets, and to be called of men, Rabbi, Rabbi.

8. But be not ye called Rabbi: for one is your Master, even Christ; and all ye are brethren.

9. And call no man your father upon the earth: for one is your Father, which is in heaven.

10. Neither be ye called masters: for one is your Master, even Christ.

11. But he that is greatest among you shall be your servant.

12. And whosoever shall exalt himself shall be abased; and he that shall humble himself shall be exalted.

13. But woe unto you, scribes and Pharisees, hypocrites! for ye shut up the kingdom of heaven against men: for ye neither go in your- selves, neither suffer ye them that are entering to go in.

14. Woe unto you, scribes and Pharisees, hypocrites! for ye devour widows' houses, and for a pretence make long prayer: therefore ye shall receive the greater damnation.

15. Woe unto you, scribes and Pharisees, hypocrites! for ye compass sea and land to make one proselyte, and when he is made, ye make him twofold more the child of hell than yourselves.

16. Woe unto you, ye blind guides, which say, Whosoever shall swear by the temple, it is nothing; but whosoever shall swear by the gold of the temple, he is a debtor!

17. Ye fools and blind: for whether is greater, the gold, or the temple that sanctifieth the gold?

18. And, Whosoever shall swear by the altar, it is nothing; but whosoever sweareth by the gift that is upon it, he is guilty.

19. Ye fools and blind: for whether is greater, the gift, or the altar that sanctifieth the gift?

20. Whoso therefore shall swear by the altar, sweareth by it, and by all things thereon.

21. And whoso shall swear by the temple, sweareth by it, and by him that dwelleth therein.

22. And he that shall swear by heaven, sweareth by the throne of God, and by him that sitteth thereon.

23. Woe unto you, scribes and Pharisees, hypocrites! for ye pay tithe of mint and anise and cummin, and have omitted the weightier matters of the law, judgment, mercy, and faith: these ought ye to have done, and not to leave the other undone.

24. Ye blind guides, which strain at a gnat, and swallow a camel.

25. Woe unto you, scribes and Pharisees, hypocrites! for ye make clean the outside of the cup and of the platter, but within they are full of extortion and excess.

26. Thou blind Pharisee, cleanse first that which is within the cup and platter, that the outside of them may be clean also.

27. Woe unto you, scribes and Pharisees, hypocrites! for ye are like unto whited sepulchres, which indeed appear beautiful outward, but are within full of dead men's bones, and of all uncleanness.

28. Even so ye also outwardly appear righteous unto men, but within ye are full of hypocrisy and iniquity.

29. Woe unto you, scribes and Pharisees, hypocrites! because ye build the tombs of the prophets, and garnish the sepulchres of the righteous,

30. And say, If we had been in the days of our fathers, we would not have been partakers with them in the blood of the prophets.

31. Wherefore ye be witnesses unto yourselves, that ye are the children of them which killed the prophets.

32. Fill ye up then the measure of your fathers.

33. Ye serpents, ye generation of vipers, how can ye escape the damnation of hell?

34. Wherefore, behold, I send unto you prophets, and wise men, and scribes: and some of them ye shall kill and crucify; and some of them shall ye scourge in your synagogues, and persecute them from city to city:

35. That upon you may come all the righteous blood shed upon the earth, from the blood of righteous Abel unto the blood of Zacharias son of Barachias, whom ye slew between the temple and the altar.

36. Verily I say unto you, All these things shall come upon this generation.

37. O Jerusalem, Jerusalem, thou that killest the prophets, and stonest them which are sent unto thee, how often would I have gathered thy children together, even as a hen gathereth her chickens under her wings, and ye would not!

38. Behold, your house is left unto you desolate.

39. For I say unto you, ye shall not see me henceforth, till ye shall say, Blessed is he that cometh in the name of the Lord.

Cross-references

JST Matthew 23:35   Mark 12:38–40
Luke 11:37–54; 18:9–14; 20:45–47

The Lord delivered this discourse in the temple during the last week of his ministry, just after his enemies presented the questions to him discussed in the previous chapter. This discourse clarifies explicitly the teachings the Lord gave earlier in his ministry. In it he delivers his farewell to the temple authorities, to the leaders of Israel, and to the chosen people.

The sermon is rare in that it is formulated in a completely logical manner, enumerating successive points of warning and reasoning, with examples to substantiate both. The Savior closes it with an expression of the deepest compassion concerning not only his people but also the Holy City and what the Holy City represents.

Although the Lord gave this discourse in the presence of a multitude, he directed it to his disciples.[1] It concerned the leadership of Israel but could be applied to religious leadership in any age.[2]

Jesus began by announcing that the scribes and Pharisees sat in Moses' seat, recognizing that in that position they in fact exercised at least a portion of Moses' authority.[3] The Lord was not seeking the positions of these men, nor was he encouraging immediate disobedience to their authority. Quite to the contrary, he acknowledged them as the authorized leaders in Israel; but he warned the people of their duplicity and directed the disciples not to emulate them. He instructed the multitude to follow the leadership's instructions, but he specifically warned them not to imitate their works.

Jesus described their evil works by declaring that they were outwardly punctilious in their observance of the Law, while privately eschewing the spirit of it. "Rabbinism had practically superseded the law in the substitution of multitudinous rules and exactions, with conditional penalties; the day was filled with traditional observances by which even the trivial affairs were encumbered; yet from bearing these and other grievous burdens hypocritical officials could find excuse for personal exemption."[4]

While acknowledging the legitimacy of the Jewish leaders' authority, the Lord instructed his audience not to imitate their false teachings and insincerity because the leaders were oppressive and ostentatious. They loved prominence and titles, and they were filled with avarice and pride. The Lord used specific examples to prove the truth of his accusations. First he said that the Pharisees bound heavy burdens upon the people that they themselves would not attempt to move with even "one of their fingers." Second, they made broad their phylacteries and enlarged the borders of their garments so as to be seen of men (Numbers 15:38). Third, they loved "the uppermost rooms at feasts, and the chief seats in the synagogues . . . and to be called of men, Rabbi, Rabbi."

The Lord next made two specific charges against Israel's leadership and warned the disciples (and all future leaders of Israel) not to be guilty of these things. First, they lacked spiritual integrity and love for the people. Second, their obedience was merely for show, for "Rabbinism [had] placed the ordinances of tradition above those of the Law,"[5] and the burdens of their demands had become intolerable. The Lord cautioned his disciples, "Be not ye called rabbi: for one is your Master, even Christ . . . and call no man your father upon the earth: for one is your Father, which is in heaven." Jesus continued by explaining what their relationship with one another should be: "He that is greatest among you shall be your servant. And whosoever shall exalt himself shall be abased; and he that shall humble himself shall be exalted."

This strong denunciation of the leaders of Israel "rolled over their guilty heads, with crush on crush of moral anger . . . [and] condemnation."[6] The spirituality of the Law of Moses had been destroyed by the Pharisees. They had reduced it to intellectualism, and the Lord warned the leadership of their errors and sins in eight specific instances, each introduced with the word *woe*.

The First Woe: Preventing Salvation. Because of their rigorous requirements and hypocritical piety, Israel's leadership had restricted entrance into the kingdom of heaven to those who possessed the knowledge they (the leaders) dictated. They had determined that anyone without this Pharisaic knowledge was ignorant; therefore, it was impossible for them to attain God's kingdom. They rejected the anticipated Messiah who stood before them, and while they themselves would not enter his kingdom, they also worked hard at preventing others from entering—a most grievous sin.

The Second Woe: Covetousness and Hypocrisy. The Lord had once before noted the ineffectiveness of the prayers of the Jewish leadership,[7] but now he specified that their prayers were hypocritical and only contained a pretense of righteousness. The Pharisees devoted more and more time to prayer until some boasted that they were praying nine hours out of every day,[8] and their personal avarice had increased to the point that they would "devour widows' houses" in an attempt to satisfy their greed.

The Third Woe: Proselyting. Although the Jews sought converts to satisfy the requirements of their Law, they seemed to denounce proselyting per se. In their pride and exclusiveness they laid strict rules upon converts as a test of their sincerity (even though they spoke of them with the same contempt they reserved for the plague of leprosy).[9] In their compulsion to convert the world to an apostate form of Judaism, they condemned themselves; and due to the added restrictions they placed on their converts, they made the convert "twofold more the child of hell than [themselves]."

The Fourth Woe: Oaths of Moral Blindness. The Lord condemned the arbitrariness of their oaths. Jewish traditions dictated that it meant nothing to swear an oath by the temple, but if the oath were sworn by the gold of the temple, a man was bound. With contempt for such distinctions based on worldliness, the Lord declared, "Whether is greater, the gold, or the temple that sanctifieth the gold?" The Jews valued the temple by its gold and riches rather than by its spiritual worth. Their oaths and vows had diminished the sanctity of the temple itself.

The Lord used a second example wherein he stated that if their oaths were sworn by the altar of the temple, they had no value; but if they were sworn by the gift upon the altar, the oath was valid. Again the Lord asked, "Whether is greater, the

gift, or the altar that sanctifieth the gift?" The Lord called them
"fools and blind" for there was no distinction between the altar
and the gifts upon it—or the temple and him who dwelled within
it. An oath sworn upon heaven was an oath sworn upon God,
since God sits upon the throne of heaven. Their distinctions
were folly and emphasized the moral blindness of the Jews of
Christ's time.[10]

The Fifth Woe: Omitting Weightier Matters of the Law. In
this denunciation the Lord used one of the laws of the Church[11]
to show how they had reduced a correct principle of the gospel
to unrighteousness and in the punctilious observance of that
principle had justified their elimination of the second great commandment. They had reduced the law of tithing (which Moses
had commanded) to a complicated, detailed burden, since they
tithed anise and mint and sometimes even the leaves and stocks
of plants.[12] While they strained out the gnat from their goblet
that their drink might remain pure, they hypothetically swal-
lowed a camel in their hearts; expending their religious zeal on
mere trifles left them no time for the weightier matters of the
Law. Tithing (as Moses prescribed it) should have been paid;
but justice, mercy, and faith were things that should not have
been left undone.

The Sixth Woe: Purification. Purification was an important
issue with the Pharisees. Jesus chose this issue to dramatize
their absurdity in applying this principle[13] (Mark 7:4). In this
discourse the Lord accused them of being outwardly punctilious about their cleanliness, while inside they were full of "extortion and excess." Outwardly they extolled their personal righteousness before the people, but their hearts were full of iniquity
and sin. He exhorted them to first cleanse that which was within
to ensure "that the outside of them may be clean also."

The Seventh Woe: Hypocrisy. To emphasize his scathing
denunciation of their ridiculous facade of righteousness, the Lord
compared the leaders of Israel to "whited sepulchres." The Jews
made a great effort to keep their burial places clean, simulating
the sanctity of the temple.[14] The Lord used the analogy of a
sepulchre to declare that they appeared outwardly clean and
beautiful, but within they were full of uncleanliness and dead

men's bones. He accused them of hiding their hypocrisy and iniquity under the cloak of their self-righteousness.

The Eighth Woe: The Rejection of Prophets. In this last woe the Lord expanded his comparison of whited sepulchres and plastered graves, noting that the Pharisees also built and garnished great tombs for the ancient prophets. They did this to extol their own righteousness, and they proudly boasted that if they had lived during the time of those ancient prophets, they would not have killed them. In this allegation (wherein they condemned their forefathers for murdering the prophets), they reflected the same obdurate spirit that their fathers had possessed. They loudly proclaimed that they would not have killed the previous prophets, even though their full intent was to take the life of their Savior.

It was the Messiah who stood before these Jewish leaders, and it was he who had sent the prophets they so revered. By rejecting him (the living fulfillment of ancient prophecy), it was as if they had rejected all of the early prophets also.[15] The Lord confirmed this when he stated that the blood of all the prophets from Abel to Zacharias (the father of John the Baptist[16] whom they had slain in the temple near the altar) was upon their heads—because they failed to accept the Lord's message.

Finally, Jesus condemned these leaders of the Jews to the same judgment that would befall those who had actually killed the ancient prophets—because they were knowledgeably killing the Son of God.[17]

In his "woes" the Lord contrasted his moral purity and humility with the sophistries and hypocrisy of the rabbis. The Jews had filled up their lives with petty details, and the Lord "abhorred all cant and insincerity, and all trading with religion; all striving after mere outward success . . . [and although exceptions existed], insincerity and immorality in the teachings of a religion can only multiply and perpetrate themselves in their disciples."[18]

The theology and hierarchy of Judaism had become what Jesus described as whitewashed sepulchres, "pure to the eye, but with death and corruption within."[19] The Jewish leaders had proved that he was right by their rejection of him. He demanded moral and religious reform, but they were wedded to falsehood and immorality and would rather kill him than let him lead them back to the Father.

At the conclusion of this discourse the Lord uttered a sad lamentation: "O Jerusalem, Jerusalem, thou that killest the prophets, and stonest them which are sent unto thee, how often would I have gathered thy children together, even as a hen gathereth her chickens under her wings, and ye would not! Behold, your house is left unto you desolate."

The Lord no longer claimed the great temple in Jerusalem as "his" temple; he had withdrawn his approval of that great edifice.[20] The House of the Lord was returned to the possession of evil men. He would leave Israel and its recalcitrant leaders for a time, but would look forward to the day when he could again return.

Judaism had chosen its own way.

"When Shall These Things Be?"

Matthew 24:1–42

1. And Jesus went out, and departed from the temple: and his disciples came to him for to shew him the buildings of the temple.

2. And Jesus said unto them, See ye not all these things? verily I say unto you, There shall not be left here one stone upon another, that shall not be thrown down.

3. And as he sat upon the mount of Olives, the disciples came unto him privately, saying, Tell us, when shall these things be? and what shall be the sign of thy coming, and of the end of the world?

4. And Jesus answered and said unto them, Take heed that no man deceive you.

5. For many shall come in my name, saying, I am Christ; and shall deceive many.

6. And ye shall hear of wars and rumours of wars: see that ye be not troubled: for all these things must come to pass, but the end is not yet.

7. For nation shall rise against nation, and kingdom against kingdom: and there shall be famines, and pestilences, and earthquakes, in divers places.

8. All these are the beginning of sorrows.

9. Then shall they deliver you up to be afflicted, and shall kill you: and ye shall be hated of all nations for my name's sake.

10. And then shall many be offended, and shall betray one another, and shall hate one another.

11. And many false prophets shall rise, and shall deceive many.

12. And because iniquity shall abound, the love of many shall wax cold.

13. But he that shall endure unto the end, the same shall be saved.

14. And this gospel of the kingdom shall be preached in all the world for a witness unto all nations; and then shall the end come.

15. When ye therefore shall see the abomination of desolation, spoken of by Daniel the prophet, stand in the holy place, (whoso readeth, let him understand:)

16. Then let them which be in Judaea flee into the mountains:

17. Let him which is on the housetop not come down to take any thing out of his house:

18. Neither let him which is in the field return back to take his clothes.

19. And woe unto them that are with child, and to them that give suck in those days!

20. But pray ye that your flight be not in the winter, neither on the sabbath day:

21. For then shall be great tribulation, such as was not since the beginning of the world to this time, no, nor ever shall be.

22. And except those days should be shortened, there should no flesh be saved: but for the elect's sake those days shall be shortened.

23. Then if any man shall say unto you, Lo, here is Christ, or there; believe it not.

24. For there shall arise false Christs, and false prophets, and shall shew great signs and wonders; insomuch that, if it were possible, they shall deceive the very elect.

25. Behold, I have told you before.

26. Wherefore if they shall say unto you, Behold, he is in the desert; go not forth: behold, he is in the secret chambers; believe it not.

27. For as the lightning

cometh out of the east, and shineth even unto the west; so shall also the coming of the Son of man be.

28. For wheresoever the carcase is, there will the eagles be gathered together.

29. Immediately after the tribulation of those days shall the sun be darkened, and the moon shall not give her light, and the stars shall fall from heaven, and the powers of the heavens shall be shaken:

30. And then shall appear the sign of the Son of man in heaven: and then shall all the tribes of the earth mourn, and they shall see the Son of man coming in the clouds of heaven with power and great glory.

31. And he shall send his angels with a great sound of a trumpet, and they shall gather together his elect from the four winds, from one end of heaven to the other.

32. Now learn a parable of the fig tree; When his branch is yet tender, and putteth forth leaves, ye know that summer is nigh:

33. So likewise ye, when ye shall see all these things, know that it is near, even at the doors.

34. Verily I say unto you, This generation shall not pass, till all these things be fulfilled.

35. Heaven and earth shall pass away, but my words shall not pass away.

36. But of that day and hour knoweth no man, no, not the angels of heaven, but my Father only.

37. But as the days of Noe were, so shall also the coming of the Son of man be.

38. For as in the days that were before the flood they were eating and drinking, marrying and giving in marriage, until the day that Noe entered into the ark,

39. And knew not until the flood came, and took them all away; so shall also the coming of the Son of man be.

40. Then shall two be in the field; the one shall be taken, and the other left.

41. Two women shall be grinding at the mill; the one shall be taken, and the other left.

42. Watch therefore: for ye know not what hour your Lord doth come.

Cross-references

Pearl of Great Price   Joseph Smith—Matthew 1
JST Matthew 24:1–46   Mark 13:1–37
Luke 17:20–37; 21:5–38   D&C 45:15–21

After Jesus had completed his last public denunciation of
Jerusalem and his terrible prediction of the judgment that would
come upon the temple (including its eventual destruction), the
little party of disciples, with Jesus at their head, left the sanctu-
ary and headed out of the city. They crossed the Kidron brook
on the trail that led up to the Mount of Olives. It was in the
late afternoon, and it may have been that as they traveled, a
turn in the road exposed the "sacred building . . . once more in
full view."[21] The sight would have been magnificent as the sun
shone brightly on the marble cloisters, terraced courts, and golden
spikes of the temple.[22] It may have been here that the Lord
paused to sit down and rest, and the view of the temple, coupled
with the Lord's recent comments concerning its destruction, may
have moved his disciples to sadly ask, "Tell us, when shall these
things be? and what shall be the sign of thy coming, and of the
end of the world?"

Their questions were not questions of doubt, but of inquiry
concerning the future of Jerusalem, the temple, Israel, and the
world at large. The conclusions Jesus had drawn in his discourse concerning the imminent destruction of the Jews,
Jerusalem, and the temple might have seemed inexplicable to
the Apostles, or perhaps their minds were still harboring some
of the Jewish beliefs concerning the coming of the Messiah.[23]
They may not have been able to imagine in their hearts that the
Holy City and its temple would perish before the Lord's second
coming and the end of the world.[24] It was Jesus' habit to pass
over such questions and substitute a moral lesson for a direct
reply. Therefore, while their questions dealt with time, the Lord's
response dealt with events.

His comments involved predictions and warnings of events
that would occur both in the immediate future, during the lifetime of the Apostles, and in the far-distant future; and he
spoke of the end of the world, which perhaps did not mean the

world's literal end, but the end of the prevailing social conditions among the people of the earth.[25]

The Lord began by warning the Apostles not to be deceived by other men, since he had foretold that false Christs would come in his name and deceive many. The prophecies uttered by false prophets could not save them from destruction in the end.[26] Such instances were hinted at or implied in several New Testament recordings (Acts 5:36; 8:9; 21:38), and Josephus records that many such seducers came prior to the destruction of Jerusalem.[27] The woes which were to come upon Jerusalem were not a prelude to his second coming, therefore the Apostles were to be on their guard.

The Lord next warned them of wars and rumors of wars. Nation would rise against nation, and there would be pestilence, famines, and earthquakes in diverse places; but all these were but the beginning of sorrows—another warning to the Apostles that they should not be misled by coming events. The second coming of the Savior would not take place during their lifetime. False Messiahs and violent disturbances in their political world would lead to the destruction of Jerusalem, the temple, and Israel as a nation.[28] These same signs would also occur prior to the Second Coming.

Between the destruction of Jerusalem and the Second Coming there was to be a period of unspecified duration when Satan would be allowed to deceive the world.[29] False prophets would arise and, because iniquity would abound, "the love of many [would] wax cold." When these tribulations should descend upon the Saints, many would lose their belief and fall away into apostasy.[30]

The Lord referred to the prophecy of Daniel regarding the desolation and abominations of Jerusalem, which "comprised the forcible cessation of temple rites, and the desecration of Israel's shrine by pagan conquerors,"[31] and he warned his followers to flee that destruction. Nothing should detain them— not possessions, employment, children, the weather, nor even the Sabbath day. He warned them that the tribulation would be so great prior to Jerusalem's destruction that if they hesitated to flee when they had the opportunity, they would surely be entrapped and perhaps destroyed. (The destruction the Lord

spoke of referred not necessarily to the physical body but possibly to the spiritual soul.)[32]

Jesus now moved beyond the immediate prophecies concerning the destruction of Jerusalem and the temple to speak of
those things that would occur after the establishment of the
Church in the meridian of time.[33] He warned the Apostles again
of false Christs and false prophets who would come and, through
their great signs and wonders, "if possible" deceive even the
"very elect." Although some individuals in isolated instances
might actually claim to be the Christ coming to save the Church,
the Lord was more likely referring to false doctrines or false
claims that would be made in his name. He warned that "So
profound and learned will be their doctrines, so great and marvelous their works—with in some instances false miracles being
done by them through the power of the Devil—that the very
elect will almost be deceived."[34] Jesus was warning the Apostles
and future members of the Church to be constantly on guard,
lest they be deceived and led into secret chambers after false
teachings.

After he had given these warnings to his Apostles, the Lord
quickly moved to the general signs of his second coming. He
reiterated the warning that the Saints should be aware of these
signs since the world would view the events of those times as
normal occurrences; but the Saints would know that his coming was nigh, and at his actual appearance—after the sun and
moon had been darkened and the stars had fallen from heaven—
they would be prepared for the great, universal sign that the
Lord had designated to tell the world of his advent.[35]

Jesus prophesied that prior to this great event the gospel
would be restored to the earth. This restoration would occur
after a long period of priestcraft and apostasy.[36] After the restoration there would be a gathering of the elect, and the times
of the Gentiles would be fulfilled.[37] To emphasize the gathering, the Lord gave a short analogy in the parable of the fig tree.
This parable also indicated to his disciples that his second coming would not be immediate or during their lifetime. Jesus told
the Apostles that no man knew the time, day, or hour except
his Father.

The fig tree analogy applied to both the immediate events

he had predicted and the future events he prophesied. The uncertainty of the exact date of the Lord's future prophecies eliminated any potential calculations pertaining to when the Second Advent would occur.[38]

The uncertainty of the date of the Lord's second coming would make men careless; he therefore warned the Apostles (as well as all future Saints) to take heed, lest they, like the people before the flood, give way to pleasures and indulgences or be so engrossed in the anxieties of life that they are unprepared for his return. This analogy was a particularly good one, since before the flood the people were "drinking, marrying, and giving in marriage." They neither anticipated nor dreaded a catastrophe, yet the flood came and took them all away. In like manner, the righteous should not be so engrossed in their daily temporal activities as to be unable to discern the signs of his second advent.[39] When the Lord comes, he will come quickly; two will be standing together and only one taken—prepared to enter the Lord's presence through membership in the Church and obedience to God's commandments.[40] But the one left in the "field" will be destroyed. Again the Lord cautioned, "Watch therefore: for ye know not what hour your Lord doth come."

The Lord noted that during the last stages of the earth's existence (prior to his second coming) the ties of companionship normally existing between people would be broken,[41] and the salvation of many would be in danger because of personal unrighteousness. He cautioned the Saints to be constantly watchful of the world, to remain faithful in the work of the gospel, and to protect themselves, lest enemies of the work come upon them. The Lord then concluded this discourse with the parable of the watching servants.[42]

The Apostles had asked when all of these things would be, but the Lord would not give them exact times; however, he did indicate what signs would precede the events he had spoken of. Whether those signs would be displayed at the destruction of Jerusalem or duplicated prior to his second coming did not matter. The discourse contained all that was necessary to warn and teach his disciples (and all future disciples) to be constantly watchful and prepared. However, whatever the age one lives in, when death approaches, it seems as though the great and dreadful day of the Lord is imminent.[43]

The Final Discourses

13

"In My Father's House"

John 14:1–31

1. Let not your heart be troubled: ye believe in God, believe also in me.

2. In my Father's house are many mansions: if it were not so, I would have told you. I go to prepare a place for you.

3. And if I go and prepare a place for you, I will come again, and receive you unto myself; that where I am, there ye may be also.

4. And whither I go ye know, and the way ye know.

5. Thomas saith unto him, Lord, we know not whither thou goest; and how can we know the way?

6. Jesus saith unto him, I am the way, the truth, and the life: no man cometh unto the Father, but by me.

7. If ye had known me, ye should have known my Father also: and from henceforth ye know him, and have seen him.

8. Philip saith unto him, Lord, shew us the Father, and it sufficeth us.

9. Jesus saith unto him, Have I been so long time with you, and yet hast thou

not known me, Philip? he
that hath seen me hath seen
the Father; and how sayest
thou then, Shew us the
Father?

10. Believest thou not
that I am in the Father, and
the Father in me? the words
that I speak unto you I speak
not of myself: but the Father
that dwelleth in me, he doeth
the works.

11. Believe me that I am
in the Father, and the Father
in me: or else believe me for
the very works' sake.

12. Verily, verily, I say
unto you, he that believeth
on me, the works that I do
shall he do also; and greater
works than these shall he do;
because I go unto my Father.

13. And whatsoever ye
shall ask in my name, that
will I do, that the Father may
be glorified in the Son.

14. If ye shall ask any
thing in my name, I will do
it.

15. If ye love me, keep
my commandments.

16. And I will pray the
Father, and he shall give you
another Comforter, that he
may abide with you for ever;

17. Even the Spirit of
truth; whom the world cannot receive, because it seeth
him not, neither knoweth

him: but ye know him; for he
dwelleth with you, and shall
be in you.

18. I will not leave you
comfortless: I will come to
you.

19. Yet a little while, and
the world seeth me no more;
but ye see me: because I live,
ye shall live also.

20. At that day ye shall
know that I am in my Father,
and ye in me, and I in you.

21. He that hath my com-
mandments, and keepeth
them, he it is that loveth me:
and he that loveth me shall
be loved of my Father, and I
will love him, and will manifest myself to him.

22. Judas saith unto him,
not Iscariot, Lord, how is it
that thou wilt manifest thyself unto us, and not unto the
world?

23. Jesus answered and
said unto him, If a man love
me, he will keep my words:
and my Father will love him,
and we will come unto him,
and make our abode with
him.

24. He that loveth me not
keepeth not my sayings: and
the word which ye hear is not
mine, but the Father's which
sent me.

25. These things have I
spoken unto you, being yet

present with you.

26. But the Comforter, which is the Holy Ghost, whom the Father will send in my name, he shall teach you all things, and bring all things to your remembrance, whatsoever I have said unto you.

27. Peace I leave with you, my peace I give unto you: not as the world giveth, give I unto you. Let not your heart be troubled, neither let it be afraid.

28. Ye have heard how I said unto you, I go away, and come again unto you. If ye loved me, ye would rejoice, because I said, I go unto the Father: for my Father is greater than I.

29. And now I have told you before it come to pass, that, when it is come to pass, ye might believe.

30. Hereafter I will not talk much with you: for the prince of this world cometh, and hath nothing in me.

31. But that the world may know that I love the Father; and as the Father gave me commandment, even so I do. Arise, let us go hence.

It was time for the Passover, and the inhabitants of Jerusalem would have been prepared for a joyous celebration; but it was a somber little band that surrounded Jesus on the night of his last supper. The Twelve were undoubtedly remorseful at the thought of the Lord's impending sacrifice and ashamed of the unknown traitor in their midst. Jesus, as if perceiving the sorrow in their hearts, bade them to be of good cheer: he could look beyond their present troubles and even beyond those that would soon come upon them. He gave them encouragement and hope when he said, "Ye believe in God, believe also in me."

This is an interesting discourse. The Lord clearly wanted to instruct the Apostles on this last evening, but they kept interrupting him with questions. Each time, he would answer their questions and then return to his instructions.

John 13:38 records the Lord's prophecy that before the cock crowed at dawn, Peter would deny him three times. The first four verses of this sermon may have been given in response to that comment, and the Lord may have wanted to reassure the Apostles that their troubles would not endure long, because he promised them that in his Father's house were "many mansions" and he was going there to prepare a place for them.[1]

Jesus was giving the Apostles a glimpse of what they had to look forward to. He undoubtedly hoped that throughout his ministry they had learned these basic truths and knew both the direction he must take and the way that they must follow. But Thomas interrupted him and asked a simple question that demonstrated once more their lack of understanding:[2] "Lord, we know not whither thou goest; and how can we know the way?"

Jesus did not reprimand Thomas but again declared his Messiahship:[3] "I am the way, the truth, and the life: no man cometh unto the Father, but by me." He thus explained to Thomas (and to the others) that there was more to life than physical existence, and that to attain the Father's kingdom, they would have to follow his teachings and commandments. Then, reiterating his relationship to the Father, Jesus stated, "If ye had known me, ye should have known my Father also."

Philip was still not convinced. "Lord," he said, "shew us the Father, and it sufficeth us." To this Jesus replied, "Have I been so long time with you, and yet hast thou not known me, Philip?" The Lord again explained that anyone who had seen him had seen the Father. They were alike in doctrine, purpose, and appearance. Mildly rebuking Philip, Jesus asked him why he wanted to see the Father, in spite of what he, the Savior, had taught him. Jesus again reminded the Twelve of the relationship that existed between himself and the Father and told them that they must believe on him to understand that relationship. He testified that he had not come to do his own works nor to speak of his own words, but to do the will of the Father. Jesus admonished the Twelve that if they could not believe his allegations, they should remember the evidence he had given them through his ministry. He concluded with the promise that, "He that believeth on me, the works that I do shall he do also." He limited, however, the great power he was leaving them by making it commensurate with their faith and belief in him.

At this point the Lord returned to his discourse and, for the first time, instructed the Apostles to pray in his name.[4] He promised them that if they would do so, he would grant their righteous petition so that the Father might be glorified in the Son.

His next instruction began with an admonition to the Apostles. Merely professing love for the Lord was not enough— it was their actions that would evidence their keeping of his commandments. The Lord promised the Apostles that if they kept the commandments, he would give them "another Comforter," which the world could not receive and did not know, but who would come and dwell with them; and so as to not leave them comfortless, he promised that he would return again. Joseph Smith commented on this passage of scripture:

> There are two Comforters spoken of. One is the Holy Ghost, the same as given on the day of Pentecost, and that all Saints receive after faith, repentance, and baptism. This first Comforter or Holy Ghost has no other effect than pure intelligence. It is more powerful in expanding the mind, enlightening the understanding, and storing the intellect with present knowledge, of a man who is of the literal seed of Abraham, than one that is a Gentile, though it may not have half as much visible effect upon the body; for as the Holy Ghost falls upon of the literal seed of Abraham, it is calm and serene; and his whole soul and body are only exercised by the pure spirit of intelligence; while the effect of the Holy Ghost upon a Gentile, is to purge out the old blood, and make him actually of the seed of Abraham. That man that has none of the blood of Abraham (naturally) must have a new creation by the Holy Ghost. In such a case, there may be more of a powerful effect upon the body, and visible to the eye, than upon an Israelite, while the Israelite at first might be far before the Gentile in pure intelligence.

The Second Comforter

The other Comforter spoken of is a subject of great interest, and perhaps understood by few of this generation. After a person has faith in Christ, repents of his sins, and is baptized for the remission of his sins and receives the Holy Ghost, (by the laying on of hands), which is the first Comforter, then let him continue to humble himself before God, hungering and thirsting after righteousness, and living by every word of God, and the Lord will soon say unto him, Son, thou shalt be exalted. When the Lord has thoroughly proved him, and finds that the man is determined to serve Him at all hazards, then the man will find his calling and his election made sure, then it will be his privilege to receive the other Comforter, which the Lord hath promised the Saints, as is recorded in the testimony of St. John, in the 14th chapter, from the 12th to the 27th verses. . . .

Now what is this other Comforter? It is no more nor less than the Lord Jesus Christ Himself; and this is the sum and substance of the whole matter; that when any man obtains this last Comforter, he will have the personage of Jesus Christ to attend him, or appear unto him from time to time, and even He will manifest the Father unto him, and they will take up their abode with him, and the visions of the heavens will be opened unto him, and the Lord will teach him face to face, and he may have a perfect knowledge of the mysteries of the Kingdom of God; and this is the state and place the ancient Saints arrived at when they had such glorious visions—Isaiah, Ezekiel, John upon the Isle of Patmos, St. Paul in the three heavens, and all the Saints who held communion with the general assembly and Church of the Firstborn.[5]

It would appear at this point in the discourse that the Lord was about to conclude. He declared that the world would see him no more, but that through his death he and others would live forever. He testified to the Apostles that "at that day" (referring to the resurrection) they would know that he was in the Father, "and ye in me, and I in you."

Jesus again admonished the Apostles to keep the commandments. He explained that he who kept them evidenced his love toward him, and then said, "He that loveth me shall be loved of my Father." But again the Lord was interrupted by a third member of the Twelve who asked a question which indicated that they still lacked understanding.[6] Judas (not Iscariot) said, "Lord, how is it that thou wilt manifest thyself unto us, and not unto the world?" Jesus responded with a simple explanation: "If a man love me, he will keep my words: and my Father will love him, and we will come unto him, and make our abode with him." Those—and only those—who truly love the Lord and keep all his commandments will receive the companionship and a testimony of Jesus and his Father.

The Lord returned to the place in his sermon where he had been interrupted, and extended to the Twelve the promise of the Holy Ghost (the First Comforter). He told them that the Comforter, "whom the Father will send in my name . . . shall teach you all things, and bring all things to your remembrance, whatsoever I have said unto you." No longer would the visible presence of the God of Israel abide with his people, but the Holy Ghost would manifest His word to their spirit as a result of their faith and obedience.

The Lord concluded this discourse with a powerful but comforting passage: "Peace I leave with you, my peace I give unto you: not as the world giveth, give I unto you." Jesus was the "Prince of Peace." He left his disciples with a knowledge of the gospel, and the assurance that he would rise from the grave and give all men the gift of resurrection. "Let not your heart be troubled," he declared, "neither let it be afraid." Through the Atonement and the corresponding law of repentance he had made it possible for mankind to renew themselves and dwell eternally with him in his Father's presence!

Finally, he warned his beloved Apostles of the coming of the "prince of this world"—or Satan; and even though the devil would temporarily conquer and Jesus would suffer death, through his death he would permanently defeat the source of all evil and bring the gift of eternal life to those who qualified to receive it. The Lord closed this discourse with his testimony: "I love the Father; and as the Father gave me commandment, even so I do." A righteous people cannot ignore this great example. To love the Lord is to serve him and keep his commandments.

"I Am the True Vine"

John 15:1-27

1. I am the true vine, and my Father is the husband-man.

2. Every branch in me

that beareth not fruit he
taketh away: and every
branch that beareth fruit, he
purgeth it, that it may bring
forth more fruit.

3. Now ye are clean
through the word which I
have spoken unto you.

4. Abide in me, and I in
you. As the branch cannot
bear fruit of itself, except it
abide in the vine; no more
can ye, except ye abide in
me.

5. I am the vine, ye are
the branches: He that abideth
in me, and I in him, the same
bringeth forth much fruit: for
without me ye can do nothing.

6. If a man abide not in
me, he is cast forth as a
branch, and is withered; and
men gather them, and cast
them into the fire, and they
are burned.

7. If ye abide in me, and
my words abide in you, ye
shall ask what ye will, and it
shall be done unto you.

8. Herein is my Father
glorified, that ye bear much
fruit; so shall ye be my
disciples.

9. As the Father hath
loved me, so have I loved
you: continue ye in my love.

10. If ye keep my com-
mandments, ye shall abide in

my love; even as I have kept
my Father's commandments,
and abide in his love.

11. These things have I
spoken unto you, that my joy
might remain in you, and
that your joy might be full.

12. This is my command-
ment, That ye love one
another, as I have loved you.

13. Greater love hath no
man than this, that a man lay
down his life for his friends.

14. Ye are my friends, if
ye do whatsoever I command
you.

15. Henceforth I call you
not servants; for the servant
knoweth not what his lord
doeth: but I have called you
friends; for all things that I
have heard of my Father I
have made known unto you.

16. Ye have not chosen
me, but I have chosen you,
and ordained you, that ye
should go and bring forth
fruit, and that your fruit
should remain: that whatsoever ye shall ask of the Father
in my name, he may give it
to you.

17. These things I com-
mand you, that ye love one
another.

18. If the world hate you,
ye know that it hated me
before it hated you.

19. If ye were of the

world, the world would love his own: but because ye are not of the world, but I have chosen you out of the world, therefore the world hateth you.

20. Remember the word that I said unto you, The servant is not greater than his lord. If they have persecuted me, they will also persecute you; if they have kept my saying, they will keep yours also.

21. But all these things will they do unto you for my name's sake, because they know not him that sent me.

22. If I had not come and spoken unto them, they had not had sin: but now they have no cloke for their sin.

23. He that hateth me hateth my Father also.

24. If I had not done among them the works which none other man did, they had not had sin: but now have they both seen and hated both me and my Father.

25. But this cometh to pass, that the word might be fulfilled that is written in their law, They hated me without a cause.

26. But when the Comforter is come, whom I will send unto you from the Father, even the Spirit of truth, which proceedeth from the Father, he shall testify of me:

27. And ye also shall bear witness, because ye have been with me from the beginning.

Cross-reference

John 13:32–35

Jesus closed the discourse recorded in John 14 by declaring to the Apostles, "Arise, let us go hence." As he was preparing to leave the upper room, he may have paused to deliver this discourse, or he may have delivered it while they walked; in either event, the discourse commenced with an allegory about a vine. The Lord used it to illustrate the relationship between the Father, the Apostles, and himself; and according to Elder James E. Talmage, "A grander analogy is not to be found in the world's literature."[7]

The object of this discourse was to encourage the Apostles in their future work. The Lord described the nature of their work, the honor they would receive from the Father, and the hardships and joys they would experience. He taught them that they would have to take his place and preach the gospel of the kingdom to all the world. The purpose of the allegory was not to cast Jesus, the Father, or the disciples in the role of a vine, a husbandman, or branches; Jesus simply used these things to explain the relationship between himself, the Father, and the disciples.

Jesus had already told the Apostles in his previous discourse that if they loved him they would keep his commandments. He now reiterated that statement, noting that those who do not believe on him and keep his commandments will be as the branch that "beareth not fruit," which will be purged from the tree. The Apostles were clean because they believed on the words Jesus taught them, yet he cautioned them that they would not continue to bear fruit unless they would abide in him, for the alternatives (according to the discourse) were to bring forth "much fruit," or to be cast out. The emphasis of this discourse was on obedience in keeping the Lord's commandments. If the Apostles did this they would abide in the Savior's love.

Next, the Lord taught the relationship between the disciples and their fellowman, commanding them to "love one another, as I have loved you. Greater love hath no man than this," the Lord explained, "that a man lay down his life for his friends." Jesus elaborated on this concept by stating, "Ye are my friends, if ye do whatsoever I command you." Perhaps few will ever be called upon to literally give their lives for someone else, but we can "give our lives" to the Lord through obedience to his commandments. We become his "friend" when we devote a lifetime of service to him. Jesus said that the Apostles were his friends rather than his servants. Throughout his ministry they had only been apprentices, but now as Apostles of his church and witnesses of his kingdom, they were his partners in the work, and he would fortify them against the suffering they would endure.

The Lord reminded his disciples that they did not choose him, but rather that he had chosen them and ordained them to the great work upon which they were embarking. Through their devotion to him they had separated themselves from the world, and the world would hate and persecute them for it. Then the

Lord comforted them. "Remember," he said, "the servant is not greater than his lord. If they have persecuted me, they will also persecute you." Antagonism toward faithful Saints has always been a characteristic of the true church[8] (2 Timothy 3:12).

Jesus had testified of his divinity to the Jews—his chosen people—and they rejected and hated him without a cause. It is possible that they might not have totally understood his words, but by observing his works, "which none other man did," they should have believed; rather they ascribed his miracles to Beelzebub and rejected him all the more.[9] In this they committed a grievous sin,[10] and they will be left without excuse at the judgment day.[11] The Lord told his Apostles that this fulfilled the Old Testament prophecy which stated that "they [would] hate [him] without a cause" (Psalms 35:19; 69:4).

Jesus closed this discourse by again testifying that the Comforter (the Holy Ghost) would be sent to the Apostles to bear testimony of him. He then charged them, saying, "And ye also shall bear witness, because ye have been with me from the beginning," referring to their future mission, which was to testify to the divinity of Jesus the Christ.

"Do Ye Now Believe?"

John 16:1–33

1. These things have I spoken unto you, that ye should not be offended.

2. They shall put you out of the synagogues: yea, the time cometh, that whosoever killeth you will think that he doeth God service.

3. And these things will they do unto you, because they have not known the Father, nor me.

4. But these things have I told you, that when the time shall come, ye may remember that I told you of them. And these things I said not unto you at the beginning, because I was with you.

5. But now I go my way to him that sent me; and none of you asketh me, Whither goest thou?

6. But because I have said these things unto you, sorrow hath filled your heart.

7. Nevertheless I tell you the truth; It is expedient for

you that I go away: for if I go not away, the Comforter will not come unto you; but if I depart, I will send him unto you.

8. And when he is come, he will reprove the world of sin, and of righteousness, and of judgment:

9. Of sin, because they believe not on me;

10. Of righteousness, because I go to my Father, and ye see me no more;

11. Of judgment, because the prince of this world is judged.

12. I have yet many things to say unto you, but ye cannot bear them now.

13. Howbeit when he, the Spirit of truth, is come, he will guide you into all truth: for he shall not speak of himself; but whatsoever he shall hear, that shall he speak: and he will shew you things to come.

14. He shall glorify me: for he shall receive of mine, and shall shew it unto you.

15. All things that the Father hath are mine: therefore said I, that he shall take of mine, and shall shew it unto you.

16. A little while, and ye shall not see me: and again, a little while, and ye shall see

me, because I go to the Father.

17. Then said some of his disciples among themselves, What is this that he saith unto us, A little while, and ye shall not see me: and again, a little while, and ye shall see me: and, Because I go to the Father?

18. They said therefore, What is this that he saith, A little while? we cannot tell what he saith.

19. Now Jesus knew that they were desirous to ask him, and said unto them, Do ye inquire among yourselves of that I said, A little while, and ye shall not see me: and again, a little while, and ye shall see me?

20. Verily, verily, I say unto you, That ye shall weep and lament, but the world shall rejoice: and ye shall be sorrowful, but your sorrow shall be turned into joy.

21. A woman when she is in travail hath sorrow, because her hour is come: but as soon as she is delivered of the child, she remembereth no more the anguish, for joy that a man is born into the world.

22. And ye now therefore have sorrow: but I will see you again, and your heart

shall rejoice, and your joy no man taketh from you.

23. And in that day ye shall ask me nothing. Verily, verily, I say unto you, Whatsoever ye shall ask the Father in my name, he will give it to you.

24. Hitherto have ye asked nothing in my name: ask, and ye shall receive, that your joy may be full.

25. These things have I spoken unto you in proverbs: but the time cometh, when I shall no more speak unto you in proverbs, but I shall shew you plainly of the Father.

26. At that day ye shall ask in my name: and I say not unto you, that I will pray the Father for you:

27. For the Father himself loveth you, because ye have loved me, and have believed that I came out from God.

28. I came forth from the Father, and am come into the world: again, I leave the world, and go to the Father.

29. His disciples said unto him, Lo, now speakest thou plainly, and speakest no proverb.

30. Now are we sure that thou knowest all things, and needest not that any man should ask thee: by this we believe that thou camest forth from God.

31. Jesus answered them, Do ye now believe?

32. Behold, the hour cometh, yea, is now come, that ye shall be scattered, every man to his own, and shall leave me alone: and yet I am not alone, because the Father is with me.

33. These things I have spoken unto you, that in me ye might have peace. In the world ye shall have tribulation: but be of good cheer; I have overcome the world.

Jesus opened this discourse with a warning to his disciples. He told them that persecutions would come to them as they taught the gospel and testified of the Savior. He told them that their Jewish colleagues would reject them, and he predicted their deaths, specifying that those who killed them would think they had done God a religious service, when in reality their cruelty would be merely a result of their ignorance of the Messiah and the Father.

Jesus spoke these things so that the disciples would not stumble, be offended, or have cause to doubt when they were assailed by these future events.[12] He realized that it might be difficult for them to continue to believe that their cause was just when their success waned and when it seemed that most of the power lay with the adversary. "But these things have I told you," Jesus explained, "that when the time shall come, ye may remember that I told you of them." The Lord was still attempting to help the Apostles better understand his death and resurrection. They had not understood before and had felt sorrow and confusion concerning these things. Jesus chided them not only for their lack of understanding but also for not asking more questions about his departure when they failed to comprehend it.[13]

Jesus continued his discourse to the Twelve by augmenting his instructions on the coming of the Holy Ghost, noting that as long as he was with them there was no need for the Holy Ghost and the Holy Ghost would therefore not come; but upon his departure, the Holy Ghost would be with them.[14] The Lord then instructed the Apostles on the mission of the Holy Ghost, indicating that this great Spirit would "reprove the world of sin and of righteousness and of judgment." He then explained further: "Of sin, because they believe not on me; of righteousness, because I go to my Father, and ye see me no more; of judgment, because the prince of this world is judged." The people did not believe in Jesus, but he fulfilled all righteousness by completing his mission and being resurrected. Because he completed his mission, the devil would be judged and totally overcome. Recognizing his Apostles' present limitations, the Lord explained that he had many more things to tell them, but that they would not be able to understand those things at that time:[15] but when the Holy Ghost came to them he would both clarify and reveal all things unto them (D&C 8:2-3), thus glorifying both the Savior and his Father.

The Lord concluded this portion of his discourse by again testifying of his impending death and resurrection and indicating that in "a little while" the Apostles would not see him; but he said that in "a little while" they would see him once more, after he had gone to the Father. Just as before, when the Lord spoke of his coming death and resurrection in metaphors, the

Apostles did not understand. Among themselves they asked, "What is this that he saith unto us?" Apparently the Lord could not hear their discussion, but he could perceive their thoughts and "knew that they were desirous to ask him concerning these things." He asked them why they were having difficulty with his teachings, and to help them better understand he defined the first "little while" to be the time that they would lament over his death (an event that would cause the world to rejoice); and the second "little while" to be the time he would have with them after he was resurrected (when their sorrows would "be turned into joy").[16] Then the Lord gave the example of a woman experiencing sorrow during the birth process, who, when delivered of the child, remembered the pain and anguish no more "for joy that a man is born into the world."

The Lord told the Apostles that after he had departed from them they should pray to the Father in his name for answers to their questions. He explained that although he had spoken to them in proverbs, in the future he would speak plainly of the Father. And, as if to keep his promise (and perhaps as a reward for their faith and love), he did speak clearly and plainly to them: "I came forth from the Father, and am come into the world: again, I leave the world, and go to the Father."

Because the Lord had perceived their thoughts without their asking him, the disciples received renewed conviction from this simple declaration. "Lo, now speakest thou plainly, and speakest no proverb," they rejoiced. "Now are we sure that thou knowest all things, and needest not that any man should ask thee: by this we believe that thou camest forth from God." To this Jesus responded, "Do ye now believe?" He then prophesied that the hour would soon come when they would be scattered, "every man to his own," and he would be left alone to face his painful trial and death. Yet he would not be alone, for his Father would be with him.[17]

In closing, the Lord strengthened the Apostles in their resolve, noting that he had spoken the things of his discourse that they might have peace: "In the world ye shall have tribulation: but be of good cheer; I have overcome the world."

The Great Prayer

John 17:1–26

1. These words spake Jesus, and lifted up his eyes to heaven, and said, Father, the hour is come; glorify thy Son, that thy Son also may glorify thee:

2. As thou hast given him power over all flesh, that he should give eternal life to as many as thou hast given him.

3. And this is life eternal, that they might know thee the only true God, and Jesus Christ, whom thou hast sent.

4. I have glorified thee on the earth: I have finished the work which thou gavest me to do.

5. And now, O Father, glorify thou me with thine own self with the glory which I had with thee before the world was.

6. I have manifested thy name unto the men which thou gavest me out of the world: thine they were, and thou gavest them me; and they have kept thy word.

7. Now they have known that all things whatsoever thou hast given me are of thee.

8. For I have given unto them the words which thou gavest me; and they have received them, and have known surely that I came out from thee, and they have believed that thou didst send me.

9. I pray for them: I pray not for the world, but for them which thou hast given me; for they are thine.

10. And all mine are thine, and thine are mine; and I am glorified in them.

11. And now I am no more in the world, but these are in the world, and I come to thee. Holy Father, keep through thine own name those whom thou hast given me, that they may be one, as we are.

12. While I was with them in the world, I kept them in thy name: those that thou gavest me I have kept, and none of them is lost, but the son of perdition; that the scripture might be fulfilled.

13. And now come I to thee; and these things I speak in the world, that they might have my joy fulfilled in themselves.

14. I have given them thy word; and the world

hath hated them, because they are not of the world, even as I am not of the world.

15. I pray not that thou shouldest take them out of the world, but that thou shouldest keep them from the evil.

16. They are not of the world, even as I am not of the world.

17. Sanctify them through thy truth: thy word is truth.

18. As thou hast sent me into the world, even so have I also sent them into the world.

19. And for their sakes I sanctify myself, that they also might be sanctified through the truth.

20. Neither pray I for these alone, but for them also which shall believe on me through their word;

21. That they all may be one; as thou, Father, art in me, and I in thee, that they also may be one in us: that the world may believe that thou hast sent me.

22. And the glory which thou gavest me I have given them; that they may be one, even as we are one:

23. I in them, and thou in me, that they may be made perfect in one; and that the world may know that thou hast sent me, and hast loved them, as thou hast loved me.

24. Father, I will that they also, whom thou hast given me, be with me where I am; that they may behold my glory, which thou hast given me: for thou lovedst me before the foundation of the world.

25. O righteous Father, the world hath not known thee: but I have known thee, and these have known that thou hast sent me.

26. And I have declared unto them thy name, and will declare it: that the love wherewith thou hast loved me may be in them, and I in them.

Jesus gave this discourse in the form of a prayer to his Father in Heaven. He gave it in preparation for his agony and the sacrifice he would make for all mankind. It marked the end of his earthly ministry and focused on the upcoming missionary efforts of the Twelve. He spoke as if his mission were totally complete, even though the betrayal and crucifixion still lay before him. Since he had a complete comprehension of the eternal plan of salvation, he prayed that his Father in Heaven would glorify him in accordance with that plan. He prayed that knowledge of the plan would bring eternal life to as many as would believe on him, and then declared, "This is life eternal, that they might know thee the only true God, and Jesus Christ, whom thou hast sent."

The promise of this great passage is clear. If, through study and prayer, we come to know Jesus and follow his teachings, we will receive life eternal: the same life that the Eternal Father has, the same kind, type, and quality of life as God.[18] (D&C 132:19-22; 29:43-44; 14:7.)

In the first part of this discourse the Savior prayed about himself. He then included the welfare of his beloved Apostles in his communication with God. The Father had given the Apostles to his Son "out of the world," the Son had manifested his Father's name to them, and they had kept the Father's word. They received the words of the Savior as if they had come directly from the Father, they gained a fervent testimony that Christ had come from the Father, and they believed implicitly that the Father had sent him.

He continued his prayer, interceding for the Apostles and pleading with the Father to bless them because of the love that he had for them.[19] While he was in the world he could protect them, but he was leaving to return to the Father, so he pleaded not only for their safety but also that they might be as Christ and the Father—"one" in all things. The Apostles had finally gained a "knowledge" testimony of his Messiahship, and they were now prepared to testify of his divinity to all the world. They would no longer be of the world, just as Christ was not of the world, and they would need the protection of the Father to shield them from the evils of men. Only eleven of the Apostles were with the Savior during these last moments before his trial and crucifixion, and he noted in his prayer that he had kept them all except the one who had betrayed him and whom the Savior now classified as "the son of perdition."

As he concluded this section of his prayer, the Savior expressed the desire that the Father would sanctify the Apostles and allow them to share in the Father's glory. Although this prayer was an intercession with the Father in behalf of the

Apostles, it was also a prophecy of the great work which they would do. Their accomplishments are testified to in the Acts of the Apostles and in the other books of the New Testament.

> The contrast between the dejected, faint-hearted, materializing Galilaean fishermen and peasants of the Gospels, and the heroic, spiritual confessors of Pentecost and aftertimes, is, itself, a miracle, great beyond all others. The illumination of soul, the grandeur of conception, the loftiness of aim, are a transformation from a lower to an indefinitely higher mental and moral condition, as complete as the change from early twilight to noon, and find their only solution in the admission that they must have received the miraculous spiritual enlightenment from above which Jesus had promised to send them.[20]

The third part of the Savior's prayer concerned all mankind. "Neither pray I for these alone," he said (referring to the Apostles), "but for them also which shall believe on me through their word." These Saints were also to be one, as the Apostles were commanded to be one, and as Christ and the Father are one. All this was to be accomplished so that the world would believe that the Father had sent Jesus Christ to be the Savior of mankind. Although the Lord interceded for and in behalf of mankind in general, the intercession for individuals was based on their belief: man could only be reconciled with God if he had faith in the Father and the Son and repented of his sins.[21] This was the work the Apostles were called to do, because as the Father had sent the Son, so the Son would now send his Apostles—in the same manner and on the same mission.

The Lord now concluded his prayer to his Heavenly Father with an expressed wish that the Apostles (and all those who would believe on him) would be with him in the Father's kingdom and "behold [his] glory" which the Father had given him. The world did not know the Father and it did not recognize the Son, but the Twelve now recognized him as the Messiah; and so the Savior declared the Father unto them, and would declare him again. He closed by praying that the great love that existed between the Father and the Son would continue to be with the

Apostles and—through them—with all the Saints who would believe.

Part Eight

The Darkness and the Light

Lest We Also Look Beyond the Mark   *14*

Jesus used his sermons and discourses to instruct his disciples concerning the kingdom of God. He was the Word made flesh, he was with the Father in the beginning when the world was made, he accepted the great plan of salvation presented by the Father and declared, "Here am I; send me" (Isaiah 6:8).

He was the God of Abraham, Isaac, and Jacob, and he guided Moses, the great Lawgiver, to prepare the chosen people for the kingdom of God; but they changed the Law and broke the covenant (Isaiah 24:5), and thus lost the promise.

The religious leaders of ancient Israel placed a hedge around the Law and contrived infinite minutia to direct the lives of the people, proclaiming that they did it to prepare them for the coming Messiah. They thought the Messiah would save them from their temporal problems, and they assumed he would restore Israel to the glory it had once known. They were concerned with their earthly positions, wealth, and all material things, rather than their spiritual needs. They rigidly observed the requirements of the Law only to reject the Lawgiver; yet in his discourses Jesus proclaimed their freedom—not on the earth, but from the evils of the earth.

During his ministry the Savior taught in parables—stories of everyday life that encompassed the marvelous truths of the kingdom of heaven. Through his parables he displayed his familiarity with every aspect of life and illustrated his great spiritual teachings. He demonstrated his consummate power with miracle upon miracle, thereby proclaiming his Messiahship and teaching his doctrine.

But it was in his discourses that he verbally announced his claim to the Messiahship and the establishment of his new kingdom. He would not put new wine in old bottles, nor would he use the pedantic leadership of his day. They could not see beyond their offices to find their own salvation, and in so doing they blocked the way for others. Instead, in all but one instance, he called his Apostles from the simple Galileans, and he ordained them to be the leaders of the kingdom of God. They worked with him from day to day, observing all that he did and listening intently to his sermons. Before his mission ended they had learned his ways and recognized him as the Savior.

He declared his gospel in the Sermon on the Mount, which opened the way for individuals to know God and love him with all their heart, might, mind, and strength. He presented to the people and rulers alike a doctrine that conflicted in almost every way with the religion of their Jewish society. To a lowly Samaritan woman by a well he declared himself to be "living water," and the ensuing discourse produced a harvest of great proportions. He used the ceremonies of the Jewish feasts and celebrations to declare himself the "bread of life," the "light of the world," and the "good shepherd," yet they sought only to stone him. He taught Nicodemus, a "Master" of Israel, about baptism (both by water and by the Spirit), and he explained the change that must come upon each individual if he is to follow the true path.

He watched as the poor widow cast in her mite, and declared her contribution greater than all the wealthy donations that had been given "in their abundance." He taught that the sanctity of the marriage vow was God-given, rather than given by man. He was questioned by Pharisees, scribes, Sadducees, and lawyers, all of whom attempted to entrap him in his words and deeds. He proclaimed John the Baptist as John had proclaimed

Him. He praised John's work and condemned those who had rejected him. He accused the Jewish leadership of being blind, and warned his disciples of their leaven. He knew the Law because he was the "giver" of the Law, yet they questioned him and asked, "How knoweth this man letters?"

In their contempt, the Pharisees brought a woman before him taken in the sin of adultery and asked him to judge her. In reply he proclaimed their Law to be accurate, for he had given it; then he required him "who was without sin" to be the first to cast a stone at her. But they were all ashamed, being smitten by their own guilt, and they left the woman alone with him. Though he could not forgive her without proven repentance, in great compassion he would neither punish nor condemn her, but warned her to go and "sin no more."

When the Lord's public ministry drew to a close, he lamented over Jerusalem and the holy temple (which he had called his house and his Father's house); yet he ultimately reassigned it to the Jews because of their disbelief. His final instructions to the Twelve included the forecast of his death and the prophecy of their future suffering. But he also promised them rewards beyond their wildest dreams, if they endured. He left them the Holy Ghost to assure them of his love and to bring to their minds the great teachings he had given them. He taught them of his Father and promised them that they would return to his presence if they would but believe. Finally, he prayed as no other man has ever prayed and, completing his mission, requested the Father to shower forth the blessings of heaven upon all those who would believe.

The Jews wanted an earthly king—but Jesus was a heavenly King. They wanted to be able to work their way back into the kingdom, but they refused to do the things the Lord required of them. They wanted to enjoy all earthly pleasures without limitations. They wanted to have all of the blessings the scriptures promised them, but they would only rely on their ancient covenant to acquire them. Even though they recognized the Lord's claims, they continually demanded signs of his divinity. They did not believe, because they would not believe.

The discourses apply to modern Saints as readily as they do the ancients. The teachings are the same and they excite the same controversies; there are still some who believe, but many who do not. The Lord's message is continuous—one eternal round—and the discourses contain all that is needed to come to a sure knowledge of the Father and the Son.

The Savior taught a message that was woven into the fabric of everyday life. He promised future rewards for righteous living and help with daily problems: he spoke of the love of God and love of our fellowman.

We can change the commandments of his law or put hedges around them. We can limit our compliance and reject not only the law but also the Lawgiver; or we can learn, accept, believe, and evidence our love of God by our obedience to his will. By so doing we either accept or reject the sermons and discourses of Jesus the Messiah.

Notes

Introduction

1. See *The Miracles of Jesus the Messiah.*
2. See *The Parables of Jesus the Messiah.*
3. Parables, chapter 1, notes 25 and 26.

Chapter 1: Discourses

1. Farrar 2:257.
2. Parables, chapter 1.
3. Miracles, chapter 1.
4. Ed 2:167.
5. Ed 2:28.
6. Geikie 2:195.
7. Ed 2:28.
8. Parables, chapter 1.
9. Miracles, chapter 1.
10. Ed 2:393.
11. Ed 2:394.
12. Geikie 2:38.

Chapter 2: The Ministry Commenced

1. The references refer primarily to Luke chapter 6; however, various elements of the doctrine are taught in the discourses recorded randomly throughout Luke.

2. Before publication of the 1979 edition of the Bible for The Church of Jesus Christ of Latter-day Saints this was known as the Inspired Version. In the Church it is now generally referred to as the Joseph Smith Translation (JST).

3. DNTC 1:212, 214; MM 2:116; Geikie 2:48; Farrar 1:25-28.

4. Some have questioned whether the Sermon on the Mount was delivered all at once or merely so recorded by Matthew. That it was likely one continuous discourse is suggested by the fact that the Lord also delivered it to the Nephites on the Western Hemisphere in one uninterrupted sequence. (See 3 Nephi 12, 13, and 14.)

5. Geikie 2:48-49; Farrar 1:250. For detail on the composition of the multitude see Ed 1:526.

6. Miracles, chapter 1; Farrar 1:261.

7. Farrar 1:260.

8. Farrar 1:260.

9. Ed 1:527–28.

10. Ed 1:527–28.

11. JC p. 232.

12. Ed 1:527.

13. JC p. 232.

14. JC p. 246.

15. Geikie 2:58.

16. Farrar 1:265–67.

17. Geikie 2:49.

18. Geikie 2:55.

19. JC p. 231.

20. JC p. 231.

21. DNTC 1:215.

22. DNTC 1:215.

23. JC p. 231.

24. JC p. 231.

25. Parables, chapter 5.

26. JC p. 231.

27. JC p. 231.

28. DNTC 1:216.

29. JC p. 231.

30. Geikie 2:56.

31. Geikie 2:61.

32. DNTC 1:218.

33. DNTC 1:218.

34. JC p. 233.

35. Geikie 2:59.

36. Geikie 2:63.

37. DNTC 1:222.

38. DNTC 1:222.

39. Geikie 2:64.

40. Geikie 2:65.

41. Geikie 2:65.

42. Geikie 2:65–66.

43. JC p. 235.

44. DNTC 1:227.

45. Geikie 2:66.

46. JC p. 235.

47. DNTC 1:228.

48. The Joseph Smith Translation modifies the automatic extension to the cloak, as indicated by Matthew, stating that if the man sues again, then we should give him the cloak also (JST Matthew 5:42).

49. Again the Joseph Smith Translation modifies the automatic extension, commanding that if then compelled to go twain, we should go the twain (JST Matthew 5:43).

50. Geikie 2:72.

51. Geikie 2:73.

52. Parables, chapter 7.

53. Ed 1:530.

54. JC p. 237.

55. Geikie 2:76.
56. JC p. 238.
57. Parables, chapter 5.
58. Ed Temple p. 338.
59. Geikie 2:77.
60. JC p. 242.
61. DNTC 1:251.
62. DNTC 1:254.

Chapter 3: New Leadership

1. MM 2:99.
2. Geikie 2:43.
3. Although divergent opinions abound as to when the call of the Twelve occurred, it would appear that it took place between two early visits of Jesus to Jerusalem. Jesus went up to Jerusalem to the "unknown feast" (John 5:1). This feast was either the Passover (MM 2:64–65) or the Feast of Purim (Ed Temple p. 332; for his further considerations see Ed 2:768). Because this feast is not named, the speculated length of Jesus' ministry varies from two and one-half to three and one-half years. These calculations involve John 4:35. If Jesus communicated with the woman at the well in December, the feast would be the Feast of Purim. The Feast of Purim (or Esther) was held between the thirteenth and the fifteenth day of the Jewish month Adar (the twelfth month), which approximately corresponds to the first of March on our present calendar (Ed Temple pp. 331–32; 207). There is no doubt that in John 6:4 Jesus went up to the Passover celebration held at the time of the spring equinox in the Jewish month Nisan, which is the first month of the Jewish calendar year and equivalent to our end of March or beginning of April (Ed Temple p. 205).
4. It is significant to note that from time to time people came to Jesus and volunteered to go with him. In most of these incidents Jesus did not accept their offer (Matthew 8:19–22). He chose to specifically select and ordain those he wanted to have with him in his ministry (John 15:16).
5. JC p. 226.
6. JC p. 226.
7. Bruce p. 37.
8. MM 2:104–5.
9. MM 2:102.
10. JC p. 218.
11. JC p. 218.
12. Smith p. 504.
13. Miracles, chapter 8.
14. JC p. 219.
15. Smith p. 277.
16. JC p. 220.
17. Miracles, chapter 7.
18. JC p. 221.
19. Geikie 2:46.

20. JC p. 221.
21. Geikie 2:47.
22. Bruce p. 6.
23. Smith p. 510.
24. JC p. 222.
25. JC p. 222.
26. Geikie 2:47.
27. JC p. 223.
28. Smith p. 693.
29. JC p. 223.
30. Bruce p. 19.
31. JC p. 223.

32. If James II, the Apostle, is the son of Alpheus Clopas (Matthew 27:56; Mark 15:40; John 19:25), and this Alpheus is the same as the one mentioned in Acts 1:13, it would make Judas, Simon, and James brothers. It is believed that Alpheus Clopas was the brother of Joseph, Mary's husband. (Smith p. 277.)

33. Smith p. 277.
34. JC p. 225.
35. JC p. 225.
36. Josephus, Wars, IV: 3, 9; Ed 1:522.
37. JC p. 225.
38. Ed 2:473.
39. JC p. 226.
40. Bruce p. 377.
41. Bruce p. 101.
42. Geikie 2:172.
43. Geikie 2:171.

44. A purse was a girdle in which money was carried; a scrip was a small bag or wallet wherein provisions were carried. (DNTC 1:326.)

45. JC p. 329.

46. Generally speaking, the serpent used in this example was an emblem of curing power, similar to that which Moses used in the wilderness when the poisonous serpents attacked the children of Israel (Numbers 21:8). The dove was symbolic of the purity of their hearts.

47. Geikie 2:173.
48. JC p. 330.
49. DNTC 1:336.

50. Perhaps the reference by Luke to "other seventy" would indicate that the first quorum of seventy had been organized. DNTC 1:433.

51. Ed 1:26.
52. Ed Temple p. 277.
53. JC p. 427.

54. See pamphlet: "History of the Organization of the Seventies" by Joseph Young, Sr., Salt Lake City, Utah, 1878.

55. Joseph F. Smith, Conference Report, 1904, p. 3.

Chapter 4: Cleansing the Temple

1. Ed 1:367. The tax was in the amount of one-half shekel and had to be paid in the temple money or ordinary Galilean shekels. It could not be paid in the money common in Palestine at that day. Many coins of different countries were used in Palestine at Christ's time, including Palestinian silver, copper coin, Persian Tyrian, Syrian, Egyptian, Grecian, and Roman. (Ed 1:367-68.)
2. Josephus, Wars, VI, IX:3.
3. Ed 1:368.
4. Ed 1:369-70.
5. Geikie 1:471.
6. Josephus, Antiquities, XX, IX:2-4.
7. JC p. 155.
8. Geikie 1:472.
9. Ed 1:374.
10. Miracles, chapters 1 and 2.
11. JC p. 155.
12. JC p. 528.
13. Miracles, chapter 8. Matthew records the miracle of the fig tree after the cleansing of the temple (Matthew 21:18-22).
14. MM 3:348.
15. Geikie 2:378.
16. JC p. 158.

Chapter 5: The Test for Those Who Followed

1. Miracles, chapter 17.
2. Geikie 2:246-47.
3. Geikie 2:247.
4. JC p. 386.
5. Geikie 2:247.
6. Bruce p. 202.
7. MM 3:82.
8. Ed 2:120.
9. DNTC 1:419.
10. Ed 2:345.
11. Bruce p. 282.
12. Previous declarations: First—Matthew 16:21; Mark 8:31. Second—Matthew 17:22-23; Mark 9:31.
13. JC p. 502.
14. JC p. 503.
15. Matthew reports that it was the mother of James and John who petitioned the Lord, whereas Mark reports that James and John petitioned the Lord directly. These were the same Apostles who had, at a former time, requested that fire be called down from heaven to consume their adversaries (Luke 9:54). John had wished to forbid the one who cast out devils with whom he was not familiar (Mark 9:38).
16. Ed 2:347.

17. Ed 2:78.
18. JC p. 361.
19. Ed 2:79.
20. Ed 2:79.
21. MD pp. 411–13.
22. TPJS p. 274.
23. JC p. 364.
24. JC p. 365.

Chapter 6: "I Know That Messias Cometh"

1. The Gospel of John is unique, and differs considerably from the treatment of the Savior's life by the synoptic Gospels; i.e., Matthew, Mark, and Luke. Generally speaking, Matthew reads like a brief summary of the life of Christ even in the more detailed reports of his discourses, miracles, and parables. Mark, the shortest of the Gospels, appears to be a succession of rapid sketches of the life of Jesus, while Luke treats the life of Jesus with deeper historical purpose. Luke, however, outlines the story rather than telling it in detail (Ed 1:394). All three of the Synoptics treat the life of Jesus in a historical setting. John alone does not profess to give a narrative of the life of Christ, but rather selects incidents from his life which characteristically describe Jesus in his ministry and his claim to the Messiahship (Ed 1:394).

2. *New Testament Commentary for English Readers*, edited by Charles John Ellicott, p. 374.

3. Geikie 1:489; Ed 1:390.

4. DNTC 1:148.

5. Josephus, Antiquities XX: 6, 1.

6. Although the scripture indicates that all of the Apostles went into the small city, leaving Jesus alone, it is highly unlikely that he was left on the road without accompaniment. In all probability John remained behind to keep him company. (Ed 1:406.)

7. Geikie 1:494.

8. Ed 1:409, including notes 2 and 3.

9. Ed 1:395.

10. Geikie 1:495.

11. Smith p. 212–13; Geikie 1:499.

12. Morris p. 266.

13. JC p. 173.

14. Josephus, Antiquities, XVIII: 2, 2. For a detailed discussion on the traditions, religion, derivation, and history of the Samaritans, see Ed 1:390–403.

15. Geikie 1:497.

16. Geikie 1:497.

17. Bruce p. 247.

18. Parables, chapter 3.

19. JC p. 174.

20. A similar occurrence had taken place when the Lord called Nathanael to the ministry—there Nathanael declared Jesus to be the King of Israel (John 1:48–49).

21. The Joseph Smith Translation states: "I who speak unto thee am the Messias" (JST John 4:28).

22. Geikie 1:503.

23. Pertaining to the time of year of this occurrence and whether the comment of Christ in verse 35 pertains to the current time of year or whether the four months spoken of were parabolic in nature, see Ed 1:419–20; Appendix XV.

24. Farrar 1:214.

25. Geikie 1:502.

Chapter 7: The Messiah They Looked For

1. For specific information on these materials see Trench p. 243; Geikie 2:86–87; Ed Temple p. 331–33.

2. Miracles, chapter 5.

3. Geikie 2:91.

4. MM 2:70.

5. DNTC 1:191.

6. MM 2:71.

7. JC p. 208.

8. JC p. 209.

9. MM 2:76.

10. Miracles, chapter 2.

11. Ed 2:25.

12. Geikie 2:179.

13. The synagogue had worship days during the week (Monday and Thursday) other than the normal Sabbath worship. It may have been on one of these days that the sermon took place. (Geikie 2:179).

14. Ed 2:29.

15. Ed 2:29.

16. JC p. 339.

17. Geikie 2:181.

18. Ed 2:28.

19. Geikie 2:184.

20. JC pp. 342, 347 note 10.

21. JC p. 342.

22. DNTC 1:358.

23. JC p. 342.

24. Geikie 2:184–85.

25. JC p. 343.

26. Bruce p. 146.

27. Miracles, chapter 3.

28. Ed 2:36.

29. Geikie 2:186.

30. Ed 2:36.

31. JC p. 344.

32. Ed Temple p. 270.

33. For detailed information on the Feast of Tabernacles, see Ed Temple pp. 268–87.

34. Ed 2:165.

35. Geikie 2:279.

36. Ed Temple p. 285; Ed 2:166.

37. The ancient Jewish explanatory commentary on the Old Testament.

38. As quoted in Ed 2:166.

39. Ed 2:165.

40. It is significant to note that in John chapter 7 the crowds in the temple are mentioned eight times, whereas they are not mentioned at all in chapter 8. For this reason Edersheim determines that the "light of the world" discourse was given on the last day of the feast, or perhaps even the day after, commonly known as the Octave of the feast, after most of the crowds, common in the normal feast days, had dissipated. If this interpretation of John were adopted, it would indicate that Jesus gave the "light of the world" discourse principally before his adversaries and not the people in general.

41. Edersheim rejects this segment of the scripture as spurious. For his detail on the matter see Ed 2:163 note 1. Although some reject the story of the adulterous woman, it would appear to be authentic for the following reasons: First the Joseph Smith Translation left the story intact and did not reject it, thus indicating that the story belonged in the sacred text. Second, Elder James E. Talmage also indicated the authenticity of the story.

42. Farrar 2:65.

43. JC p. 405.

44. Ed 2:165.

45. DNTC 1:452.

46. Ed 2:168.

47. Ed 2:169.

48. Ed 2:169.

49. Farrar 2:75.

50. Ed 2:167.

51. Geikie 2:286.

52. Ed 2:173.

53. DNTC 1:461.

54. Ed 2:175.

55. Ed 2:176.

56. DNTC 1:462–64.

57. Miracles, chapter 4.

58. The Feast of Dedication was first instituted by Judas Maccabees in the year 164 B.C. to celebrate the rededication of the temple. (Ed Temple p. 334.)

59. JC pp. 417–18.

60. JC p. 418.

61. Miracles, chapter 5.

62. Ed 2:229.

63. JC p. 488.

64. Miracles, chapter 4.

Chapter 8: Principles

1. Ed 1:366–67; MM 1:469.
2. Farrar 1:196.
3. Farrar 1:196–97.
4. JC p. 159.
5. Ed 1:381.
6. Geikie 1:481.
7. Ed 1:382.
8. Miracles, chapters 1 and 2.
9. Ed 1:381.
10. JC p. 160.
11. Geikie 1:479.
12. Geikie 1:479.
13. MM 1:478.
14. Miracles, chapter 14.
15. Ed 2:328.
16. Farrar 2:227–28.
17. JC p. 473.
18. Geikie 2:347.
19. Ed 2:332.
20. Ed 2:332 note 5.
21. For detail on the grounds for divorce practiced by the Jews at the time of Christ see Ed 2:332–34; Geikie 2:347.
22. JC p. 474.
23. JC p. 474.
24. Ed 2:335.
25. JC p. 475.
26. JC p. 475.
27. JC p. 475.
28. MM 3:293.
29. DNTC 1:547.
30. DNTC 1:547.
31. This appears to be a duplication of a previous similar experience (Matthew 18:3).
32. Ed 2:336.
33. Ed 2:387.
34. Ed 2:387.
35. Josephus, Antiquities, XIV: 7, 1 and 2.
36. DNTC 1:628.
37. JC p. 561.
38. Ed 2:389.
39. Parables, chapter 10.
40. Parables, chapter 8.
41. DNTC 1:691.
42. Ed 2:792–94.
43. Topical Guide: Service.
44. JC p. 585.
45. Ed 2:792.

Chapter 9: Questions

1. JC p. 194.
2. Ed 1:514.
3. Geikie 2:27.
4. Geikie 2:30.
5. Geikie 2:32.
6. Geikie 2:31.
7. Ed 1:508.
8. DNTC 1:182.
9. Ed 1:520.

10. If the question posed by the disciples of John the Baptist, as recorded in Matthew 9:14, is viewed in this manner, then there is no conflict between the Matthew verse and the events as recorded in Mark 2:18 and Luke 5:33 (JC p. 195.)

11. Ed Temple p. 338.

12. For example, a fast commemorated the destruction of Jerusalem by the Chaldeans, and others were connected with the incidents of the siege, the troubles of the first period of captivity, or the day which commemorated the translation of the scriptures. (Geikie 2:35.)

13. Ed 1:662.
14. Geikie 2:35.
15. Geikie 2:35.
16. JC p. 196.
17. DNTC 1:186.

18. The Joseph Smith Translation adds to the Matthew text a third question posed by the Pharisees. They asked Jesus why he did not accept their baptism, as they claimed to be keeping the whole law. Jesus declared to them that they did not keep the Law because if they had kept it they would have received him, and he stated, "For I am he who gave the law." This insertion (JST Matthew 9:18–21) comes before the old cloth/old wineskins analogy, but only in the Matthew text; it does not appear in either Mark or Luke.

19. Miracles, chapter 3.
20. Ed 1:576.
21. DNTC 1:280.
22. MM 2:226.
23. Ed 2:339.
24. Ed 2:339.
25. JC p. 476.
26. DNTC 1:556.
27. Geikie 2:355.
28. Ed 2:298.
29. Geikie 2:342.
30. JC p. 445.
31. Ed 2:301.
32. JC p. 446.

Chapter 10: Enemies

1. DNTC 1:261.

2. The Lord's comment that they return and testify to John of his miracles and words could possibly indicate that John did not have a full comprehension of what the spiritual kingdom of God comprised. (JC p. 256.)

3. MM 1:382.

4. TPJS pp. 275-76.

5. TPJS p. 276.

6. Ed 1:670.

7. Geikie 2:110.

8. We know that Jesus taught extensively in Capernaum and worked many miracles there, even making it his own community. (See Matthew 9:1; Mark 9:33; Matthew 8:5-17; Mark 2:1-12.)

9. DNTC 1:469.

10. DNTC 1:504.

11. Ed 2:305; DNTC 1:503.

12. Ed 2:305.

13. Ed 2:305.

14. This quotation is taken from "Lecture Sixth," *Lectures on Faith.* The *Lectures on Faith*, first known as *Lectures on Theology*, were given to the early elders of the Church at the School of the Prophets in Kirtland, Ohio (HC 2:175-76). Joseph was active in the preparation of these lectures on theology during this period of time (HC 2:180). The lectures were later published in the first editions of the Doctrine and Covenants under the title, *Lectures on Faith*, and although the same were noted as "judiciously written and compiled," there was a marked difference between the *Lectures on Faith* and the revelations given in the first editions of the Doctrine and Covenants. The *Lectures on Faith* were later dropped from the Doctrine and Covenants. (See HC Index under Faith, Lectures on.) For a complete text of the *Lectures on Faith*, including a historical sketch by Elder John A. Widtsoe, see *Discourses on the Holy Ghost*, compiled by N. B. Lundwall, Bookcraft, Inc., Salt Lake City, Utah 1959, fifth printing 1967. The quotation inserted is taken from this text, pages 143-44 and footnote.

15. Ed 2:7.

16. Ed 2:8.

17. Geikie 2:191.

18. Miracles, chapter 3.

19. Ed 2:8.

20. Miracles, chapter 5.

21. Ed 2:8.

22. Ed 2:10. For detail of the ritualistic requirements of washing and the sins associated with lack of observance, see Geikie 2:191-92.

23. Ed 2:21.

24. DNTC 1:368.

25. JC pp. 353-54.

26. Miracles, chapter 10.

27. Geikie 2:216.

28. MM 3:27.

29. MM 3:28.

30. Only John records this appearance of Jesus at Jerusalem. From this period of the ministry until its end John records three appearances of Jesus in the Holy City. The first (the one now under discussion) at the Feast of Tabernacles; the second, at the Feast of Dedication (John 10); and the third was his final entry before the Crucifixion (which all the Evangelists agree upon).

Luke, during this same period of the Lord's ministry, also records three journeys to Jerusalem (but does not record the events of the visits) and it would follow that the three journeys to Jerusalem described by Luke fit into the three appearances at Jerusalem described by John. Luke describes what took place in Christ's ministry before and after the appearance, while John describes only what took place at Jerusalem. (Ed 2:127.)

31. Ed Temple p. 270.
32. Ed Temple p. 269.
33. MM 3:111.
34. DNTC 1:438.
35. Geikie 2:263.
36. This denial of hospitality produced the story of James and John's requesting that lightning be called down from heaven to destroy some Samaritan villages, resulting in their nicknames, "sons of thunder" (see Luke 9:54; Mark 3:17). Apparently they, too, had not come to the total understanding and comprehension that the kingdom of God would not be expanded by violence. By their attitude they also displayed their Jewish training, believing that everyone other than Israel was their enemy. Jesus rebuked their foolishness and passed on to another village.

37. Ed 2:148.
38. Ed 2:151.
39. Ed 2:151.
40. DNTC 1:441.
41. Miracles, chapter 5.
42. JC p. 404.
43. DNTC 1:444; Ed 2:154.
44. MM 3:128.
45. Ed Temple pp. 278–81.
46. Ed 2:160.
47. Ed 2:160; DNTC 1:445.
48. DNTC 1:449; Geikie 2:278.

Chapter 11: The Last Controversies

1. Geikie 2:392.
2. JC p. 544.
3. JC p. 545.
4. Ed 2:385.
5. Ed 2:385.
6. JC p. 545.
7. Ed 2:385.
8. Geikie 2:395.
9. Geikie 2:397.

10. Ed 2:397.
11. Farrar 2:235; DNTC 1:605.
12. Farrar 2:235.
13. Geikie 2:398.
14. JC p. 548.
15. For detail on the Sadducean belief concerning the resurrection see Ed 2:397–99.
16. DNTC 1:612.
17. Ed 2:405.
18. JC p. 518.
19. Proselytes to the Jewish faith from Greece were pledged to the seven commandments of Noah. (1) The avoidance of murder; (2) the avoidance of bloodshed; (3) the commitment not to rob; (4) the rejection of idolatry; (5) the worship of Jehovah; (6) the obedience to Jewish courts in matters of religion; (7) to eat no freshly killed or still-bleeding flesh. In addition to these covenants they submitted to the law of circumcision; however, they could not pass beyond the court of the Gentiles in the temple. (Geikie 2:409.)
20. MM 3:411.
21. JC p. 518.
22. JC p. 520.
23. JC p. 520.
24. Ed 2:393–94.

Chapter 12: "Farewell, I Will Come Again"

1. Farrar 2:244.
2. DNTC 1:615.
3. TPJS pp. 272–73, 318–19.
4. JC p. 553.
5. Ed 2:407.
6. Farrar 2:244.
7. Parables, chapter 9.
8. Geikie 2:403.
9. Ed 2:411.
10. Ed 2:412; JC p. 556; MM 3:396.
11. DNTC 1:619.
12. Ed 2:412.
13. DNTC 1:620.
14. Farrar 2:246.
15. TPJS pp. 221–23; DNTC 1:623.
16. TPJS p. 261.
17. MM 3:405.
18. Geikie 2:406-7.
19. Geikie 2:407.
20. MM 3:408.
21. Ed 2:431.
22. Josephus, Antiquities, XV: 11, 3.
23. Geike, 2:416.

24. Geikie 2:416.
25. DNTC 1:640.
26. Ed 2:446.
27. Josephus, Wars, II: 13, 4, 5; Antiquities, XX: 5, 1; 8, 10. For information on the Jewish belief of the anticipated Messiah see Ed 2:434–35.
28. JC p. 571.
29. JC p. 572.
30. DNTC 1:641.
31. JC p. 571.
32. DNTC 1:644–45.
33. DNTC 1:647.
34. DNTC 1:647.
35. TPJS pp. 286–87; DNTC 1:660; MM 3:448.
36. JC p. 573.
37. DNTC 1:656.
38. JC p. 574.
39. DNTC 1:675–76.
40. DNTC 1:668–70.
41. JC p. 575.
42. Parables, chapter 10.
43. MM 3:462.

Chapter 13: The Final Discourses

1. TPJS p. 366.
2. Geikie 2:451; JC p. 602.
3. JC p. 602.
4. JC pp. 602–3.
5. TPJS pp. 149–51.
6. DNTC 1:739.
7. JC p. 604.
8. DNTC 1:751.
9. Miracles, chapter 3.
10. Ed 2:523.
11. JC p. 606.
12. JC p. 607.
13. DNTC 1:753.
14. DNTC 1:753.
15. DNTC 1:754.
16. JC p. 608.
17. JC pp. 608–9.
18. DNTC 1:761.
19. JC p. 610.
20. Geikie 2:470.
21. DNTC 1:764.

Scriptural Appendix to the Sermon on the Mount

Subject:	Matthew	Luke	3 Nephi	JST
Setting	5:1–2	6:12–19	12:1–2	5:1–4
Poor in spirit	5:3	6:20	12:3 .	5:5
They that mourn	5:4	6:21	12:4	5:6
The meek	5:5		12:5	5:7
Hunger and thirst	5:6	6:21	12:6	5:8
Merciful	5:7		12:7	5:9
Pure in heart	5:8		12:8	5:10
Peacemakers	5:9		12:9	5:11
Persecuted	5:10	6:22–23	12:10	5:12
Revile you	5:11–12		12:11–12	5:13–14
Salt of earth	5:13	14:34–35	12:13	5:15
Light of world	5:14–15	8:16; 11:33	12:14–15	5:16–17
Let light shine	5:16		12:16	5:18
Law fulfilled	5:17–20	16:17	12:17–20; 12:46–47	5:19–22
Anger	5:21–26	12:58–59	12:21–26	5:23–28
Adultery/lust	5:27–30		12:27–30	5:29–34
Divorce	5:31–32	16:18	12:31–32	5:35–36
Oath/Honesty	5:33–37		12:33–37	5:37–39
Eye/eye; cheek	5:38–42		12:38–42	5:40–44
Love enemies	5:43–47	6:27–36	12:43–45	5:45–49
Be perfect	5:48		12:48	5:50
Alms	6:1–4		13:1–4	6:1–4
Prayer	6:5–15	11:2–4	13:5–15	6:5–16
Fasting	6:16–18		13:16–18	6:17–18
Treasure	6:19–34	11:34–36; 12:22–34; 16:9–13	13:19–34	6:18–39
Judgment	7:1–5	6:37–38; 6:41–42	14:1–5	7:1–8
Holy as pearls	7:6		14:6	7:9–11
Ask/seek	7:7–12	11:9–13	14:7–14	7:12–21
Narrow way	7:13–14	13:22–24	14:13–14	7:22–23
False prophets	7:15–20	6:43–44	14:15–20	7:24–29
Do Father's will	7:21–23	6:46; 13:25–30	14:21–23	7:30–33
Rock/sand	7:24–27	6:47–49	14:24–27	7:34–35
Taught/authority	7:28–29			7:36–37

Subject Index

—A—

Adultery, sin of, 24; woman accused of, 117

Almsgiving, teaching on, 30

Andrew, description of, 48

Anger, not justified in showing, 24

Apostles, admonished in Sermon on the Mount, 20; all Galilean except one, 44; Andrew, 48; ask when Second Coming will be, 214; Bartholomew/Nathanael, 49; call of, 43; called before Sermon on the Mount, 11; charge to, 54; compared to light of the world, 21; compared to salt, 20; concerned at bread of life discourse, 112; concerned over discourse on divorce, 142; death of predicted, 232; disciples prior to call, 43; disputing over glories, 77; groups of, 44; James, (James II), 51; Jesus prays for welfare of, 236; John, 47; Judas/Lebbaeus/Thaddaeus, 52; Judas Iscariot, 53; Matthew/Levi, 51; meaning of word, 44; needs and comforts of, 58; number twelve significant, 45; order in Quorum, 44; Peter, 45; Philip, 49; promised mansions, 222; results of first mission, 59; seen by New World prophets, 45; sphere of first mission, 57; Simon Zelotes, 52; startled at rich not attaining kingdom, 162; testimony of, 83; Thomas/Didymus, 50; thoughts of aggrandizement of, 82; trouble interpreting Christ's metaphors, 180; warned not to be deceived, 28

—B—

Baptism, discourse on, 133

Bartholomew/Nathanael, description of, 49

Beatitudes, contrasts new kingdom with old, 15; followed by series of woes, 18; hunger and thirst, 16; meek, 16; merciful, 16; peacemakers, 17; persecuted, 17; poor in spirit, 15; pure in heart, 17; teachings of, 14; those that mourn, 15;

"Beware the Leaven of the Pharisees," discourse on, 178

Blind Lead the Blind, discourse on, 175

Bread of Life, discourse on, 104

—C—

Call of the Twelve, discourse on, 43

Capernaum, discourse on bread of life at, 108; upbraided with other cities, 170

Charge to the Twelve, discourse on, 54

Children, kingdom compared to, 77; punishment for offending, 78

Christ, discourse on, 194; discourse on farewell of, 203

Comforter, first is Holy Ghost, 223; second is Jesus Christ, 223

Controversies, discourses on last, 189

—D—

Devil, adopted father of Jews, 122; Jesus accused of being, 122

Disciples, admonished in Sermon on the Mount, 20; life of portrayed in Sermon on the Mount, 13; test for those who followed, 75. See also Discipleship Prevented

Disciples Indeed, discourse on, 75

Discipleship Prevented, discourse on, 171

Discourses (general): Jesus announced Messiahship by, 242; generally, 7; like conversations, 7; most common method of teaching, 9; problems similar to those of parables and miracles, 7; used familiar scenes and objects in, 9; test of faith, 111

Discourses (specific): A Charge to the Twelve, 54; A Question on the Resurrection, 193; Baptism, 133; "Beware the Leaven of the Pharisees," 178; Christ's Farewell, 203; Disciples

pated, 7; people astonished at teaching of, 40; perceived thoughts of Apostles, 77; personality of characterized, 72; questioned by Pharisees, 154; rejected by those he sought to save, 9; rejection of a result of Jews' religious development, 8; relationship to the Father, 102; testimony of the Twelve concerning, 83; witnesses his divinity, 103

Jews, accused of adding to word of God by Samaritans, 95; all but impossible to believe, 8; Apostles to admonish leaders of, 36; ask for Messianic sign, 179; claim Abraham as father, 121; concept of divorce among, 25; expected temporal kingdom, 8, 170; formal prayers of, 31; had abrogated second great commandment, 29; had endless oaths, 26; had no need for a Savior, 7; made hasty retaliation the rule of the day, 28; hated Samaritans, 96; Jesus confronts leaders, 101; killed Jesus knowledgeably, 210; misunderstood second great commandment, 148; put questions to Jesus, 153; restrictions on women, 98; retaliation of under Law of Moses, 27; teaching of destruction of, 79; three great charges against Jesus, 176; traditionalism of incompatible with the scriptures, 178; unbelief of, 199; wanted powerful Messiah, 121; warned at cleansing of temple, 71; why Jesus was rejected by, 200

John, description of, 47; never to taste of death, 87; requests glory, 82; special friendship with Jesus, 77

John the Baptist, disciples of question Jesus, 156; discourse on, 166; greatest of prophets, 169; John the Apostle an early disciple of, 48

Judas/Lebbaeus/Thaddaeus, description of, 52

Judas Iscariot, description of, 53; son of perdition, 237

Judgment, difference between JST and KJV on, 36; relates to second great commandment, 147; teaching on, 35

—K—

Kingdom of heaven, acceptance of, 37; Apostles vie for position in, 76; as portrayed by the Beatitudes, 18; chil-

dren compared to, 77; citizenship requirements, 29; means of teaching, 13; qualification for, 77; rich can hardly attain, 162; "what must I do to gain?" 161

—L—

Law of Moses, compared to new gospel, 21; contrasted with the Beatitudes, 15; demanded obedience by fear, 12; gospel superior to, 23; hedge around condemned, 19; Israel observed only letter of, 20; Jesus fulfilled, 12, 22; Samaritans rigidly attached to, 95; teaching tool to prepare for Messiah, 12; woe to those secure in, 19

Leadership, Jesus establishes new, 42

Leaven, beware the Pharisees', 179

Light of the World, discourse on, 112

Lord's Prayer, pattern for prayer, 31; teaching emphasis of, 32

Love, replaced fear in gospel, 28

—M—

Marriage and Divorce, discourse on, 138

Matthew/Levi, description of, 51; gives dinner for Jesus, 154

Messiah, belief in origin of, 186; Jesus not the one anticipated, 7; Law of Moses teaching tool to prepare for, 12; Samaritans looked forward to coming of, 96; type Jews looked for, 109, 121

Miracles, brought multitude together for Sermon on the Mount, 11

Mother, discourse from question on who is, 158

Murder, sin of, 23

Mysteries, not to teach, 37

—N—

Nicodemus, defends Jesus, 188; discourse to, 135

—O—

Oaths, of moral blindness, 208; Jews had endless, 26

Scripture Index

OLD TESTAMENT

Malachi		3:1–3	69
3:1	169		

NEW TESTAMENT

Matthew		15:1–20	175
4:13	68	16:1	193
4:18–19	49	16:4	86
4:23	7	16:5–12	178
4:23–24	11	16:13–19	46
5, 6, 7	10	16:13–28	83
5:3	15	16:18	46
5:4	15	16:21	249n12
5:5	16	17	76
5:6	16	17:1	46
5:7	16	17:1–2	47
5:8	17	17:9	86
5:9	17	17:22–23	77, 249n12
5:10	17	18:1–11	76
5:13	20	19:1–15	138
5:14–15	21	19:9	26
5:16	21	19:16–24	81
5:17–20	21	19:16–30	160
5:21–26	23	19:28	81
5:27–30	24	20:17–28	80
5:31–32	25	20:21	47
5:33–37	26	21:12–17	71
5:38–48	27	21:18–22	247n13
6:1–4	30	22:15–46	189
6:4–13	30	23:1–39	204
6:14–15	32	24	49, 146
6:16–18	33	24:1–42	211
6:19–34	33	25:31–46	145
7:1–5	35	26:36–37	47
7:6–8	36	26:37	46
7:9–14	37	26:49	54
7:15–23	38	26:69–75	86
7:24–29	39	27:5	44, 54
8:5–17	255n8	27:56	248n32
8:14	46	27:63	70
8:19–22	247n4	28:19	57
9:1	68, 255n8		
9:9–13	51, 153	Mark	
9:13	177	1:16–20	46
9:14	254n10	1:29	46
9:14–17	156	2:1–12	255n8
9:15	86	2:13–17	51, 154
9:16–17	42	2:18	254n10
10:1–42	54	2:18–22	156
10:37	159	3:6	191
10:42	43	3:13–19	57
11:1–30	166	3:31–35	158
12	176	3:17	47, 256n36
12:7	177	5:37	46, 47
12:46–50	158	6:3	52
13:55	52	6:7–13	57